Perspectives on Richard Ford

Perspectives on Richard Ford

Edited by

Huey
Guagliardo

University Press
of Mississippi
Jackson

www.upress.state.ms.us

08 07 06 05 04 03 02 01 00   4 3 2 1

Library of Congress Cataloging-in-Publication Data

Perspectives on Richard Ford / edited by Huey Guagliardo.
    p. cm.
  Includes bibliographical references and index.
  ISBN 1-57806-233-0 (alk. paper) – ISBN 1-57806-234-9 (pbk. : alk. paper)
  1. Ford, Richard, 1944—Criticism and interpretation. 2. Alienation (Social
psychology) in literature. 3. Existentialism in literature. 4. Identity in literature. I. Guagliardo, Huey.

PS3556.O713 Z85 2000
813'.54—dc21

                                                              99-045448

British Library Cataloging-in-Publication Data available

For Deborah, Ethan, and Joshua

Contents

First, I wish to thank my wife, Deborah, and my sons, Ethan and Joshua, for their patience and support. My special thanks to Lewis Simpson, Eddie Dupuy, and Elinor Ann Walker for their encouragement and helpful suggestions. I am also very grateful to Richard Ford for opening his home to me and agreeing to be interviewed for this volume. Finally, I would like to acknowledge the original publishers for permission to reprint the works listed below.

The Marginal People in the Novels of Richard Ford" by Huey Guagliardo first appeared in *The Southern Quarterly* 37.2 (1999): 16-32. Reprinted by permission.

"The Confessions of an Ex-Suicide: Relenting and Recovering in Richard Ford's *The Sportswriter*" by Edward Dupuy first appeared in *The Southern Literary Journal* 23.1 (1990): 93-103. Reprinted by permission.

The Sportswriter: Post-Faulkner, Post-Southern?" by Fred Hobson is a revised version of an essay that first appeared in *The Southern Writer in the Postmodern World* by Fred Hobson, University of Georgia Press, 1991: 41-72. Reprinted by permission.

Richard Ford's Postmodern Cowboys" by Jeffrey J. Folks first appeared in *Southern Writers at Century's End*, edited by Jeffrey J. Folks and James A. Perkins, University Press of Kentucky, 1997: 212-25. Reprinted by permission.

"A Conversation with Richard Ford" by Huey Guagliardo first appeared in *The Southern Review* 34 (1998): 609-20. Reprinted by permission.

There can be little doubt that Mississippi author Richard Ford will find a secure place in the canon of American literature. As of this writing, Ford has published five novels: *A Piece of My Heart* (1976), *The Ultimate Good Luck* (1981), *The Sportswriter* (1986), *Wildlife* (1990), and *Independence Day* (1995). Ford first gained widespread critical acclaim for *The Sportswriter*, the story of suburbanite Frank Bascombe's struggle to survive loneliness and great loss. The novel clearly struck a chord with readers and reviewers alike. The *New York Times* referred to *The Sportswriter* as "a devastating chronicle of contemporary alienation" (Kakutani 21), and *Newsweek* described Ford as "one of the best writers of his generation" (Clemons 82). Frank Bascombe's narrative continued in *Independence Day*, the sequel for which Ford won both the Pulitzer Prize and PEN/Faulkner Award. As its title suggests, the novel is unquestionably American in spirit, capturing the experience of life in America's suburbia (its landscape as well as the fears and dreams of its inhabitants) as few other novels have; yet it derives universal appeal through its deft depiction of one man's meandering journey down life's freeway. In Ford's version of the great American road novel, Frank Bascombe's quest for freedom and independence requires him to negotiate a labyrinthian way that is anything but free. Frank encounters many twists and turns along his way, not to mention a loopy and confusing network of on-ramps and off-ramps as he enters into or exits from various relationships, all of which force him to pay close attention to the meaningful signs and signals, that is, the right language, that might lead him toward the important human connections that he seeks.

Although Ford (who is also the author of *Rock Springs* [1987], a well-received volume of short stories, and *Women with Men* [1997], a collection of three related novellas) now has a significant body of work and several important literary honors to his credit, it would seem that he has merely reached the midpoint of his career. Born on February 16, 1944, in Jackson, Mississippi, he is currently in his midfifties and at the height of his literary powers. As Richard Ford emerges as a major figure among American writers of the post-World War II generation, the time is certainly ripe for a serious critical appraisal of his work.

Perspectives on Richard Ford offers a collection of nine essays examining Ford's fiction, as well as an interview with the writer himself. While the essays employ a variety of critical perspectives, they all place Ford's texts within the framework of the literature of alienation—a tradition with which Ford has associated himself since the very beginning of his career. As Kenneth Holditch points out, Ford's first novel, *A Piece of My Heart*, is uncompromisingly dark in its treatment of characters suffering through various degrees of desperation and despair; and much in the novel "is reflective of French humanistic existentialists, particularly Albert Camus." This early novel is certainly Ford's most pessimistic, but his later works of fiction continue to explore issues of human loneliness, isolation, and despair. In his analysis of Ford's second novel, *The Ultimate Good Luck*, Robert Funk examines the way in which the author uses the framework of the American detective/adventure novel and that genre's lonely hero in order to dramatize the individual's alienation from society. Funk observes that Ford's lonely protagonist, Harry Quinn, has much in common with Ernest Hemingway's existential hero, Harry Morgan. Both characters are caught up in the absurd randomness of modern life. Like Hemingway, argues Funk, Ford intends for his readers to empathize with his character's experience of displacement and alienation. For Elinor Ann Walker, Ford's story "Great Falls" and his short novel *Wildlife* "provoke a Sartrean examination of loneliness and ways of redeeming that state." Walker finds in Ford, as in Jean-Paul Sartre, a "fascination with being, knowing, and nothingness."

Clearly, the writers who served as major influences upon Ford's work included not only the trio whom the author lionized in his 1983 *Esquire* magazine essay as "the three kings" of modern American literature—that eminent fellow Mississippian, William Faulkner, and those most extraordinary members of Gertrude Stein's "Lost Generation," Hemingway and F. Scott Fitzgerald—but the French existentialists and more recent practitioners of the novel of alienation such as John Barth, Donald Barthelme, Raymond Carver, John Cheever, Frederick Exley, and, especially, Walker Percy. Several of the essays in this volume, in fact, most notably Fred Hobson's and Edward Dupuy's, find fascinating echoes of Percy in Ford's texts. For Dupuy, Frank Bascombe's narrative voice in *The Sportswriter* calls to mind Percy's concept of "the ex-suicide," that is, the person who chooses suicide but then decides not to go through with it. Because the alternative of death is available, the ex-suicide is free to embrace the mystery of everyday life. Like a castaway washed up on an island, a familiar image in Percy's writings, Bascombe overcomes his dreamy alienation to view life anew, becoming fully open to what Percy and Ford would call the "pure possibility" of experience. For his part, Hobson concludes, at least with respect to *The Sportswriter*, that Percy (not Hemingway, Faulkner, or Fitzgerald) is the writer whom Ford most resembles, particularly in terms of the creation of character (Frank Bascombe's way of "facing the abyss" invites comparison to Binx Bolling's "Little Way" in *The Moviegoer*) and also in demonstrating a southerner's unique view of alienation in contemporary American culture.

There is indeed a tendency in many of these essays to examine Ford's narratives of alienation in a cultural context. Focusing on such issues as the impoverishment of human relationships, especially male/female and parent/child relationships, as well as the inner emptiness, detachment, and solipsism which characterize so much of life in the dangerous and uncertain world—the secular late-twentieth-century world—which is Ford's milieu, the essays demonstrate that Ford, like few other writers of his generation, powerfully depicts what it feels like to live in such a world. Of course, this is precisely why modern readers respond so readily to Ford's fiction. Priscilla Leder's, William Chernecky's and Jeffrey J. Folks's essays, as well as my own piece, all emphasize the large-scale cultural implications of Ford's fiction. Leder offers an astute analysis of gender relations in *Rock Springs*, showing various ways in which the relationships between men and women in the short stories dramatize "the isolation and loneliness of modern experience." Chernecky explores the Frank Bascombe novels as reflections of a "contemporary American cultural climate where people no longer yearn for personal salvation, let alone any return to some earlier epoch, but for the sense, the ephemeral illusion, of personal well-being, good health, and psychic security." Folks examines why Ford, a southerner, chose to write about "the alien and marginal culture" of the American West in works such as *Rock Springs* and *Wildlife*. Folks concludes that the western settings of Ford's stories allow the author to create "a more blatant representation of alienation," for "[t]he mountain West offers a convenient symbolic landscape . . . expressing the rootlessness of an increasing number of Americans." Furthermore, argues Folks, "the social and economic dilemmas of America as a whole are not escaped but only magnified by the desolate, ecologically damaged New West." Finally, my essay points out that Ford's works dramatize the breakdown of such cultural institutions as marriage, family, and community, the very institutions which give meaning and purpose to one's life. I assert that his marginalized protagonists often typify the rootlessness and nameless longing so pervasive in a highly mobile, present-oriented society in which individuals, having lost a sense of the past, relentlessly pursue their own elusive identities in the here and now.

This sense of rootlessness is a feeling which Ford, perhaps, understands even more keenly than most writers today. In a series of memoirs written for *Harper's*, Ford provides details of his family's history, although he admits that he was "forced to piece together" many of the details, because, as he says, "We were not a family for whom history had much to offer" ("My Mother, in Memory" 44). When combined, however, these memoirs offer a revealing glimpse of Ford's literary journey, truly providing a piece of his heart.

A traveler from a family of travelers, Ford learned early on that "Home is finally a variable concept" ("Accommodations" 43). Ford's father, Parker Carrol Ford, was a traveling salesman for the Faultless Starch Company. When Richard was eight years old, Parker suffered a heart attack, and the family moved into the Marion Hotel in Little Rock, Arkansas, which was run by Richard's grandfather, Ben Shelley. As a younger man, Ben had also been a traveler, "a boxer and roustabout" who would later work for the railroad, moving "wherever the railroad would take [him]" ("My Mother, in Memory" 45). Growing up in Ben Shelley's hotel, "detached from normal residential lives" ("Accommodations" 42), provided an important formative experience for young Richard. Among other things, living in the hotel taught him "a cool two-mindedness: one is both steady and in a sea that passes with tides. Accommodation is what's wanted, a replenished idea of permanence and transience; familiarity overcoming the continual irregularity of things" ("Accommodations" 39). As pointed out by several of the essays in this volume, the characters in Ford's fiction are certainly in quest of accommodation. Not only do they desire accommodation in the sense of achieving a feeling of locatedness, that is, the sense of feeling at home in the world (in *Independence Day*, for example, Frank Bascombe, a realtor, seeks homes for others even as he searches for a "homey connectedness" of his own), but they must also learn to accommodate themselves to life's uncertainties.

Ford learned at an early age to accommodate himself to uncertainty. Life in the Marion Hotel, he says, came with the knowledge that "if my grandfather lost his job . . . we lost it all" ("Accommodations" 43). When Richard was only sixteen, his father had a fatal heart attack. In a way, it might be said that Ford's adult life, the life of the son independent of his father's authority, began at that point. As an adult, Richard Ford has been a traveler whose life has embodied the permanence amid transience that he experienced as a boy. Ford and his wife, Kristina, to whom he has been married for over thirty years, have lived in at least fourteen different states, yet they always seem to return to the Deep South where the author spent his youth. For Ford, those early years spent in his grandfather's hotel serve as a metaphor for the permanence and transience that is life itself, a metaphor that expresses Ford's own existentialist worldview: "In the hotel there was no center to things, nor was I one. . . . I simply stood alongside. . . . And what I thought about it was this: this is the actual life now, not a stopover, a diversion, or an oddment in time, but the permanent life, the one that will provide history, memory, the one I'll be responsible for in the long run" ("Accommodations" 43).

As I point out in the essay that immediately follows this introduction, the marginalized and alienated characters in Ford's fiction also discover that there is "no center to things," and they typically find themselves standing alongside the edge of an emotional abyss, alone and isolated, looking back at an often uncontrollable life. Only by accepting some aspects of their predicament as part of the natural human condition and by gaining a sense of solidarity with others can these characters recover themselves and learn to live successful lives. In the final analysis, affection felt for and received from other human beings may offer the only redemption (albeit a kind of secular redemption) possible for Ford's characters, the only way to survive alienation in an age lacking the belief in a divine presence which once provided a framework for human existence.

In a piece called "Where Does Writing Come From?" Ford quotes Wallace Stevens, who wrote that "in an age of disbelief . . . it is for the poet to supply the satisfactions of belief in his measure and his style" (255). Like Stevens, Ford looks to art, rather than religion, to provide consolation and redemption in a chaotic time. When Stevens, in his poem "The Idea of Order at Key West," writes of "The maker's rage to order words of the sea" (52), he is saying that the poet is driven to bring order to the chaotic world ("the sea") through his use of language. For Ford, Stevens's "blessed rage for order" (51) is fully realized in the very act of telling a story. Ford drives home the importance of telling by quoting from Frank Kermode's *The Sense of an Ending*: "It is not that we are connoisseurs of chaos, but that we are surrounded by it, and equipped for coexistence with it only by our fictive powers" ("Where Does Writing" 255).

Over and over again Ford's works exhibit the author's belief in those "fictive powers," in "the good to be got from telling" ("Reading" 61), that is, in the power of language to order experience, to console and to heal, to bridge the gap between self and other. At the same time, the author expresses his concern for the devaluation of language in the modern world. His fiction demonstrates that while language often fails us, when it succeeds in connecting two human beings on the lonely margins of existence, it can serve to reverse feelings of alienation and dislocation. In the last of his memoirs for *Harper's* (its subtitle, "One More Writer's Beginnings," is a nod to fellow Jacksonian Eudora Welty), Ford describes writing as "an existential errand" involving "dark and lonely work" ("First Things First" 76); and he explains that the main goal of writers is "to discover and bring to precious language the most important things they were capable of, and to reveal this to others with the hope that it will commit an effect on them—please them, teach them, console them. Reach them" ("First Things First" 75). In this way, of course, Ford locates and connects with today's readers as they stand on the lonely edge of a new millennium. A number of the essays in this collection, especially Dupuy's, Walker's, and Folks's, examine the way in which the author makes language, and its power to redeem human loneliness, a central concern of his fiction.

My interview with Ford concludes this volume. Many of the issues discussed in the essays are dealt with in that conversation with the author. Thus, after offering a variety of critical perspectives on Richard Ford's work, *Perspectives on Richard Ford* will allow the writer himself to have the last word.

Huey Guagliardo

1944	Richard Ford born on February 16 in Jackson, Mississippi.
1952	Ford's traveling salesman father, Parker Carrol Ford, suffers a heart attack. As a result, the Fords move into the Marion Hotel (managed by Richard's grandfather) in Little Rock, Arkansas
1960	Ford's father dies of a heart attack on February 20, four days after Richard's sixteenth birthday.
1962	Enrolls at Michigan State University majoring in hotel management but changes major to English.
1966	Teaches junior high school in Flint, Michigan. Enlists in United States Marine Corps, but receives discharge after contracting hepatitis.
1967	Attends Washington University Law School for one semester.
1968	Marries Kristina Hensley and decides to pursue a career as a writer.
1970	Receives M.F.A. degree in creative writing from the University of California at Irvine where he studied with Oakley Hall and E. L. Doctorow.
1974-76	Teaches at the University of Michigan.
1976	*A Piece of My Heart* is published.
1981	Teaches at Princeton University. *The Ultimate Good Luck* is published. Ford, discouraged by his inability to find a significant readership, quits writing fiction to work for *Inside Sports*

magazine.

1982   Ford's mother, Edna, dies. *Inside Sports* ceases publication. Ford begins work on *The Sportswriter.*

1986   *The Sportswriter* is published.

1987   *Rock Springs* is published.

1989   Richard and Kristina Ford move to New Orleans where Kristina now serves as executive director of the New Orleans City Planning Commission.

1990   *Wildlife* is published.

1995   *Independence Day* is published.

1996   Wins Pulitzer Prize and PEN/Faulkner Award for *Independence Day.*

1997   *Women with Men* is published.

Perspectives
on Richard
Ford

In his novels Richard Ford explores the lives of characters who are desperately searching to locate themselves in a world that is often unpredictable and beyond their control. Ford's major novels are tales of betrayal, loss, loneliness, and the search for meaning. The Ford protagonist is a man living on the edge of intimacy, unable to commit to a relationship, and typically estranged from those he loves and who love him. From Robard Hewes and Sam Newel, the alternating centers of revelation in *A Piece of My Heart* (1976), Ford's first novel, to Harry Quinn, the emotionally disabled Vietnam veteran of *The Ultimate Good Luck* (1981), to Frank Bascombe, the narrator and protagonist of both *The Sportswriter* (1986) and *Independence Day* (1995), the only novel ever to be awarded both the Pulitzer Prize and PEN/Faulkner Award, Ford presents his readers with fascinating studies of the modern consciousness.

One of Ford's central themes is perhaps best expressed by Carlos Bernhardt, the philosophical Mexican lawyer of *The Ultimate Good Luck*, who points out that "Everyone is marginal." In other words we are all, metaphorically at least, like the bands of Indians in the novel whom Bernhardt calls the "Marginales" or "Marginal people" (106), scratching out a precarious existence on the "edge of the city" (105) while death always lurks in the shadows. Of course, it is how we deal with our marginality that is of ultimate importance. The phrase "marginal people" fits Ford's spiritually and emotionally impoverished characters in at least two ways. Living in an age which is absent the religious faith

The Marginal People in the Novels of Richard Ford

Huey Guagliardo

3

that once served as a centering force, an age in which the presence of even a "lonely, faraway and inattentive god" (*Independence* 292) is seldom felt, the characters in Ford's novels are relegated to the shadowy margins of existence where much is uncertain and uncontrollable. They often fall victim to life's sheer randomness, but they also choose to live another kind of peripheral existence, on the edge of affection, because they become so caught up in the obsessive struggle to control their lives that a fully human interaction with others is lost to them. They must learn to cope with chance, change, and the heavy finality of death without surrendering their humanity. Only when they find themselves on the farthest edge of loneliness and despair, however, do they reach out to another in the darkness.

Undeniably, a certain ambivalence concerning the issue of marginality is inherent in Ford's texts. While the individual struggles of Ford's characters for control and for a more centered existence convey the notion that marginality is a condition that human beings should strive to overcome, in a broader sense the novels suggest that the marginality resulting from life's uncertainty is an inevitable part of the human predicament. Indeed, there is often the sense in Ford's work that not only should marginality be accepted, but it might even be beneficial in leading one toward discovery and growth. Although his texts dramatize the individual's search for wholeness, locatedness, and centeredness (implying that it is possible for a person to move out of marginality into a more "central" or controlled existence), at the same time these texts depict a culture in which fragmentation and dislocation are pervasive states, a culture in which, to borrow a well-known line from Yeats's "The Second Coming," "Things fall apart; the centre cannot hold." Human beings are often relegated to the margins because what center there is has become a "calamitous center" (*Piece* 45), a maelstrom. Ford's power as a writer derives, in part, from his depiction of this existential dilemma, this struggle to reconcile the irreconcilable. The strength of Ford's writing also derives from the fact that, in spite of his ambivalence about the nature of marginality, he is constant in expressing the view that life on the lonely edge is best survived through a sense of connectedness with others. Again and again, the survivors in Ford's fiction not only learn to accept the precarious re-

Marginal People in Ford's Novels

ality of the human condition, but ultimately they come to know one another. In keeping with the twentieth-century tradition of the novel of alienation, Ford's end-of-the-century fiction depicts the modern human predicament as a struggle to come to terms with one's fate and with the surrounding chaos.

Ford's works also offer a penetrating commentary on contemporary culture. Individually and cumulatively, these works document the failures of our culture by displaying so well the peculiar afflictions which have spread so rapidly through life in the modern world: the individual's sense of alienation, restlessness, displacement, and fragmentation; the sense of rootlessness, of being cut off from the past, which so often characterizes life in an increasingly mobile society; the disintegration of community; the breakup of the family; and the impoverishment of all human connections. Ironically, the more Ford's exiled and rootless characters pursue their own identities and struggle to gain independence and control of their lives, the more marginalized they become, the more estranged from others and from themselves. They must journey toward the discovery that genuine self-realization, freedom, and wholeness can be attained, not by disconnecting from others, but by bonding with others. Such is the key to surviving a life on the margins.

It is interesting to note that the image of marginality, so pervasive a metaphor in Ford's fiction, is also used by the author to express his view of the writer's role in modern society, as well as his view of literature in general. In an article entitled "What We Write, Why We Write It, and Who Cares," he again expresses ambivalence about a life on the margins by asserting that writers "accept—even if [they] don't exactly relish—marginality in our culture" (52). He believes that the writer must resist cultural and political threats to artistic freedom even if in doing so he risks "being ignored and castigated" (49). Perhaps the writer is willing to accept, even to choose, a certain form of marginalization—social, economic, aesthetic—because, as Ford, alluding to Robert Browning, explains:"the nature of art is to be on the 'dangerous edge of things'" (53). In art, as in life, it is on the precarious edge that new discoveries are made and growth becomes possible; and, Ford insists, literature's "high aim" is "discovering something important" (52). In this same essay, he expresses his belief that it is "literature's spirit" to allow for "the possibility of a change for the better," for "as writers we're not so much devoted to those qualities in humans which are merely subject to change, as we're devoted to those more precious qualities subject to growth, to whatever can be altered by events but not destroyed by them" (44). In Ford's own novels, discovery and growth are most likely to occur when the individual is pushed to the very brink of alienation and despair.

Ford has often expressed his belief in literature's potential to release readers from their isolation and lift them out of their despair by helping them to connect with other human beings. "I want my stories," he says, "to affect readers in the way great literature has affected me: to be the ax for the frozen sea within us; to be as Durenmatt wrote, a rebel against death" ("What We Write" 52). In an essay in which he discusses Sherwood Anderson's "Death in the Woods," Ford writes that the story concerns "the ways by which we each nurture others" and "the good to be got from telling" ("Reading" 61). For Ford, literature can help one to survive feelings of marginalization largely through the affirmative power of language, which has the capacity to reverse alienation and help the individual to locate himself or herself in the world by establishing a sense of connectedness with others. This is especially evident in *Independence Day*, in which Ford has former writer Frank Bascombe echo the same "ax for the frozen sea" (320) metaphor quoted above, and in which Frank often expresses his faith in the power of language to console and to heal. In an *Esquire* essay, Ford explains that "the singular value of written words, and their benefit to lived life" did not become clear to him until he read William Faulkner's *Absalom, Absalom!*, "which . . . sets out to testify by act to the efficacy of telling, and to recommend language for its powers of consolation against whatever's ailing you" ("The Three Kings" 581). Although Ford believes in the "efficacy of telling," at the same time he recognizes that language is often ineffective. Frank Bascombe, for example, is a character who understands the importance of language in reaching others as well as its limitations. In *The Sportswriter*, Frank, who accepts the fact that sometimes there is "Just nothing to say" (369), also understands that "Some things can't be explained. They just are. . . . [that] Literature's consolations are always temporary, while life is quick to begin again" (223). Nevertheless, it is clear that Ford regards language as essential to surviving on the margins, for often it succeeds in creating a redemptive link between two human beings on the lonely edge of life.

In the allegorical *A Piece of My Heart*, Robard Hewes and Sam Newel are desperately alienated characters whose quests to recover passion in their lives return them to their roots in the Deep South. Robard, driven by "a kind of ruinous anxiety that just one thing will satisfy" (15), leaves his wife of eight years and his job in California to travel three thousand miles in order to indulge his lust for Beuna, a woman, now married, with whom he had a torrid affair twelve years earlier. The suicidal Sam leaves his girlfriend and law school in Chicago, hoping to reenter the world and find a reason to go on living. The lives of Sam and Robard converge on an uncharted island in the state of Mississippi, an island formed over a century before when the Mississippi River abruptly changed its course.

The island and the river are clearly the central metaphors in this novel. Ford suggests that there is much in human experience which, like the river, cannot be fully understood or controlled. *A Piece of My Heart* contains many references to the unpredictable meandering of the river. These references serve as expressions of life's randomness and of the marginality inherent in human experience. In addition, they serve to foreshadow the novel's many ironical twists and turns. One key passage concerns a story that Robard heard while working in the Helena switchyards. After the river suddenly changed course one night, so the story goes, the townspeople gradually began to move down off the kudzu bluff where the original town was located and to settle where the river had once flowed. When everyone had moved down off the bluff, they decided to change the name of the new town in the bottom to Helena and to call the original town on the bluff West Helena. According to the men who worked in the switchyards, this movement became known as "The Great Comedown," and they "swore that the town, by coming off the bluff, had exercised bad judgment and would have to suffer misfortune because . . . the town now existed at the pleasure of the river, and they believed anything that owed to the river would have to pay, and when it paid, the price would be steep." When Robard relates this story to Beuna, she responds with "a pained look" and says, "Ah, shit, Robard. We're all dying sooner or later. Them assholes think they figured the reason. But I'm satisfied there ain't no reason" (54-55). Beuna is obviously much more accepting of life's absurdities than Robard, and she is much less concerned with being in control.

While the imagery of the meandering river emphasizes life's randomness and impermanence, the uncharted island represents human beings' futile attempts to control their destinies by cutting themselves off from the flow of humanity. As old man Lamb, the owner of the island, declares when it is pointed out to him that he has been shooting deer out of season: "It's *my* land. It's open season on anything I take a notion to shoot. Piss on deer season and every other season. I'll shoot what I want to shoot. . . . This here is *my* island and I don't care about nobody but myself, by God . . ." (130). But the old man is more dependent on others (such as his wife, his black servant, T.V.A., and occasional hunting companions) than he cares to admit; and, as the reader discovers later, Mr. Lamb merely holds a fifty-year lease on the island, a lease which, like Mr. Lamb himself, is soon to expire.

Clearly, Sam Newel is obsessed with trying to understand his life, while Robard Hewes is obsessed with trying to control his. Each typifies the alienated, fragmented man of the modern world trying to recover his sense of wholeness. Sam's girlfriend, Beebe, who sends him to her grandparents' island to "compose" (84) himself, tells him that he has a "poor tolerance for ambiguity" and a tendency to "make things terrible when they're only slightly confusing" (71). The overweight, hypochondriacal Sam, however, sees himself as "flying apart a mile a millisecond" (72) and as suffering an "inventory of afflictions" (182). He searches through his childhood memories of his traveling salesman father for clues that will help him to solve the puzzle of his own fractured existence, but he is unable to put the pieces of the puzzle together to form a coherent picture. Lyrical memory passages appear throughout the novel as italicized snapshots of isolated scenes from Sam's childhood, accentuating Sam's sense of fragmentation. As he puts it, "I . . . end up thinking about just parts all the time. There's something easy about them I don't understand, and I can't hold them together well enough to figure out what it is" (80). For Robard, however, contemplating the past is of little use in managing the present. According to Robard, "[T]hings just happen. One minute don't learn the next one nothin" (230). His sense of life's randomness makes him determined to live in the moment, for that is his only hope for control; but living in the moment precludes commitment, making it impossible for him to sustain a relationship with another: "He didn't like the idea that whatever had turned [Beuna's] life into a hurricane had turned his the same way and made a part of his own existence sag out of control down into the sink of unmanageables" (157). His inability to control his feelings for Beuna causes him to view her "as an impediment or as something to be survived" (15-16). Robard's desire for control, for "managing everything" (197), as Sam puts it, causes him to resist genuine intimacy with others, and will not permit him to make a commitment to another human being, either to his wife or to Beuna. A typical Ford protagonist, Robard has erected a protective emotional barrier between himself and others. When Beuna asks, "Do you love me?" he responds by saying either "All right" (11) or, if he is in a less intimate mood, "I can't talk about that" (46). The language of intimacy eludes him, and he finds himself facing a terrible dilemma. He can remain isolated on the margins where he deceives himself about being in control, or he can allow himself to be sucked into "the calamitous center," into the maelstrom that is hurricane Buena. Either way, he feels "alone and unprotected" (45).

Neither Sam nor Robard has learned to appreciate or to participate fully in everyday life, nor can they accept what cannot be understood or controlled. As Mr. Lamb tells Robard in explaining why the birds wake up singing: "Because . . . they're happy to be alive one more day. You can't count on that, Hewes. Them little birdies know it, too. That's why they're out there singing all the time. They're trying to tell us something. 'Tweet, tweet, you're alive, you ignorant asshole'" (142). In a later scene, the old man relates to Sam the enigmatic story of the late Johnny Carter's hopelessly marginal existence. Carter, who was Mrs. Lamb's "half-wit" (213) cousin, married a Choctaw girl who died while giving birth. After his wife's Indian relatives absconded with the infant, Carter confronted them in their Mississippi hometown, emblematically named Rough Edge, where he murdered four of the relatives with a shotgun and retrieved the baby, which he then brought to his father to raise. Mr. Lamb points out that after the shooting he allowed Carter to hide out on the island in a little cabin behind the Lambs' own house. According to Mr. Lamb, Carter would remain in that location until his death forty-five years later. Sam reacts to the story with shocked disbelief that the law was never brought into the matter: "Four people get blown up because some psychopath cousin wants his old man to take care of his baby, and you deprive the law the chance to settle with him" (215). Mr. Lamb, emphasizing the fact that Carter, although "nuttier'n a pet coon" (215), nevertheless was family, asks Sam what he would have done in the same situation. Sam replies: "I'd have gotten him a good lawyer . . . had him plead dementia praecox, put him on the stand, and told him to act crazy" (216). The old man, who sees his own very human solution as superior to Sam's bureaucratic one, tells the overly analytical Sam, "You're a fish, Newel, by God. You belong back up in Lake Michigan where it's cold and wet, not down here where people's got blood" (216).

Their quests for understanding and control keep Sam and Robard on the periphery of life. A shattered heart, as the novel's title suggests, makes it difficult to form connections with others; yet each man seems to understand the other better than he understands himself. "Just cause you think up some question don't mean there's an answer" (230), Robard tells Sam; and Sam, who detects a "Heartbroken" (262) quality about Robard, says to him: "If you like things so goddamned manageable, just what're you doing down here?" (197). "Down here," of course, might refer to our mutable planet as well as to the state of Mississippi. Ironically, Robard ends up being killed, not by the jealous husband whom he has planned so carefully to avoid, but by a boy who takes him to be a poacher on the very land that Robard himself has been hired to protect. The precarious and random nature of human existence is further demonstrated when, near the end of the novel, Sam watches helplessly as Mr. Lamb accidentally electrocutes himself while fishing. The old man's demise is reduced to the indignity of his final utterance of surprise: "Oops" (249). Sam ultimately realizes that he has reached the edge of his despair. He is appropriately on the "edge" of his cot when he decides that, even though he hasn't solved the puzzle of his life, he will return to Chicago, to Beebe

Marginal People in Ford's Novels

and law school "and get started in the way he felt fated," sensing "a squeamish serenity in . . . choosing the only thing left, when everything else was eliminated and not by any act, but just by the time and place." He is said to feel the "compromise satisfaction" of a person "washed up on the beach of some country after spending weeks floating around on a tree limb, too far from home ever to be deposited *there*, and satisfied to be on land, no matter really which land it happened to be" (225). This passage epitomizes the existential dilemma so often at the heart of Ford's narratives, for it implies that while Sam is better off once he accepts his situation, he is no less marginalized. The beach, after all, represents another kind of margin; and Sam is but a castaway far from home, far from the center, if such a place even exists. Ford has described adult life as "a poor, compromised state of being" ("Reading" 61); and, of course, it was Freud who said that the satisfactions of adulthood are to be achieved primarily through love and work, which for Sam Newel may be found in Beebe and the law. Perhaps Ford is suggesting in his first novel that it would be foolish of any human being to expect much more.

The protagonist of *The Ultimate Good Luck* is another alienated character living his life on the edge and, like Robard Hewes and Sam Newel, finding himself "on the periphery without a peripheral perspective" (36), that is, without the insight necessary for coping with life's uncertainties. Harry Quinn is a Vietnam veteran in Mexico trying to free his ex-girlfriend Rae's cocaine-smuggling brother from prison. Harry's life can be measured by a series of one-night stands. Like Robard Hewes, Harry is obsessed with controlling his life, and he prides himself on living in the present, for "In the present, he knew precisely how it would all feel every time: the contact, then the being alone, then somebody else coming in to fill up the space. That was manageable, and you felt lucky and not anxious" (10). Just as for Robard, it is a woman who interferes with Harry's ability to manage things: "Rae had left a space he couldn't quite manage anymore. And he'd come down for Sonny [Rae's brother] just to get Rae, since Rae seemed essential to the present, and since he was tired of being alone with himself" (11). Through his plan to free Rae's brother, Harry hopes to change both his luck and his life, at least for the moment.

Because of his desire for control, Harry finds it as difficult as did Robard Hewes to tie himself to commitments or to risk intimacy. Not surprisingly, his life of "efficiency" is revealed as a pattern of false starts and failures in those two most significant areas of human experience, work and love. After the horror of Vietnam he worked at a series of dead-end jobs, from supplying pipe to oil fields in Louisiana, to repossessing cars in Los Angeles, to running a deer tag station in Michigan. His failed relationship with Rae is encapsulated in the following exchange:

"Do you love me?" she said. She had begun to cry. "You don't like to say it, do you?" she said. "It scares you. You don't want to need it."

"I can take care of me," he said. (69)

Harry believes that "the only dangerous lie to being in love was that it was permanent. . . . He knew love's limits, and that was the key to everything" (80). His desire to live for the moment, which he can control, is incompatible with the kind of commitment necessary to achieving an intimate relationship. For Harry, "Intimacy just made things hard to see, and he wanted things kept highly visible at all times" (21). Harry's cynical detachment from others, his attempt to avoid emotional entanglements, keeps him on the periphery of life.

Harry's effort to stay in control is seriously challenged by the situation which he encounters in Mexico. Mexico, in fact, serves as a metaphor for chance, for life's randomness, in *The Ultimate Good Luck*: "Mexico was like Vietnam or L.A., only more disappointing—a great trivial abundance of crap the chief effect of which wasn't variety but sameness. And since you couldn't remember the particulars from one day to the next, you couldn't remember what to avoid and control. And the only consolation finally was that you didn't have any stake in it, and Quinn didn't figure to be around long enough to earn one" (15). The problem for Harry is that there is more at stake than he realizes.

Harry hires a Mexican attorney, the philosophical Carlos Bernhardt, to help him bribe Sonny out of prison, but Harry and Carlos soon find themselves on "the periphery of things out of control" (15-16). The bribery scheme is doomed to failure, entangled as it is in an elaborate web of greed and deceit. Bernhardt is murdered, and it is clear at the end of the novel that Sonny has met the same fate. Shortly before his death, however, Bernhardt, a man who desires intimacy as strongly as Harry resists it, decides, in what is clearly the novel's central scene, to share his philosophy of life with Harry. "I will show you a thing," says Bernhardt as he drives Harry and Rae to "the edge of the city" (105) where bands of Indians live a scavenger existence. These are people who have little control over their own lives, who "have no rights, only needs." Bernhardt describes the Indians as "Marginales" or the "Marginal people," and we are told that for him the sight of these people camped in their makeshift cardboard hovels constituted "an understatement of a much more illuminating truth." When the significance of the scene seems lost on Harry, Bernhardt explains that "Everyone is marginal," and when Harry still refuses to understand Bernhardt's lesson, the lawyer is more direct: "You see in a tunnel. Outside what you see, things are not one way, but other ways at once. You need to be tolerant" (106). In other words, Harry fails to recognize the essence of his predicament, that is, his intolerance for the uncertainty that is a necessary part of the condition of being human. He lives on the periphery of intimacy because he cannot tolerate the uncertainty of another's love.

The "Marginales" episode is preceded and followed by scenes that are designed to emphasize Harry's detachment from others. In the earlier incident, Bernhardt takes Harry beyond "the peripheral boulevard at the boundary of the slum barrios" (91) to see the body of a murdered boy who had sold cocaine to Sonny. As they drive back toward town, Bernhardt shares some details of his personal life with Harry: "My father is dead, now, two years . . . . I have to leave my government career to come and support my mother and my brothers. I am like you in that way. I don't want to. But I am involved." Harry's only reply is, "I don't know what the fuck you're talking about." When Harry, referring to the dead boy, asks: "So why do I have to see that? Just for laughs?" Bernhardt explains: "You will know what I am trying to do for you now . . . . You see what I have to see. You are involved" (96-97). In the later scene, Bernhardt takes from his desk drawer the picture of a half-nude woman and shows it to Harry as a sign of trust. "That doesn't mean shit to me," says Harry. For Bernhardt, however, "It is an intimacy . . . . As if we were friends" (124). Bernhardt tries to help Harry to understand the importance of intimacy and the importance of being involved in the lives of others.

Through Bernhardt's death and through his love for Rae, Harry gradually comes to recognize the wisdom of the lawyer's philosophy. From Bernhardt he learns that "everybody lives in some relation to the luckless," and that "when you *tried* to protect yourself completely and never suffer a loss or a threat, you ended up with nothing. Or worse, you ended up being absorbed right into nothing, into the very luckless thing you were most afraid of" (127). After witnessing Bernhardt's being murdered by a young man with a machine gun, Harry and Rae walk away from the scene quickly in order to avoid the soldiers and the police who will soon be swarming the area. Harry recognizes Bernhardt's killer standing under a street light a few blocks from the murder scene. Although he feels the impulse to shoot the man, Harry's desire to protect Rae from harm is stronger than his desire for revenge:

He held her and pressed her shoulders against the [shop's] window glass, and put his face close to hers for a long time, trying to join her breathing to his breathing, and calm her, staring through the cheap pane into an empty barbershop, at the chair and the white walls and the mirrors where he could see his reflection. And then by degrees he heard the soft suspiring night sigh of the city begin again, and Rae became erect and cool in his arms, and he could smell her breath hot and not sweet, and for a moment, with her close to him, his cheek on the cold glass, he felt himself fully located for once, and in a world in which time couldn't pass. (157)

A short time later, Harry muses about Bernhardt's death: "Bernhardt's absence made him feel marooned close to the clean, satisfied edge of exhausted possibility, beyond affection or sorrow, the stalemate edge of all loses, the point where time froze on whatever was present, and nothing could be longed for or feared or protected against, where luck was not the thing you played" (161). Harry's feeling of being "marooned" can be compared to Sam Newel's identification with the castaway who, after weeks floating in the ocean, is satisfied to be anyplace, no matter how far away from home. Both men come to accept the marginal nature of human existence, and, in doing so, learn to give themselves up to another. Harry realizes that his being driven to the edge of possibility by

Marginal People in Ford's Novels

events beyond his control "was the best luck there was," the ultimate good luck, for it allows him to surrender himself to Rae's love and to locate himself in the world: "And sometime in the afternoon he'd get on the plane with Rae, then that would be all that mattered anymore, an intimacy that didn't need an outside frame" (161).

Significantly, *The Ultimate Good Luck* concludes on Harry's birthday, a symbol of his rebirth. Rae reminds Harry that it is his birthday, and she asks: "Do you think you're old enough to live your life now?" For Harry, the castaway, "Love seemed to him like a place to be, a place where nothing troublesome could come inside." The novel ends with this exchange:

> "Do you think you're old enough to live your life unprotected, Harry?" she said. "You can't back off from what scares you."
> "Nothing scares me," he said.
> "Happy birthday, then," she said. "Happy birthday to you." She got out of bed to come with him. (201)

In a 1987 interview, Ford, in responding to a question about the characters in one of his short stories, offers some insights which apply just as well to the major characters in his novels. He says that what interests him most about his characters is that they are "people on the edge; things could really get worse, or things could get a little better." He goes on to explain that the people in his stories are ultimately redeemed by affection: "Without that affection, without making that little crucial contact, that day passes and the next day starts and then things may go from bad to worse. I believe, in my heart of hearts, that it's just those little moments of time, those little, almost invisible, certainly omittable, connections between people which save your life or don't, and that if your life has a habit of seizing those little moments, then, I think, life can go on for you, have the possibility of being better" (Bonetti 95-96).

Such a connection with another human being makes redemption possible not only for Harry Quinn, but for all of the other marginal people in Ford's fiction.

Although the central characters in Ford's first two novels are roundly developed and interesting enough in themselves, none of them can match the "truth of a lived life" (*Sportswriter* 360) that is Ford's greatest achievement in the creation of Frank Bascombe, the narrator and protagonist of both *The Sportswriter* and *Independence Day*. Another one of Richard Ford's "marginal people," Frank lives a "normal applauseless life" (*Sportswriter* 10) in the prosperous suburban community of Haddam, New Jersey, on the city's edge, where "the rule that *location is everything* gets taken seriously" (*Sportswriter* 50). Certainly Ford's Frank Bascombe novels effectively dramatize the impoverishment of human relationships in contemporary culture, for, like Harry Quinn, Frank has chosen his own location on the periphery of life. He maintains a protective distance from others and resists genuine intimacy. The first-person narrative structures of both novels serve to emphasize Frank's somewhat self-absorbed, peripheral view of the world and to record his psychological and spiritual journey.

In *The Sportswriter*, Frank explains to the reader how he finally "faced up to a great empty moment in life" (369) and learned in the process to accept, rather than to resist, the mystery at the heart of human experience. More than any of Ford's major characters, Frank has learned to accommodate himself to life's uncertainties, and he has had more than his share of bereavement. He has suffered the loss of his young son, has endured a painful divorce from "X" (as he refers to his ex-wife throughout his narrative), and is adjusting to being separated from his two remaining children. Furthermore, before the end of the novel, he is forced to deal with the suicide of a troubled friend. Yet, Frank "Faced down regret. Avoided ruin" and survived "to tell about it" (4). Ford's observation that "as writers we're not so much devoted to those qualities in humans which are subject to change, as we're devoted to those more precious qualities subject to growth, to whatever can be altered by events but not destroyed by them" ("What We Write" 44) is especially relevant to Frank Bascombe, whose growth and development span two novels and exceed that of any of the author's previous characters.

The Sportswriter is a novel about death, life's "one certain closure" (374), but it is also a novel about the possibility of rebirth. While *The Ultimate Good Luck* ends, symbolically, with a reference to the protagonist's birthday, *The Sportswriter* begins, symbolically, with references to two birthdays. The novel opens on Good Friday, the day of Christ's death on

Marginal People in Ford's Novels

the cross, but this Good Friday also happens to mark the thirteenth birthday of Frank's son Ralph, who died at the age of nine. Frank also mentions that his own birthday is only two weeks away. Equally significant is the fact that roughly half of the story takes place on Easter Sunday. These juxtapositions of death and birth, of the crucifixion and resurrection that represent the Christian paradox that we must lose our lives in order to gain them, provide the background for this secular tale of loss and recovery in suburban America.

Frank, who was once said to have "a promising literary career" (4), retreated from "the ambiguous stuff of complex literature" (42-43) to take refuge in the literalness of sportswriting and New Jersey. He claims that he turned to sportswriting because he "didn't know with certainty what to say about the large world and didn't care to risk speculating" (51-52). He asserts that sportswriting has taught him that "there are no transcendent themes in life. In all cases things are here and they're over, and that has to be enough" (16). Like Ford's other protagonists, Frank opts for the here and now and prefers not to dwell on the past: "All we really want is to get to the point where the past can explain nothing about us and we can get on with life. . . . In my view Americans put too much emphasis on their pasts as a way of defining themselves, which can be death-dealing" (24).

Although Frank became a sportswriter in order to get back into the world, he was only partially successful. In Ford's novel, sportswriting is used to represent yet another type of peripheral existence. A sportswriter, of course, always observes from the sidelines, never actually getting involved in the action. Frank himself, in fact, has come to regard sportswriting as a peripheral occupation—"not as a real profession" (312)—that allows him to maintain a safe distance from those around him. As he puts it, "To be a sportswriter, sad to say it, is to live your life mostly with your thoughts, and only the edge of others'" (348). Frank's ex-wife considers him to be "a loner" (12), and his relationships with others tend to be superficial. "I don't have any relationships at all" (328), he confesses at one point. He is a member of a small group called the Divorced Men's Club, but admits that the five men in the club "hardly know each other and sometimes can barely keep the ball moving before a drink arrives" (79). When one of those men, Walter Luckett, insists on unburdening himself to Frank, it is with great reluctance that Frank decides to listen, afterwards concluding that the true measure of friendship is "the amount of precious time you'll squander on someone else's calamities and fuck-ups" (97). Even Frank's romance with Vicki Arcenault, whom he claims to love, is based on little more than a superficial physical attraction. Their relationship is a type of shallow and transitory affair that has become commonplace in modern life.

Frank often refers to a period of "dreaminess," or alienation, that he endured after his son's death. He defines that dreaminess as "a state of suspended recognition, and a response to too much useless and complicated factuality" (42). Indiscriminate sex was a symptom of Frank's alienation during this period of dreaminess, and it was his way of avoiding emotional commitments. He admits that during his "wandering two-year period" of dreaminess, he "must've slept with eighteen different women" (128) in a desperate attempt to reenter the world by bridging the gap between immanence and dreamy transcendence. At that time he also had an obsessive desire to immerse himself in the lives of the women he was dating, to demand full disclosure. But that, he now realizes, was a terrible mistake: "What I was doing . . . was trying to be within myself by being as nearly as possible *within* somebody else. It is not a new approach to romance. And it doesn't work. In fact, it leads to a terrible dreaminess and the worst kind of abstraction and unreachableness." Frank's attempt to substitute factuality, what he calls "full-disclosure" (130) for real intimacy was merely an exercise in self-deception which allowed him to "simulate intimacy" (129) with another human being while remaining on the margins of meaningful involvement.

Now that Frank has emerged from the state of dreaminess, he opts for mystery as opposed to full disclosure. "I have relinquished a great deal," he says. "I've stopped worrying about being completely *within* someone else since you can't be anyway—a pleasant unquestioning mystery has been the result" (132). "Mystery," he says, "is the attractive condition a thing (an object, an action, a person) possesses which you know a little about but don't know about completely. It is the twiney promise of unknown things (effects, interworkings, suspicions) which you must be wise

Marginal People in Ford's Novels

enough to explore not too deeply, for fear you will dead-end in nothing but facts" (101-102). Frank is a man "always vitally interested in life's mysteries" (42). Mystery and her sister anticipation, "the sweet pain to know whatever's next" (43), are, for Frank, what make life worth living. "I hate for things to get finally pinned down," he says, "for possibilities to be narrowed by the shabby impingement of facts—even the simple fact of comradeship. I am always hoping for a great surprise to open in what has always been a possible place for it—comradeship among professionals; friendship among peers; passion and romance" (83). But, as Frank eventually realizes, an appreciation for mystery does not negate the need for an intimate life, even though his peripheral existence as a sportswriter makes such a connection difficult to attain.

Frank's peripheral life is jolted, however, when his friend Walter Luckett commits suicide on Easter Sunday, a day traditionally representing promise and renewal. Although the two men were not particularly close, Frank is sent reeling when he learns that Walter is dead. Just as when his son Ralph died, "awful, mealy factual death" (351) once again intrudes its presence upon Frank's life. In desperation he reaches out to Vicki Arcenault, even though he knows that their relationship is about to end. She punches him in the mouth as he tries to put his arms around her. While heading home, after being rejected by Vicki, he stops at a phone booth to call Selma Jassim, a woman with whom he had an affair during the worst depths of his dreaminess; but this ends up being another exercise in futility. Frank finds himself on the "outer edge" (305) of a town at ground zero, literally "Ground Zero Burg" (300), a burger joint near the phone booth, "sunk in the secular aimlessness of Sunday that Easter only worsens for the lonely of the world" (305). His only successful human contact on this day is with Debra Spanelis, the seventeen-year-old carhop at Ground Zero who ministers to him by bringing him a root-beer float after he is injured in a freak accident with a grocery cart. "Who would've thought a root-beer float could restore both faith and health" (307), he says. Ground Zero seems to suggest a new starting point for Frank in terms of his relationships with others. The man who insists that he is "*not* a problem solver" (300) even offers some fatherly advice to Debra, who, like himself, is "available for an improvement" (311).

With the feeling that his future "remains unassured" (313), Frank drives home to Haddam, visits X and his children, then goes with X to see Walter's apartment in search of a better understanding of "the complicated human dilemma" (338). Frank and X seem on the edge of renewed intimacy. When X asks Frank if he understands Walter's suicide, Frank replies, "I think so" and goes on to explain that "Walter gave himself up to the here and now, but got stranded" (334). Obviously feeling a bit stranded himself, Frank impulsively suggests to X that they make love in Walter's apartment. Horrified by the suggestion, X walks out. "Left alone in the cool silence of dead Walter's yard," Frank sees himself as "a man with no place to go in particular" (338). Then feeling "as invisible as Claude Rains in the movie," as invisible as God himself in the modern world, Frank drives the "post-Easter streets of Haddam" with the knowledge that "God does not help those who are invisible too" (339). Frank's feeling of invisibility is reminiscent of Harry Quinn's sense of being "absorbed into nothing," a sensation which Quinn learns is the result of protectively insulating himself from others. Frank drives to the train station and hurriedly boards the night train to New York, just as a woman (whom he incorrectly imagines to be Walter's sister) is about to ask his assistance. He justifies his reluctance to make this connection by convincing himself that "it's better not to take a chance. You can take too many chances and end up with nothing but regret to keep you company through a night that simply—for the life of you—won't end" (346). While on the train, however, Frank recalls a "perilous dream" that he often had during his worst period of dreamy alienation. The dream involved his being in bed with a strange woman whom he could not touch but whom he had to "lie beside for hours and hours on end in a state of fear and excitation and scalding guilt." Frank remembers that he would wake from this dream "on the edge of the bed . . . cramped and achy as though clinging at the edge of a lifeboat on a vast and moody sea" (351), familiar Ford images representing the marginal nature of existence. Craving human contact when he arrives in the city, Frank goes to the office of the sports magazine where he works, for "Writers—all writers—need to belong" (354).

Significantly, Walter Luckett is buried on Frank's thirty-ninth birthday. "Walter's death," asserts Frank, "had the effect on me that death means to have; of reminding me of my responsibility to a somewhat larger world" (366). Indeed, after Walter's funeral Frank gives up his peripheral life as a sportswriter and travels to Florida in an attempt to grant a request that Walter had made in his suicide note. While in Florida Frank meets some of his relatives; he discovers that he is "glad to have a past" (371) and that having a past "is not a burden" (371) after all. By the end of the novel, Frank Bascombe is still a work in progress. He is a man who, through "a good whacking loss" (9), comes to understand that "Some things can't be explained. They just are" (223), and that "Some life is only life, and unconjugatable, just as to some questions there are no answers. Just nothing to say" (369). By relinquishing his desire for complete understanding and control, that is, for full disclosure, and yielding to life's uncertainties, Frank remains open to the possibility of his own resurrection and renewal, realizing that "A life can simply change the way a day changes—sunny to rain, like the song says. But it can also change again" (107). Once again, Ford is suggesting that we must surrender to life in order to live it. The novel concludes with an image of rebirth, as Frank, whose birthday has come and gone, describes the sensation that a person sometimes has of shedding the skin of his regrets and beginning anew with that "feeling of wind on your cheeks and your arms, of being released, let loose, of being the light-floater" (375).

The psychological and spiritual journey of Ford's suburban Everyman, Frank Bascombe, progresses further in *Independence Day*, the author's most richly developed novel. Five years have passed, and Frank is now forty-four, and his son, Paul, briefly introduced in *The Sportswriter* as a tenderhearted ten-year-old who tries to contact his dead brother by carrier pigeon, is now a troubled teen who has been arrested for shoplifting. Paul is also prone to emit "unexpected barking noises" (13), and he spends a great deal of his time "thinking he's thinking" (14), that is, monitoring his thoughts in an attempt to gain understanding and control of his life. Like *The Sportswriter*, this novel also takes place over a holiday weekend. Its events begin on a Friday and end on Monday, the 4th of July, 1988. This time it is the nation's birthday that marks an important passage in the life of a Ford character. As Frank says, it is "a weekend when my own life seems at a turning or at least a curving point" (226). The 4th of July/election year setting also provides Ford with ample opportunity to render the state of American culture in the latter half of the twentieth century; and *Independence Day* is clearly the novelist's most insightful commentary to date on contemporary life, with particular emphasis upon the dissolution of those important human connections long sustained by families and communities. A major portion of the plot involves an automobile trip that Frank and Paul take to the basketball and baseball halls of fame as part of the absent father's attempt to bond with the son he feels is rapidly slipping away from him. That Frank chooses this quintessentially American pilgrimage—the 4th of July, the possibilities of the open road, the halls of fame—as his means of bonding with Paul demonstrates the extent to which Ford's protagonist embraces suburban America's ideals even as his own experiences reveal the culture's many failures and breakdowns.

Frank's own life has changed considerably over the five-year period. His ex-wife, Ann (he now uses her first name), remarried and moved with Frank's two children from Haddam, New Jersey, to Connecticut, after which Frank moved into the house formerly owned by Ann and quit his job as a sportswriter to become a "Residential Specialist" (91) for a real estate firm. As a result of these events, Frank has entered a phase of his life that is even more passive than his life as a sportswriter. He refers to this phase as "the Existence Period," which implies, among other things, a midlife willingness "to let matters go as they go and see what happens" (10-11). In *Independence Day*, Frank's "relocation"—new home and new point of view—as well as his new job in an industry that supposedly stresses the notion that "location is everything" are extremely significant in expressing Ford's concern with the question of what it really means to locate oneself and gain one's independence in a complex and often dangerous world.

As the novel begins, we see that life in still-quite-prosperous Haddam has been somewhat devalued, along with its real estate. Crime and violence have spread even to this once-quiet suburb. The modern world is a dangerous place, and there seems to be no escape from life's randomness. Frank himself has been mugged, his neighbors burglarized, and a colleague/ex-girlfriend raped and murdered. Haddam, in short, has

Marginal People in Ford's Novels

failed to protect its residents from the violence and uncertainty of the world. It is a community on the edge; or, as Frank expresses it: "there's a new sense of a wild world being just beyond our perimeter, an untallied apprehension among our residents, one I believe they'll never get used to, one they'll die before accommodating" (5). As in Ford's other novels, there is once again a strong sense of the marginality of human existence, a marginality that Frank, once a writer, understands more keenly than most of his neighbors. The Existence Period is Frank's newest way of coping with life's unpredictability and with his own feeling of being "*waaaay out there at the edge*" (111).

According to Frank, selling real estate is the "ideal occupation" (111) for someone gliding along in the Existence Period. Frank regards the real estate profession, like sportswriting, as a peripheral occupation, as "being on the periphery of the business community" (115). Frank explains that "the one gnostic truth of real estate" is "that people never find or buy the house they say they want." Instead, "The premise is that you're presented with what you might've thought you didn't want, but what's available, whereupon you give in and start finding ways to feel good about it and yourself." To Frank, this scheme makes perfect sense: "Why should you only get what you think you want, or be limited by what you can simply plan on? Life's never like that, and if you're smart you'll decide it's better the way it is" (41). Being a realtor also provides Frank with the perfect position from which to observe the "dislocatedness" (55) so prevalent in modern suburban life. As a realtor he must constantly deal with people who, like himself, are trying to find their place, to locate themselves; but he soon discovers that no one is really at home, that in a sense we are all homeless nomads searching desperately for what he refers to as that "homey connectedness" (93). Always an astute observer of contemporary American society, Ford finds the realty profession to be the ideal vehicle for commenting on the rootlessness and sense of longing that are characteristic of an increasingly mobile population.

Frank's view of reality and of realty, his Existence Period philosophy that we seldom get what we plan on and might as well learn to accept the fact, is dramatized in a comical episode involving a couple from Vermont, Joe and Phyllis Markham, who are searching for a dream house that does

not exist in the Haddam market. The episode also points to the disintegration of families and communities in American culture, as well as to
a general pattern of rootlessness. The Markhams' lives have followed an
all-too-familiar pattern in a society in which families and communities
are dissolving. They were each married to another, but "spouses wan-
dered off with other people's spouses; their kids got busily into drugs, got
pregnant, got married, then disappeared to California or Canada or
Tibet or Wiesbaden" (36). The middle-aged Joe and Phyllis reinvented
themselves, found each other, married, and built comfortable lives in
Vermont; but, like so many restless Americans, they eventually decided to
pull up stakes in search of a dream. Now they find themselves living in a
motel and running out of money. Their "predicament of homelessness"
(55) is emphatically suggested by their beat-up, borrowed Nova with the
"muddy bumper sticker that says ANESTHETISTS ARE NOMADS" (45).
On a "rainy summer morning" with "the seeds of gloomy alienation sown
in" (57), Frank prepares to show his clients a house "in the Haddam area"
(59), a suburb of a suburb, so to speak. Joe Markham, however, makes
clear just how important location is to him: "I don't want to live in an area.
. . . Nobody ever said the Vermont area, or the Aliquippa area . . . . They
just said the places" (59). Frank views Joe as a man "who's come to the
sudden precipice of what's left of life a little quicker than he knows how
to cope with" (52). Frustrated after showing the Markhams forty-five
houses, Frank tries to convince them to see things from his point of view
and to settle for a house which, while below their expectations in a number of ways, realistically represents the best that they can expect for their
money. However, the house is not actually in Haddam, the most desired
location, and, to make matters worse, it has a minimum security prison in
its backyard. Selling "the positive aspects of close-by prison living" (74)
requires the realtor's best attempts at "pseudo-communication" (76).
Although the prison behind the fence is an all-too-real reminder of the
dangers lurking just beyond the perimeters of suburban life, Frank tries
to minimize its importance with the less-than-comforting reminder that
"No one knows his neighbors in the suburbs anyway. It's not like
Vermont" (75). In spite of himself, the cantankerous Joe Markham seems
ready to surrender to the influence of Frank's Existence Period philoso-

Marginal People in Ford's Novels

phy. Even before being shown the house, he ironically announces: "I've completely quit becoming. . . . I'm not out on the margins where new discoveries take place anymore" (50). His poor wife, Phyllis, perhaps realizing that they have, in fact, reached the edge of their possibilities, unenthusiastically resigns herself to the thought that "maybe no one gets the house they want" (76).

Although Frank's passive, stoical life in the Existence Period may help him to cope with disappointment and uncertainty, and in so doing provide him with a false sense of independence from life's travails, such a view of the world definitely has its drawbacks. Most notably, as he is well aware, the view can result in "physical isolation and emotional disengagement . . . which cause trouble equal to or greater than the problems" (390) which it solves. As he explains, "[I]t is one of the themes of the Existence Period that interest can mingle successfully with uninterest . . . intimacy with transience, caring with the obdurate uncaring" (76). Later, he confesses that "intimacy had begun to matter less to me" (96). A certain disinterest or uncaring is often evident in Frank's dealings with others, particularly the homeless Markhams. Even more significantly, however, his emotional detachment is shown by his willingness to allow a satisfying romantic relationship with his lady friend, Sally Caldwell, to end without the least bit of resistance on his part. In fact, he admits to Sally that at times he feels "beyond affection's grasp" (171). Most important, Frank may even sense and fear that, in addition to physical distance, an emotional distance is gradually separating him from his son, Paul. His ex-wife, Ann, views him as a "half-hearted parent" and suggests that he should think of his children "as a form of self-discovery" (247). By the end of the novel, Ann's advice proves prophetic.

Frank plans the 4th of July/halls of fame weekend trip in order to connect with Paul and help the boy to find his way in the world, but the trip ends up being more a journey of discovery for the father than it is for the son. Frank has brought along two "key 'texts' for communicating" (8) with Paul on this "voyage meant to instruct" (263), Emerson's "Self-Reliance" and Carl Becker's *The Declaration of Independence*. Frank explains: "The impulse to read *Self-Reliance* is significant here, as is the holiday itself—my favorite secular one for being public and for its implicit goal of leaving us only as it found us: free" (7). Believing that "independence is ... what [Paul] lacks—independence from whatever holds him captive: memory, history, bad events he struggles with, can't control, but feels he should" (16), Frank hopes to initiate his son into some of the more useful tenets of his own Existence Period philosophy. But perhaps it is Frank's own gradual emergence from the Existence Period, his growing realization that "laissez-faire is not precisely the same as independence" (177), that "independence and isolation [are] not the same" (369), which allows him to embark on this journey that will take both Paul and himself "From Fragmentation to Unity and Independence" (259).

Frank's pairing of the words "unity" and "independence" is an important one, for it is evidence of his intuitive understanding that true freedom requires strengthening, not severing, ties with others. In fact, Frank tries to drive this point home to Paul by explaining that the founding fathers "wanted to be free to make new mistakes, not just keep making the same old ones over and over as separate colonies.... [Thus] they decided to band together and be independent and were willing to sacrifice some controls they'd always had in hopes of getting something better—in their case, better trade with the outside world" (260). The importance of strengthening ties, of "establishing a greater sense of connectedness" (27), is further emphasized in the novel in a variety of subtle ways: by the pair of tiny ribbon bows which Clarissa, Frank's daughter, gives to her father and brother before they embark on their journey; by the bow tie pasta which Sally Caldwell prepares especially for Frank; and by a seemingly offhand reference which Frank makes to "the poignant line" (95) in Thornton Wilder's nostalgic *Our Town*. Wilder's decidedly American play, of course, is also about making connections—to a family, to a community, and to a nation—and the importance of such connections is expressed by that play's leitmotif, "Blessed Be the Tie That Binds." While *Our Town* depicts a simpler life in the past, Ford's equally American novel depicts "the perilous character of life" (202) in the present time when the ties are becoming frayed, that is, when the most important human connections are in a state of dissolution.

If true independence requires solidarity with others, it also requires

Marginal People in Ford's Novels

surrendering the desire for control and accepting one's connection to the past as a useful guide to living in the present. In his own life, Frank has had his difficulties in all three areas. He maintains a posture of detachment from others; he vacillates between a desire to control life and a desire to surrender to it, and he would like to jettison much of his past. As Frank puts it, "[W]hen you're young your opponent is the future; but when you're not young, your opponent's the past and everything you've done in it and the problem of getting away from it. (My son Paul may be an exception.)" (95) In *The Sportswriter*, Frank had observed that "You can get detached from your beginnings . . . just by life itself, fate, the tug of the everpresent" (24). There is a scene at the Deerslayer Inn in Cooperstown in which Frank discovers a link to the past of which he, as much as Paul, is a captive. The bad memories of a failed marriage and of other events which he regrets and would like to forget all return when he finds an old copy of a book of short stories that he once published. He looks at the photograph on the dust jacket depicting an image of himself as a young writer, an image which may remind the reader of Harry Quinn, a man who chose to reject the past and to live in the moment, and which also serves as a reminder of Ford's view of the writer's "marginality in our culture": "I take a look at the . . . author photo . . . a young man, though this time with a completely unwarranted confidence etched in his skinny mouth, ludicrously holding a beer and smoking a cigarette (!), an empty sun-lit (possibly Mexican) barroom and tables behind, staring fixedly at the camera as though he meant to say: 'Yep, you just about have to live out here in the wild margins to get this puppy done the way God intended. And *you* probably couldn't hack it, if you want to know the gospel.' And I, of course, *couldn't* hack it; chose, in fact, a much easier puppy on a much less wild margin" (320).

Although Frank's peripheral, Existence Period life in the suburbs of New Jersey is considerably "less wild" than either Harry's Mexico or the young Frank's marginalized life as a writer, it is, in its own way, fraught with perils; and Frank is only deceiving himself when he refuses to acknowledge the fact that he is as much a captive of events beyond his control as is his son.

For much of the novel father and son cannot seem to connect. Frank frets about "[n]ot owning the right language" (17) to communicate with a boy who has erected his own protective barriers—his periodic barking noises and his habit of wearing headphones—against human contact. Indeed, in *Independence Day*, there is a great deal of emphasis upon the role that language plays in helping one to achieve or avoid connections with others. As Frank looks over the copy of his old collection of short stories, he takes some satisfaction in the knowledge that the book is "still striving to the purposes I meant it to: staging raids on the inarticulate, being an ax for the frozen sea within us, providing the satisfactions of belief in the general mess of imprecision" (320). As he tries to connect with Paul the next morning, Frank expresses his faith in the affirmative power of language: "My trust has always been that words can make most things better and there's nothing that can't be improved on. But words *are* required" (353). Of course, Frank is also experienced in using language to distance himself from others. The pride that Frank takes in his skillful use of "a form of strategizing pseudo-communication" (76) as a realtor comes to mind, along with his attempts at "pseudo-intimacy" (169) with Sally Caldwell. With Paul, however, Frank's failure to find the right language is quite painful, leaving him as "lonely as a shipwreck" (265). At times even their "oldest-timiest, most reliable, jokey way of conducting father-son business" fails, and their "words get carried off in the breeze, with no one to care if [they] speak the intricate language of love or don't" (265-66).

After a visit to the Basketball Hall of Fame and a night spent at the Deerslayer, father and son finally begin to make some progress toward meaningful communication; but just as the two seem on the verge of connecting, the trip ends abruptly when Paul is injured in a batting cage accident. The boy steps face-first into a fastball from a pitching machine, a device that represents the many things in life over which we have little or no control. Frank has tried to teach Paul to "let some things go" (351) and surrender to life's uncertainties: "you're trying to keep too much under control, son, and it's holding you back" (329). Ironically, though, Frank himself must relearn that very lesson, and it is the injured Paul who sends his father the message: "Tell my dad he tries to control too much. He worries too much too" (381). Indeed, although Frank has been will-

Marginal People in Ford's Novels

ing to give in to uncertainty in many areas of his life, he has been as unwilling as Robard Hewes or Harry Quinn to surrender to the affection of another.

As Frank ministers to his injured son, a connection from the past steps from a crowd of onlookers to minister to Frank. It is Irv Ornstein, a stepbrother whom he has not seen in twenty-five years. Interestingly, in *The Sportswriter* it was Irv Ornstein who, in a roundabout way, was responsible for helping Frank to connect with his relatives in Florida. Irv offers to drive Frank to the hospital as Paul is taken away in an ambulance, and Frank surrenders to Irv's "full authority" (365). At the hospital where Paul's injuries are treated, Irv and Frank become reacquainted. Irv, it seems, is "going through an 'odd passage' in life" (388) which, in many ways, mirrors Frank's own experience. A designer of flight simulators, Irv feels as if he is living a simulated existence. Like Frank, he is unable to commit to a relationship. As Frank puts it, "[Irv] complains of feeling detached from his own personal history, which has eventuated in a fear . . . that he is diminishing; and if not in an actual physical sense, then definitely in a spiritual one." Once again we have the idea, also expressed by Harry Quinn, that the person who tries to protect himself from life's uncertainties ends up with nothing and, in fact, runs the risk of being absorbed into nothingness. Frank, who himself has occasionally experienced a "'fear of disappearance'" (388), can easily relate to such feelings; and he concludes that "Irv is entering his own Existence Period, complete with all the good and not-so-good trimmings, just as it seems I'm exiting it in a pitch-and-tumble mode" (392). It is, of course, possible that Frank is merely experiencing an illusion, what he himself refers to as "one of the Existence Period's bedrock paradoxes . . . that just when you think you're emerging, you may actually be wading further in" (193). Nevertheless, Paul's accident and the chance meeting with "Irv-the-solicitous" (368) seem to provide the impetus needed for Frank finally to exit from and advance beyond the Existence Period. As Irv says, "Incidents we can't control make us what we are" (371). Or, as Frank himself says, "[T]here's nothing like tragedy or at least a grave injury or major inconvenience to cut through red tape and bullshit and reveal anyone's best nature" (406). Frank's encounter with Irv might be compared to the reader's encounter with Ford's novel, for just as the feeling of solidarity with the sympathetic Irv seems to release Frank from his isolation, so the reader may be freed from his or her own isolation by the same feeling of solidarity with the author and his characters.

The novel ends on Independence Day, with Frank's having gained independence from his self-imposed isolation and from his fear of emotional engagement. He makes progress toward improving his strained relationship with his ex-wife, Ann, and he proposes that Paul change locations and come to live with him. He even manages to find a suitable location (one of his own rental houses) for the wandering Markhams. "What more can you do for wayward strangers than to shelter them?" (424) he says. More important, Frank reconciles with Sally Caldwell, after a long and intimate telephone conversation during which they discuss "possibilities for commitment" (406). He looks with hope toward the future, to a possible marriage with Sally, and to the "Permanent Period" (450) of his life, which will surely be marked by that "greater sense of connectedness" (27) for which he has been searching.

Frank's reference to the "Permanent Period" echoes a passage from one of Ford's own essays, entitled "Accommodations," in which the author reminisces about spending a large part of his childhood in his grandfather's hotel. "In the hotel," writes Ford, "there was no center to things, nor was I one. . . . I simply stood alongside. . . . And what I thought about it was this: this is the actual life now, not a stopover, a diversion, or an oddment in time, but the permanent life, the one which will provide history, memory, the one I'll be responsible for in the long run" (43). According to Ford, this type of marginalized life, a life without a center, taught him that "Home is finally a variable concept" (43). Such a life, he says, "promotes a cool two-mindedness: one is both steady and in a sea that passes with tides. Accommodation is what's wanted, a replenished idea of permanence and transience . . ." (39). Like Ford himself, Frank Bascombe seems to have developed a certain ambivalence, or "two-mindedness," with respect to his feelings of marginalization. The "Residential Specialist," whose job it is to find accommodations for others, seems to have accommodated himself to the notion that being truly at home may not be possible in a world where human beings so often feel like homeless

Marginal People in Ford's Novels

nomads or castaways. Perhaps a clean, newly renovated "rental" is the best accommodation one could hope for in either a fluctuating realty market or a chaotic world. Indeed, the house that Frank offers to the Markhams, with its "new white metal siding and new three-way windows with plastic screens glistening dully in the sunlight" (30), might be compared to Hemingway's little café, that symbol of light and order in "A Clean, Well-Lighted Place." While Frank may seem as resigned to his fate as any Hemingway hero, at the same time he discovers that a "homey connectedness" (93) with others might be available even on the wildest margins, and that whatever permanence is possible in this impermanent world derives more from that sense of connectedness than from any sense of place. Frank asks: "[Is] there any cause to think a place—any place—within its plaster and joists, its trees and plantings, in its putative essence *ever* shelters some spirit ghost of us as proof of its significance and ours?" His answer: "No! Not one bit! Only other humans do that . . ." (442).

The final scene of *Independence Day* suggests that the best way to deal with life's marginality is to reach out to the other marginal people in the darkness. The novel's closing calls to mind a scene toward the conclusion of Walker Percy's *The Moviegoer*, in which Binx Bolling, when asked what he plans to do with his life, replies: "There is only one thing I can do: listen to people, see how they stick themselves into the world, hand them along a ways in their dark journey and be handed along, and for good and selfish reasons" (233). In what is perhaps the most moving passage in Ford's fiction, and the author's own testament to the "efficacy of telling" ("The Three Kings" 581), Frank is awakened from a sound sleep in the middle of the night by a ringing telephone. Most likely it is Paul on the line, but the caller is less important than the fact that Frank responds with healing words and with what he once referred to as "the real stuff," the "*silent intimacies* . . . of the fervently understood and sympathized with" (96). The passage clearly shows how far Frank's journey has taken him. And for the Ford reader who may also take consolation from the healing words of a gifted writer at the height of his power, it represents a fitting culmination to everything that the author has written thus far:

And when I said hello from the darkness, there was a moment I took to be dead silence on the line, though gradually I heard a breath, then the sound of a receiver touching what must've been a face. There was a sigh, and the sound of someone going, "Ssss, tsss. Uh-huh, uh-huh," followed by an even deeper and less certain "Ummm."

And I suddenly said, because someone was there I felt I knew, "I'm glad you called." I pressed the receiver to my ear and opened my eyes in the dark. "I just got here," I said. "Now's not a bad time at all. This is a full-time job. Let me hear your thinking. I'll try to add a part to the puzzle. It can be simpler than you think."

Whoever was there—and of course I don't know who, really—breathed again two times, three. Then the breath grew thin and brief. I heard another sound,"Uh-huh." Then our connection was gone, and even before I'd put down the phone I'd returned to the deepest sleep imaginable.

And I am in the crowd just as the drums are passing—always the last in line—their *boom-boom-boom*ing in my ears and all around. I see the sun above the street, breathe in the day's rich, warm smell. Someone calls out, "Clear a path, make room, make room, please!" The trumpets go again. My heartbeat quickens. I feel the push, pull, the weave and sway of others. (451)

In his dream, Frank is no longer alone on the periphery of life. Instead, he is a bystander among bystanders, a castaway among castaways, immersed in the great current of human experience and excited by the infinite possibilities that it offers. The dream is another sign that the Existence Period of his life has ended, and the Permanent Period has begun.

Marginal People in Ford's Novels

Richard Ford's first novel, *A Piece of My Heart,* is for a variety of reasons an anomaly in relation to his later work. It is considerably more pessimistic than much of the other fiction, and it is the only one of his works of fiction to date set in the Deep South in which he was born. The uncompromising darkness of the novel emanates from various states and degrees of despair in several of the characters. At a crucial time in both their lives, the protagonists, Robard Hewes and Sam Newel, come simultaneously to a strange, uncharted island in the Mississippi River between Arkansas and Mississippi, a domain ruled over by a cantankerous, eccentric, and paranoid old man, Mark Lamb, who lives there with his wife, Fidelia. The couple and T.V.A. Landrieu, their servant, are the island's only permanent inhabitants. Robard comes to this microcosmic spot ostensibly to take the job as a guard against poachers, Newel to escape complications of his city life and try to find a direction for the future. Both exemplify philosopher Søren Kierkegaard's famous axiom that "the specific character of despair is precisely this: it is unaware of being despair," although Newel is closer than Robard to sensing his condition.

The young men differ markedly in their backgrounds, their educational levels, their attitudes, and their approaches to life. Newel, a law student, is from an upper-middle-class family, while Robard, essentially uneducated, is a laborer, who has grown up without many of the advantages Newel has taken for granted. Despite the dissimilarities, however, the two are alike in one way: both come to the island on quests, one physi-

"On the Fine Edge of Disappearing"

Desperation and Despair in *A Piece of My Heart*

W. Kenneth Holditch

cal, the other philosophical or emotional; both are desperate, Newel for an answer to life's problems, Robard for fulfillment of his lust; and both are in despair, Newel consciously, Robard unconsciously. Robard's mission is driven by his sexual obsession for Beuna, a married woman. Newel thinks that he can leave his problems behind him and that Mark Lamb, because of his advanced age, might provide him some answer so that he could "be part of something happening, not something I remembered" (229). Robard's beliefs, fatalistic and deterministic, are related to those exemplified in the attitudes and actions of protagonists in novels by Albert Camus and Jean-Paul Sartre and their followers, while Sam Newel's search for meaning and order is more reflective of the protagonists of Walker Percy.

The disparity between the ideologies results in a remarkable series of discussions, often developing into arguments, with the taciturn and private Robard, as an unwilling participant in the dialogue, endeavoring to escape the net of Newel's persistent and probing inquiries. Newel considers Robard "fastidious," possessed of the ability to keep a "life apart and private," a trait Newel himself has "never been lucky enough to cultivate" (162). When Newel states that his girlfriend, Beebe, an airline stewardess and the granddaughter of Mark Lamb, believes they should just have sex and forget everything else, Robard replies sardonically that it was not a bad idea, that Newel might "get accustomed to it" (231). Newel chides Robard for committing adultery, as a result of which Beuna's husband is gunning for him, a circumstance that should never have occurred unless, Newel says, "you believe the whole world just boils down to a piece of mysterious nooky" (271). There is, Robard acknowledges to himself, a mystery to Beuna, something besides sex that draws him to be near her, makes him want to be a part of her, while she desires only sex to such an extent that she would willingly sacrifice "all that he wanted to save" (276).

As a fatalist, Robard believes that "you had to be ready to glide in the wake of fate sooner or later . . ." (200), that forces at work in a person can grow into "a life separate and sometimes as complete and good as your own" (11). His fatalistic view seems to have been born of, or at least intensified by, his father's accidental death in a flash flood while sitting in his car, a fact of his history that has left Robard believing that he might

Desperation and Despair in *A Piece of My Heart*

anytime feel "the impact and the long slow daze that ended by dying" (39). His father had been "a planner and a conniver," who believed, wrongly in Robard's view, that things were the way they should be (201).

Robard's cynicism surfaces when he learns of the death of Buck Bennett, who, along with six surgeons, was asphyxiated by gas jets in the hunting cottage he managed. Robard thinks that perhaps Buck in "a kind of weariness" deliberately left the gas jets on, having recognized the futility of life and so decided that "the best thing to do was to go to sleep." Robard, trying to understand what Buck's death means to him personally, concludes that although he was sorry for it, it "didn't affect his life at all" (54). Convinced that "decisions got made ahead of time," he envisions scales in which "the sides were weighted and one got chosen in the balance," although he does acknowledge that "the unforeseen"—presumably such an event as his father's accidental death—can disrupt the balance at any time (57). Near the end of the novel, when the owner of the Two Ducks Motel tells him that the occasional postcard he receives from people who have stayed there makes him hopeful, Robard's response is a cynical and curt "Yeah" (278).

By the time he comes to the island, he has reached a point in his life at which "time felt against him now" (139). For Robard there always exists a sense of impending doom, and in the scene which gives the novel its title, he sees on a truck a sign which reads "take another little piece of my heart" and wonders what it means (30), one of the questions that, in a sense, the rest of his narrative is involved in answering. (The quotation is, of course, from a 1960s song of Janis Joplin's.) Whenever Robard speaks to Beuna on the phone, the world disappears into the background and he realizes that he is close to the edge of doom. On the day when he plans to meet Beuna for the "new" variety of sexual encounter she has promised, he goes to the dining table in the Lambs' lodge carrying a pistol and is accused by Mark of trying to kill him. Robard feels "giddy and out of control" (200) and storms out because it seems that life had brought him to a place where he did not want to be. (The word *control*, particularly as it regards the loss of same, recurs again and again in the course of the narrative in connection with both the protagonists and other characters.)

The contrast Ford draws between Robard and other characters helps to underscore the character's fatalistic view. After Mark Lamb says that birds sing to remind us that we are alive, Robard cannot hear them and feels that he himself was, because of some character flaw, "missing something going on close to him" (142-43). When he sees Mrs. Goodenough in her store, staring at the sunset as if "locked away in a solace nothing would ever disturb," he feels frenzied, and her optimism, reflected in the aphorism "we make mistakes, but we're still here" is countered by his cynical observation that he hopes "I'm here tomorrow" (145).

When Sam Newel, in his search for someone with an answer, suggests that perhaps Robard may be a man he can rely on, Robard bitterly assures him that would be a mistake, for Robard's past experiences have led him to believe that there is no one to rely on and no reason to think that the island or its inhabitants "would turn out any better or kinder or any more understanding than they had been when he tried to make it honest . . ." (43). Although there is in his makeup more than a touch of the Calvinistic belief in predestination that was in the past and to a large extent still is part of the character of residents of the Deep South, Robard believes that whatever order exists in his life is a result of his "diligence or intuition," dependent on nothing and no one but his own "good instincts" (157). Newel feels that there is in Robard "a little fugitive terror that wanted everything just so and couldn't keep still till he had it that way" (162). Nevertheless, with the southerner's typical attachment to the place from which he came, Robard, despite having inured himself against dependence on people or locations, is convinced that Helena, Arkansas, because it was his birthplace, will allow him to fulfill his quest—to sleep with Beuna. Recognizing this belief in himself, however, he thinks that he should turn around and go in the opposite direction (44).

Other than his vague acknowledgement of some degree of fate or predestination, however, Robard seems disinclined to seek any rational order in the tangle of his accrued experiences, does not believe that anything can be learned from the past, and, indeed, lives almost totally in the present. When Newel inquires if he thinks the best solution to a problem is ignoring it, Robard replies, "If you're to where there ain't nothing else, it is" (268). He has no desire to return to any part of the past, even seeing

Desperation and Despair in *A Piece of My Heart*

his mother again, although he professes to miss her. But a visit from him would upset her, he says, since "I couldn't fit in nothin" (118). His philosophy of life seems to be, in his own words, "One minute don't learn the next one nothin," (230), and nothing ever ends but only changes and grows "into something else" (11-12). Life for him is full of "beginnings," between which exist "vacant moments when there was no breathing and no life" (8). It was these moments separating what went before and what was beginning that "had to be gotten used to" (8). His belief is reminiscent of the condition of Will Barrett in *The Last Gentleman,* who did well on tests, "but couldn't think what to do between tests" (9). After a while, Robard believes, life became cluttered with such beginnings until a man had to step back and allow life to conclude on its own "momentum" (15). This attitude, albeit expressed in Robard's unlettered way, is also remarkably parallel to Binx Bolling's observation in *The Moviegoer* that it was difficult just to get through an ordinary Wednesday (23), although Walker Percy's character certainly lacks the total cynicism of Robard.

Within the limited sphere of his existence, Robard dismisses what is not possible and quietly accommodates himself to whatever option is left (230). For the most part, he has drifted with the current, symbolically represented by the mighty river that flows past the lost island. Images of uncontrollable currents abound in the narrative: the death of Robard's father in a flash flood, Newel's early encounter with the Mississippi River, the suicide of Beebe's father in the same river, and the death of Robard himself, who does not drown but falls into the river after being shot. Robard feels himself "caught in some commotion he needed to control but couldn't quite make slow down" (45), and there is always an impending sense of doom as the action proceeds. Early in his story he begins to feel "things sliding away from him," to experience a loss of control and a sense of being trapped (31). The Mississippi River itself is a major symbol and an ever-present background to much of the action as exemplified by the events described above and others in the novel. In a remarkable set piece, Robard remembers old residents of Helena, Arkansas, originally built on a bluff above the river, telling how, after the Mississippi moved five miles east, the town was moved down to the newly created plain. Some referred to the action as "The Great Comedown" and predicted that residents of the town were destined to suffer, because "anything that owed to the river would have to pay, and when it paid, the price would be steep" (55).

So doggedly single-minded is Robard in his sexual quest that he responds to Newel's tortured search for meaning by insisting that "Life ain't *that* difficult . . ." (228). Totally caught up in the flow of events, he has fallen into a seemingly inescapable pattern: when one job ended, he went with his fellow workers to the next place where work was to be found, without any conscious decision on his part. When he determined to leave his wife and go to Beuna, since he was not yet "finished with this part of his life" (16), he for the first time makes a choice that alters the flow of events in which he feels trapped. Later he experiences the existential realization that making a choice is being alive: "one day you think you never even made a choice and then you have to make one, even a wrong one, just so you're sure you're still able" (276). Even after choosing a direction, however, he finds himself in Arkansas in a rented room above a country store trying to understand how he reached that point but unable to figure out what force is moving him (33). Despite his fatalism, Robard is troubled by this because he likes to "keep my business manageable"(119), a phrase that becomes something of a refrain in the narrative. His passion for Beuna is tainted only by fear that whatever force it is in her that is beyond control has drawn him into a situation over which he has no power.

For Robard, clearly, that force is his love for Beuna, a consuming passion that has closed most other avenues of life to him. Ford employs as symbols natural forces and disasters—storms and floods—to exemplify Robard's relationship to Beuna. In her presence, he is excited, "suddenly like a man in a tornado" (150), but his pleasure is mitigated by his fear of being swept away, for he feels that something "had turned her life into a hurricane" into which he had been pulled (157). When Newel, who seems to have convinced himself that Robard is involved in the same sort of spiritual quest that he is, insists that there are more important things than sex with a woman, Robard replies that the only thing more important than "a piece of tail" is another "piece of tail." The persistent Newel insists that Robard does not mean that, but Robard replies, "You know I believe it" (140).

Robard, disturbed by the bizarre sexual act Beuna proposes to him, finally faces the fact of her corruption and the mistake he has made in lusting for her at the expense of his marriage and determines to return to his wife and explain that "everything comes down to a choice" (276), that, in effect, to make a choice is to be alive. Robard seems to be the character that undergoes the most development in the course of the action, and his final choice is a moral one. It is a choice, however, that proves to be his undoing, for whatever power that he has had, or imagined he had, over his fate is swept up in the "hurricane" that Beuna represents, and he is trapped in what Ford calls "the calamitous center," involved "in some commotion he needed to control but couldn't quite make slow down" (45). His own death in the river is foreshadowed by his reflections at the time of Mark Lamb's death on "situations that draw you in and wring you like a rag, and let you go in the rain when the use was out of you and you weren't good for anything" (265).

A set piece in the narrative, in which Robard remembers as a boy watching the stationmaster at Helena, Arkansas, dominate with switches the movement of trains, becomes a metaphor for Robard's entanglement with Beuna. Robard wonders if the man, after doing this job for many years, would ever despair "sitting alone in the dark with all the trains and all the switches and the engineers and the conductors and the passengers facing you through one tiny light after another" so that finally "the pressure was too great, and you'd fall to the temptation, one night, of letting it all run together, of opening every switch and watching lights converge in a slow series of blinks and snaps, until they all were together and there was nothing left to dispatch" (147). When Robard asked the stationmaster how he could do it, the man responds that he has a "Mind like a moon," and says that if you look at it long enough, the moon is all you'll see. As an adult, returning to Helena in his obsessive quest for Beuna, Robard looks at the stationmaster's house and in a passage that relates him to the existentialists draws a comparison between himself in his present situation and the man who directs the trains: "Here it all was, he felt, the time when there wasn't any holding out, the one true last time, and he didn't want to do it halfway, since halfway was as good as nothing" (147-48).

As Beuna's husband, ironically named W. W. Justice, gives chase, bent on killing him, Robard perceives the irony of his situation: W. W. is unaware that Robard has already rejected Beuna and is returning to his past life. Furthermore, Robard has freed himself of Beuna but has not faced the possibility of "getting swept off exactly like his old man" (292) in a flash flood. For Robard, the choice comes too late, and as he prepares to leave, fleeing the evil that Beuna represents and in which she wants to entangle him, he is shot. Ironically, he dies not at the hands of the wronged husband but is killed by the boy hired by Gaspareau to keep intruders away from Mark Lamb's island. A further irony lies in the fact that in trying to evade W. W.'s pursuit, Robard is heading not away from but *toward* the island, which seems to offer sanctuary.

Sam Newel, the other protagonist of *A Piece of My Heart*, is a man who thinks much and, in contrast to Robard, does not see the past as a combination of beginnings and "vacant moments" from which nothing is learned. Newel attempts to find his way through the tangle of accumulated experiences, to find an order in them, and, by understanding the past, learning perhaps what to do in the future. The past, he is convinced, "is supposed to give you some way of judging things"(83), a decided contrast to Robard's belief that there is nothing to be learned. Newel's quest for order and meaning began when he was in law school in Chicago and experienced troublesome physical pains, after which "All that had seemed nicely parsed out began muddling into obsessions about starting the future with the past completely settled" (182). Like both Binx Bolling in *The Moviegoer* and Will Barrett in *The Last Gentleman*, Newel exemplifies the "many young men in the South," who, according to Walker Percy, "had trouble ruling out the possible" (*The Last Gentleman* 10). This receptivity to possibilities is a trait often commented on in existential philosophy and the fiction inspired by it.

As events progress on the island, Newel feels whatever ability to manage life he ever had to be degenerating, and one day as he listens to Mark and Fidelia Lamb argue, he perceives that now he has "lost control of everything" and can do nothing but wait "while whoever *did* have control decided how to exercise it" (211). One of his memory episodes from his childhood involves his seeing two drunken women naked in a room at the Monteleone Hotel in New Orleans. When young Sam asked his father what would make the women do such a thing, the elder Newel replies that *"now and then things get away from you and you couldn't control events anymore..."* (186). When Fidelia Lamb asks him if he has several plans, Newel responds that he does and they are "All divergent." In her typically cryptic manner, Fidelia says that "Everyone's plans are diverging now. There's no reason yours should be different" (164). Newel thinks of his relation to Beebe that "Everything was based on a nonchalance that didn't include *plans* in any customary sense. Though there was something to it all that made him feel dreary, and that made him believe it would lead to something bitter, and that it would all sweep over him one day without his knowing it was happening" (177). Unlike Robard, he is not committed to one direction but seeks some sort of external guidance.

After a while, Newel becomes almost clinically obsessive in his search for order, wanting to "stitch" everything he knows—not only serious ideas but also the mass of trivia that clutters all our minds: past moments, names, pictures, "random" pieces of this and that, memories of his father—"into some reasonable train of thought . . ." (228). He ponders the varying attitudes of his parents toward life: while his mother "knew the limits to things," his father never discovered those limits "because he adapted" and at some point his "pleasures somehow just got grafted on his pains" (82). Newel's own attempt to discover a unifying pattern seems doomed, however, for he can only think of parts, not the whole. Although he concludes that he is somehow missing some simple aspect of the parts and "can't hold them together well enough to figure out what it is" (80), he persists in the quest, convinced, like John Updike's eponymous protagonist in *Rabbit, Run,* "that somewhere behind all this . . . there's something that wants me to find it" (127).

Newel is always attempting to get to know and understand people, their past, their motives, in his eternal quest for the key to his own salvation. Newel thinks Robard may be "my chance" for an answer to his dilemma, an idea to which Robard replies, "There's lots of people in the world would run jump in the river if they thought I was their chance at anything. Sometimes I think I'm one of them" (107). Beebe, Newel's girl-friend, commenting on his desire to find answers in other people in order to direct his own quest, inquires what he is doing about it, and Newel replies that he is worrying. When she accuses him of having "a poor tolerance for ambiguity" (71) and he asks what she means, she says, "To continue what you're doing when nothing is very clearly defined" (71). This comment, interestingly, reflects what John Keats calls "nega-tive capability," the quality he terms essential in "a man of achievement": that ability to be "in uncertainties, mysteries, doubts, without any irritable reaching after fact and reason" (*Selected Letters of John Keats* 92).

Of Newel's tendency to analyze, or as she sees it, to overanalyze, every experience, Beebe insists that "You make things terrible when they're only slightly confusing" (71). His response—"Everything I think I know is ambiguous" (72)—has the potential for two interpretations, depending on emphasis. Even though his quest for an answer is for the most part un-successful, at least insofar as the limits of the novel are concerned, Newel concludes that he must find "a plainer view" of existence (228). Despite the seriousness of Newel's quest, by the way, there is a strong thread of humor that runs through his narrative, serving both to relieve and to heighten the tension in his experiences.

This intellectual—and spiritual—curiosity is demonstrated often in Newel's actions, as when he is heading south to the island inhabited by Beebe's grandparents. In Chicago, hearing from Beebe the story of her father's having committed suicide by jumping off the bridge into the Mississippi at New Orleans, Newel "decided that nothing less than two thousand miles would be safe enough to keep him off the bridge" (176). In Memphis, he plunges his hand into river water and realizes that he has never felt the Mississippi before: "It seemed now like a vast and impon-derable disadvantage, and made him feel like he needed to know" (87). Then he dives into the river, without any definite intention of self-de-struction, and is swept downstream until he is rescued by two men on a barge. Later, when he and Robard are on the island south of Memphis, Sam falls into the river and, with his characteristic habit of self-analysis, ponders what has happened in thirty-six hours: "the situation now was all out of control and there was no one there to see if he stayed down for good" (184). Always present as a backdrop to the novel's action is the sense of how quickly any degree of mastery in any situation can be lost by the human being, how thin and fragile is the crust that separates any rational progression of events from chaos.

Much of the narrative centered on the consciousness of Newel involves the contrapuntal memory passages, printed in italics, many of which are devoted to his childhood, his relationship with his parents, their relationship to each other, their travels as his father sold starch around the South. These memory sections serve to dramatize Newel's desire, cited above, to "be part of something happening, not something I remembered" (229). The reader discovers that even as a child, Newel was always observing and questioning, well on his way to becoming, to use Walker Percy's phrase in *The Last Gentleman*, the "watcher and listener and wanderer" (10) that he is in maturity. Robard's memories, in marked contrast, are sparse, many of them connected with Beuna.

While Robard has a "a kind of life apart and private," Newel is unable to live in such a way, instead, in ancient-mariner fashion, revealing to all with whom he comes in contact, whether or not they are willing or interested listeners, the confusing ideas that battle in his consciousness. In contast to Robard, who has made one major choice in his life, Newel has "divergent plans" and sees himself as open to all sorts of choices. During his years in law school, he became obsessed with "starting the future with the past completely settled" (182), but the recurrent memory passages reflecting his childhood and youth make it clear that such has not been the case. Although Newel, unlike Robard, wants to and believes he can find a pattern to his accumulated experiences, he does not seem capable of ordering his past and consequently cannot function positively in the present.

The contrasts between the two protagonists are effectively exemplified by the fact that Robard, whose existence is centered in the physical, is lean and fit, while Sam, obsessed with the mental, even the spiritual, is fat and acknowledges that he has abused his body (139). While Robard sleeps soundly at night, for Newel, "the miseries commenced" in the darkness, and he lies awake, allowing "the emptiness to inhabit him and for an airy moment release his mind to everything" (132). The differences are further developed in the scene in which the two men are on a boat headed toward the island for the first time and see a swimming deer suddenly disappear beneath the surface of the water, an event that hints at forces under the facade of reality over which the human being has no control. Although Robard fatalistically describes the deer as a "victim" of himself, Newel endeavors to "make sense" of the death, to which Robard responds that it just "happened, so I suppose I made sense out of it already" (107). When he has finally become annoyed by Newel's persistent questioning, Robard demands to know if Newel does not "get tired and want to think just whatever comes in your head" (117). Near the end of the novel, Newel decides to return to Chicago, enroll in a cram course, and "get started in the way he felt fated, if for no other reason than that was the only way left. There was a squeamish serenity in that, of choosing the only thing left, when everything else was eliminated and not by any act, but just by the time and place" (225). It is the same satisfaction, he thinks, that one would feel if, after having floated on a limb for a long time, he landed somewhere, satisfied just to be on land, though not at home. This appears to be a positive step, since Newel has chosen among the possibilities available to him and seems to have found a direction. The reader is left to guess from the ambiguous conclusion to the novel, an italicized memory passage in which Newel recalls seeing a man who committed suicide in a hotel room, as to Newel's own subsequent life.

An impending sense of doom, of death waiting just around the next corner, down the next street, hangs darkly over the events of the novel. There are sudden and unexpected deaths: the drowning of Robard's father, Lamb's accidental electrocution while he is illegally fishing with a battery, and the death of Robard, who is, ironically, shot not by his enemy but by the amoral boy. The deaths of animals—the killing of a rabbit by a bobcat, the disappearance of the deer into the depths of the river, the story Newel remembers his father telling him of the Peabody Hotel duck poisoned by cyanide, as well as his memory of a friend's killing an owl that "lost everything in one instant" (76)—serve as paradigms for the fate of the characters themselves. Several of these episodes involving death, animal and human, result from people's viciousness or amorality, but oth-

Desperation and Despair in *A Piece of My Heart*

ers are purely accidental, suggesting human beings' lack of any power over their lives. When Robard tells Beuna the story of the Great Comedown, she, even more cynical than he, replies, "We're all dying sooner or later. Them assholes think they figured the reason. But I'm satisfied there ain't no reason" (55).

Despite the differences between the two characters, there are marked similarities. Like all of Richard Ford's protagonists, Robard and Newel are essentially decent, good men, trying to get through the muddle of living in the present without hurting anyone. The nature of their despair differs in that Newel is aware of the condition and Robard is not. Newel has been sensitized to the philosophical questions that often plague intelligent human beings, while Robard seems for the most part ignorant of any meaningful possibility other than his next sexual encounter with the dangerous Buena.

The motif of existential despair is underscored in the novel with multiple images of entrapment, beginning with the scene in which an ill-fated rabbit is locked in a cage with a bobcat by a truly frightening and seemingly amoral teen-aged girl, Mona Nell, and culminating with the island, lost between two states, of which Robard says, "everything's trapped right here" (230). As he stands by the cages at the service station, looking at the caged animals, he feels himself just as cornered, "like he ought to get away, and at the same time . . . helpless to maneuver a way to go about it" (29). He is worried that the girl has never been taught what is wrong, but concludes fatalistically that it is not his job to try to instruct her. Later, when Robard states that he must be free, even though it may involve the dangers he tries to avoid, Newel offers the solution of going inside something and never coming out. Robard rejects this form of entrapment: "I always want to get out. It makes me itchy, like something was about to happen I didn't know about" (100).

Not only are they physically trapped, but the two men are also pinned, both physically and symbolically, between vindictive young people on the one hand (the sadistic girl with the animals and a boy with a gun guarding the island, who ultimately kills Robard) and old people on the other (Gaspareau, who guards the island from the mainland of Arkansas, and Mark Lamb, the island's proprietor, who is bitter and suspicious of everyone). This contrast between youth and age suggests a somewhat natural-ist view of human beings in young adulthood as moving without a priori values or direction between an animalistic nonage and a disappointed senility in which whatever once mattered has turned to ashes. Among Mark Lamb's complaints about life is the fact that young people are no longer taught about dignity, a rather ironic comment coming from such a character.

Although Newel and Robard are the protagonists of the novel, other characters are of major significance, each with his or her own unique form of despair, notably Robard's lover Beuna and Fidelia and Mark Lamb on their mysterious island. Newel, in his continuing search for an answer, has come to the island because he believes, from what he has heard of Mark Lamb, that Beebe's grandfather may provide the counsel he needs, may function as his Jungian wise old man. The island itself, however, when he first sees it, "looked to him like a reproach . . ." (96), and when he meets Lamb, Newel wishes that he could disappear, and later even comes to believe the old man to be crazy. Lamb's advice to the needy Newel is to suggest that perhaps he needs a purgative, then, seeing that he has upset the young man, solicitously to tell him not to worry, that here "We don't take ourselves serious" as they do in the North (117). The remark is typical of the acid humor with which the old man faces what-ever happens to him in life.

Lamb's philosophy is summed up in his remark that one "can't count on" living another day and that birds sing to remind us that we are alive, which he seems to imply is the only thing that matters (142). Picking up the medicine bottles the old man has dropped, Newel realizes that Lamb fears approaching death: "as if he just felt the ballast of his life going off, and couldn't stop it, and an abstraction had come on him for the first time ever and scared him and made him go after cures, which he knew in advance wouldn't work, since he knew there wasn't any way in the world to end it now. Since everything you were lonely for was gone, and every-thing you were afraid of was all around you" (219). The last sentence is an acute description of the state of despair in which Newel finds himself. Newel realizes that he lacks the "outrage" that makes it possible for the old to fight, a battle that he himself thought it not important to fight or to win (219). The strange story Lamb tells about the paralyzed Peewee McMorris, who can stick his hand in a wasp nest and feel nothing indicates Lamb's fear of pain and his desire to be free of it. Implicit in the anecdote as well is the existential notion, expressed by Dostoevsky, among others, that the origin of consciousness is suffering.

Lamb's despair takes the form of anger, even outrage, as he refuses to "go gentle into that good night." Newel realizes that he cannot best "the old man's ferocity," lacking in his character "whatever the old man had stored up in never-ceasing abundance" and therefore, perhaps, could not himself fight death as Lamb does. If he ever had such ferocity, Newel believes, it is now "directed inward," unlike Lamb's fury, which is "pointed out like ordnance at the armies of contravention and deceit that had him under constant siege" (216). Newel thinks of Lamb as "justifying himself a mile a minute" (161) because the old man "cares more than I do. It's right up in his face all the time" (229).

Mrs. Lamb asks Newel if he believes that "history runs to cycles," and when he says no, she says that her husband hates to give up the past but she disagrees: "Gone is gone to me" (163). Lamb, who is in some ways reminiscent of Shakespeare's Prospero in *The Tempest* as well as King Lear, views himself as a god of his small domain and is offended by many things, including the fact that he is required to meet once a year with inspectors sent by the owners of the island, which he never bothered to purchase. Lamb is in many ways the most outlandish character in the book, and his cynical, waspish views of life provide most of the humor; for example, his attitude toward modern behaviorist theories of crime is that one's actions are not controlled by "your childhood or whether your mother was scared by a goat, or what kind of neighborhood you live in, or if your mother dressed you up like a girl—none of that baloney" (132). Kristina Ford recalls that when her husband was working on *A Piece of My Heart*, he informed her one morning, "Well, I'm going to kill off Lamb today." At the end of his writing day, she inquired if he had indeed finished off the old man and he replied, "No, I decided to give him a couple of more jokes."[1]

Fidelia, in contrast to her husband, is a quiet, stoical, even stately woman, whose major interest centers on the shortwave radio through which she establishes a very limited degree of communication with the rest of the world. She worries about whether or not the house will collapse, but philosophically tells Newel that "It's hedonistic for us to suppose we should perplex the world by lasting on it forever . . ." (179). She perceives clearly the peculiarities of her husband, but she tolerates them, for the most part in silence, and when he is gone, she quickly takes charge of matters on the island.

Beuna, on the other hand, is a total hedonist, who is not interested in having children because "I'll just have me a good time and let the next bunch take care of theirselves without adding to the misery" (152). In episode after episode her self-centeredness surfaces, as when she says that her husband W. W.'s not having a baseball career may not make him happy, but it makes her happy, and "That's who I watch out for" (155). After Beuna prays in the Gospel Nook in the country, Robard asks what she prayed for and she says for her soul: "if I got one, I want it took care of right." For him, she says, she has prayed to St. Jude, "the one for lost causes." Why does it matter to him, she asks, and when he replies that it does not, her typically perverse reply is "That there's why I done it" (158).

Even though Robard, recognizing her nature, feels that he should leave, he knows that "whatever it was she had, badness or disappointment or meanness, was the thing that was indispensable now, and he wanted to draw in to her and glide off in infinitude and just let loose of everything" (153-54). Thinking of her in terms of a natural force, he believes that "whatever had turned her life into a hurricane had turned his the same way and made a part of his own existence sag out of control down into the sink of unmanageables" (157). Trying to figure out what is wrong with Beuna, what has ruined her, he determines that it has to do with her having reached "the point of perfect control, which was the point of purest despair" and then having "lost it all and suffered as if something indispensable had been grabbed away so quick she didn't know she had had it or ever could have controlled it" (157). Beuna insists that the difference between her and Robard is that they both want to have sex with whomever they desire, but while "It don't bother me" he has "a dead-dog look, like you was afraid of something." Irritated, he replies that he is not bothered, but she says she can hear it in his voice, even on the phone (156).

In terms of the existentialistic views reflected in *A Piece of My Heart*, Robard's attitude toward life, his cynical belief that things merely happen, that there is no underlying meaning, is reflective of French humanistic existentialists, particularly Albert Camus. Sam Newel, on the other hand, in his search for meaning and order, is much closer to heroes in the Kierkegaardian mold, John Updike's Rabbit Angstrom, or Walker Percy's Binx Bolling in *The Moviegoer*. For Newel, the lost island serves a similar purpose to that provided by Elysian Fields Avenue for Binx, a place in which he is not required to be committed to only one plan, one direction, unlike Robard, whose every action is directed toward his sexual unions with Beuna. It should be noted in regard to Percy, however, that Ford's work lacks most of the religious implications apparent in all of Percy's fiction. None of Ford's characters except Frank Bascombe in *The Sportswriter* express interest in religion, and there only peripherally as Frank enters a church lobby—but not the sanctuary—only because it is Easter Sunday.

Another prevalent motif with existential overtones relates to the lack of communication between people and its consequences, which often involve despair. Sam Newel's attempts to give voice to his views or discuss his problems with Robard are repeatedly rebuffed. When Newel complains that he himself is "the only person who'll take me seriously," Robard replies, "You'd think that'd teach you something," then adds, "I'm afraid nobody ever took me serious in their life" (119). In the rare moment of self-revelation described above, Robard admits that he misses his mother, but that they have their own lives and do not keep in touch. There is little communication between Fidelia Lamb and her husband, and she spends much of her time listening to her shortwave radio, seemingly keeping in touch with "a faraway country behind each tiny window," establishing "audio contact with the rest of the world" (119-20), though many of the programs she listens to are in Spanish, a language she does not understand. Ironically, her one-way relationship with the radio is the only communication between the island and the rest of the world. Fidelia says that her husband believes that because the island is not plotted on the Corps of Engineers map, "it has ceased to exist for the rest of the world" (164). This "lostness" is further underscored by the fact that it is in the middle of the river, a part neither of Arkansas nor of Mississippi.

Yet another motif frequently employed in the novel is that of the void, reflected in Robard's belief that life is filled with vacant moments that must be lived through. After they have had sexual relations, he sees disappointment in Beuna's eyes, "like some dead zone in her had uncovered all at once" (10), as if there existed in her "a vacancy she was beside herself wondering how to fill" (13). The motif of nothingness is sounded again and again, as when Robard tells Newel his name and adds, "You don't have to remember it. It won't mean nothin if I've got anything left to say about it" (63). Newel, who thinks "nothing good lasts very long" (67), remembers being in Chicago and yearning for darkness to envelop him: "[H]e had never thought until this very moment that he could long for it, want whatever erroneous comfort it had, making him invisible. And for a moment, in the natural order of things, he felt large and frail and brought down out of place into a painful light that made him want to hulk away back in the dark" (116). At one point, Beuna, hearing a hawk in air, "looked up, as though she were hung on the fine edge of disappearing" (156).

The despair of the novel is intensified by the setting in which most of the action occurs. Beebe describes Lamb's uncharted island as "Mississippi in its most baronial and ridiculous." She views it, nevertheless, as "a very good place to go to compose yourself, or do whatever you like" (84) and in the novel it functions as an isolated microcosm where characters attempt to find or reinforce meaning in their lives. It is significant that it is located halfway between Mississippi and Arkansas, the two states in which Richard Ford spent his childhood and youth, and the novelist states that there are several such islands in the area. "My first one to visit," he says, was above Memphis and "was owned by a Faulknerian old man," but the one in the novel Ford describes as an "amalgamation" of at least two. Significantly, one of them is actually named Mark Ham Island.[2]

Repeatedly the sense of place, not only the island but other locations as well, is woven into the narrative and the thoughts of characters. Beebe theorizes that "the strongest" as well as the "stupidest" urge of animals is

Desperation and Despair in *A Piece of My Heart*

remaining "faithful to their own wretched unpromising territory—past when the food had depleted and they were impoverished and falling over to predators" (185). Robard's ironic faith that his birthplace, Helena, Arkansas, will allow him to sleep with Beuna again exemplifies Beebe's notion. Of the state of Mississippi Newel thinks that if he were at the bridge where Beebe's father committed suicide, he would either jump himself, or worse, "he might just make all the necessary adjustments to imbecility and boredom and unreasonable gentility that everybody there seemed to make, but that nobody seemed to care much about" (176).

The ending of the novel is bittersweet, in that both protagonists have achieved some understanding, but what the benefits of the change in their lives may be is open to question. Robard has wisely decided to turn his back on Beuna and the evil he believes her to represent, but he is destroyed nonetheless. Newel has decided on a course of action, has indeed to some extent fulfilled his quest, and will presumably return to Chicago to resume his life, but the last memory scene from his childhood, the passage that ends the novel, concerns the suicide of a young man in a hotel room in New Orleans, an appropriate conclusion to a work of fiction in which death plays a most important part.

Richard Ford shares with William Faulkner a unique ability to experiment with form and language so that each novel in his canon has been distinctive in its own way. Certainly *A Piece of My Heart* differs markedly from the work that succeeded it, *The Ultimate Good Luck*, as well as from *Wildlife* and the two Frank Bascombe novels, in subject matter, character, and narrative methods. Yet within the pages of his first novel are to be found the motifs and themes that have continued to concern Ford for more than two decades.

Richard Ford is a curious figure in contemporary American literature. While he is frequently included in the canon of southern writers, he picks most distinctly unsouthern locales in which to set his fiction. His two most renowned works, *The Sportswriter* and its Pulitzer Prize-winning sequel, *Independence Day*, are set primarily in New Jersey, and only his first novel, *A Piece of My Heart*, is set in the South. Ford himself grew up in the South but has spent the greater part of his adult life living in places north and west of what are considered the southern states. Through the convergence of his background, travels, and education, he infuses his writing with an awareness of his literary progenitors, both remote and immediate. One continuing thread in Ford's work is the individual's sense of displacement in a chaotic modern world. This concern with the individual's struggle can be traced through much of southern writing since Reconstruction, where, as one commentator has noted, "the heroic . . . falls before a modern order universally acknowledged to be powerful but morally and culturally bankrupt" (Kreyling 5). This sensibility, he goes on to say, remains vital one hundred years after Appomattox in the work of Walker Percy, whose protagonists find that "their success is confounded" in a malignant world where "actions and intentions seem garbled" (173). But where Percy clings to his southern heritage, and where Ford is aware of his southern roots, Ford is also conscious of being an American writer, and hence he incorporates the regional concern with the influences of the larger popular culture.

"The Tissue of Everyone's Loneliness"

Expectation, Reality, and Alienation in *The Ultimate Good Luck*

Robert N. Funk

The concern with heroic action in a world with little real use for it fuels the plot and form of *The Ultimate Good Luck*. It seems at first consideration a seriously flawed effort at a detective/adventure novel of the type popularized by Dashiell Hammett, Raymond Chandler, and John D. MacDonald, a type which had become an established genre by the time Ford wrote his own novel. Although Ford provides all the trappings of the genre as his war-toughed hero encounters a world of violent intrigue while trying to free his girlfriend's brother from a Mexican prison, Harry Quinn remains a curiously impotent protagonist, and Ford fails to account ultimately for the plot's machinations. Yet to view the work as a failed attempt to produce a novel of this type is to miss the work's intention. Ford's purpose is not to spin an entertaining adventure yarn but to instill in the reader an intimate appreciation for the circumstances of his characters, who inhabit a violent and existential world in which human agency is a meager construct.

Ford is a writer who has a demonstrable understanding of the literary arena in which he has chosen to work. Not only was he an English major in college, but he has written a number of essays examining American literature. Two of these are contemporaneous to the composition of *The Ultimate Good Luck* and suggest his concerns and interests at the time. The first of these is a review of Walker Percy's work that appeared in 1977, after the publication of his first novel and during the time he had begun writing what would become *The Ultimate Good Luck*. In it he delineates those characteristics of Percy's work that identify him with the southern tradition. Ford writes that the novels are "set in the south yet . . . point us convincingly toward the rest of the country, watching through the eyes of lonely, wondering narrators stranded in the contemporary and slightly ludicrous malaise between orthodoxy (the Catholic Church, the stock market, the family, the south) and complete culturization; men and women stuck between transcendence and immanence, between engagement and cynicism; folks out of phase with what one of Percy's characters calls the 'actuality of themselves.'" ("Walker Percy" 558).

It is just such characters whom Ford himself will depict in his own novel, characters who are disconnected from the society that surrounds them and who struggle to control their own lives. But it is another discus-

Expectation, Reality, and Alienation in *The Ultimate Good Luck*

sion that points to the novel's complete structure. Six years after this piece and two years after the publication of *The Ultimate Good Luck*, he writes in "The Three Kings: Hemingway, Faulkner, and Fitzgerald" of these authors' contributions to American letters. Of particular interest here are Ford's comments about Hemingway: "Hemingway . . . aimed for the 'sequence of motion and fact which made the emotion.' . . . Think of 'Hills Like White Elephants,' a story I admire and that students love because it seems so modern. No one says abortion in it. Yet the feeling of abortion—loss, puzzlement, abstraction—informs every slender, stylized gesture and line, and the story has a wonderful effect" (581).

This passage presents the key to understanding what Ford's goals are in his own novel—instilling the characters' experiences in the reader. The fact that Hemingway's influence is almost palpable in the novel, as Fred Hobson has noted while commenting on Ford's use of "backwoods country, unsentimental tone, and low-life characters, some running from the law, others running for other reasons" (*The Southern Writer* 44), suggests more than that Ford was experimenting with Hemingway's style. It indicates that he is deeply influenced by Hemingway's artistry and gives one leave to speculate that this influence goes beyond appropriation of style to deeper concerns that Ford has clearly recognized.

The Hemingway novel that bears the greatest resemblance to Ford's own is *To Have and Have Not*. Superficially, one hears echoes of Hemingway's work not only from the coincidence that Ford's Harry Quinn shares his Christian name with Harry Morgan, but also from the Latin American setting and the portrayal of a blue-collar protagonist caught up in international intrigue and a randomly violent world. But the similarity between the two novels runs even deeper. Just as Harry Quinn is searching for "the ultimate good luck," Harry Morgan is only too aware of the impotence of human agency, a view that Morgan articulates with his last words: "No matter how a man alone ain't got no bloody fucking chance" (225). The novel abounds with comments concerning luck and chance; Eddy tells the treacherous Mr. Johnson that he is just unlucky (19), and Morgan at several points calculates the odds of a current enterprise, wondering all the time whether he has a chance. While Morgan does try to engineer his own success, he is ultimately helpless before a malign cosmography. While Morgan has heroic qualities, as Delbert E. Wylder has observed—his aggressiveness, animal vitality, virility, and individualism—these are eclipsed by his limitations so that "there are no heroes in *To Have and Have Not*, [even as] the novel seems obviously structured for a hero" (98-99). In this regard, Ford's own hero is drawn from the same deck—a figure who seems to be a hero, but whose heroism is open to debate.

Ford's novel shares characteristics with Hemingway's in another respect, and that is in the form of the plot. The most frequent criticism of *To Have and Have Not* is that its narrative is bogged down in extraneous sub-plots: Richard Gordon's, the financier's, Dorothy Hollis's, Henry Carpenter's, and the drunken veterans'. While Ford's novel does not exhibit a series of lengthy distractions from the main plot, it does incorporate several minor episodes contributing little or nothing to the plot. Quinn's encounter with the homeless girl would be one of these, the bombing of the ice-cream store another. In addition is Ford's failure to account for the twists that seem related to the plot but that are not finally explained; perhaps the most significant of these is the role that Deats plays. I would argue that these similarities suggest not that Hemingway has *influenced* Ford, but that Ford has acutely diagnosed Hemingway's work and has manipulated its strengths and weaknesses to his own end. Recognizing that so many readers have been alienated by the hero's failure to conform to standards of heroism and the plot's failure to conform to standards of unity in *To Have and Have Not*—a result that, perhaps, Hemingway did not intend—Ford employs these aspects in order to consciously achieve the same effect on his audience, having recognized Hemingway's propensity for successfully achieving the same result elsewhere.

Ford's aim in the novel is to alienate the reader from what is familiar just as his own characters are alienated in their world. And in such an enterprise, the detective genre works perfectly. It is perhaps the most formal of literary genres, and, hence, among the most recognizable:

Narrative structure . . . manipulates the reader's desire for closure, and usually satisfies that desire with recognition scenes, epiphanies, denouements, and an accompaning catharsis. Every narrative element either leads to an ending or prevents one from happening, while some plot developments imply one denouement, and some another. By thus creating suspense about whether and how conflicts will be resolved, every narrative exploits a constant tension between meaning (the anticipated revelation of a coherent narrative pattern) and meaninglessness (the fear that no such pattern exists). Detective fiction, which is concerned with the gap between a crime and its solution, follows this inherent narrative structure more closely, and more explicitly, than any other fictional form. (Sweeney 4)

As a result of the genre's formalism, any major deviation can be calculated to engender in the reader anxiety, to divorce expectation from conclusion.

Of course, by the late seventies the detective genre had come to permeate popular culture. But this popularity also makes defining the genre difficult, as its many practitioners bring unique variations on the basic plot of detection of those pulp stories that launched Hammett's career—the first flourishing of the genre's viable integrity. Of course, that even Hammett was writing "true" detective novels has long been called into question. Raymond Chandler writes in "The Simple Art of Murder" that "there are still a number of people around who say that Hammett did not write detective stories at all—merely hard-boiled chronicles of mean streets with a perfunctory mystery element dropped in like the olive in a martini" (16). In the thirty years between Chandler's comments and Ford's novel, it has become even more difficult to define the detective novel, but certain elements do recur. The novels' essence swirls about the loner hero and his (and sometimes her) actions in a world in which, to cite Chandler again, "gangsters can rule nations and almost rule cities, 'in which a man may be killed for little reason' and his death should be the coin of what we call civilization" (17). But the plots now may or may not involve mystery. While Ross Macdonald's detectives unwrap layers of mystery to uncover a deed lying in the past, John D. MacDonald points Travis McGee in the direction of a problem, and the reader reads not so much to uncover the mystery but to savor the hero's methods and personality as the plot unfolds. Even Robert B. Parker's Spenser novels demonstrate how far removed from the element of mystery the novels may be. Parker is perhaps the author most consciously working in the genre; his dissertation considered the novels of Hammett, Chandler, and Ross Macdonald, and his novels display the machinery of the convention and frequent allusions to the landmark authors and works. Yet he, too, sees the flexibility of the genre. For instance, his 1978 novel *The Judas Goat* has Spenser not solving mysteries per se, but stalking terrorists across Europe and North America. And it should be pointed out that Hammett's first novel, *Red Harvest*, sees his Continental Op not solving mysteries but using brute force and guile to destroy the corrupt power structure of a western mining town.

The most obvious link between Ford's novel and the genre is the opacity of the plot, and his only significant deviation from the genre is his failure to adequately resolve the plot's machinations. But even in this respect, Ford can be seen employing established trends to underscore his own purpose. As the American vein of detective fiction in the twentieth century has emphasized the actions of the hero over the Byzantine plot itself, the novels have delineated a modernist world through which the hero moves. In this world the hero is a loner—not only isolated from the mass of humanity, but also isolated from the narrative's players, whose agendas, vis-à-vis the novel's mystery, are contrary to the hero's. A most articulate argument linking the detective genre with the modernist movement comes in Scott R. Christianson's comparison of Chandler's fiction and Eliot's poetry. Christianson states that the "Tiresian posture" of the "isolated modern hero sitting before a spectacle of modern chaos and trying to make sense of it all . . . is the posture of the autonomous and lonely hard-boiled detective" (142). To illustrate his position, he employs Chandler's hero:

Marlowe proceeds almost blindly, at the mercy of disparate and unconnected experiences, now hitting upon something which might be a clue to some part of the mysteries he has encountered, then getting beaten up, shot full of "dope," kidnapped and imprisoned, at once helped and hindered by the nefarious characters he encounters. . . . Like Hamlet, the only thing Marlowe knows is that there is something rotten in the state of Denmark—or rather, California. Like Prufrock, however, Marlowe knows he is "not Prince Hamlet, nor was meant to be"; while he is the protagonist in his own story, he's just a bit player in the social drama of the L.A. underworld. The "denouement" in Chandler's novels offers

Expectation, Reality, and Alienation in *The Ultimate Good Luck* only the return of the detective to the same place he began. . . . In a pattern repeated throughout the novels, Marlowe is no richer and has no fuller understanding of the world except for a wider experience of its discontinuity and futility. (143)

While Christianson limits his discussion to Chandler, his observations are germane to the greater portion of the genre, with each of the major authors and a legion of the minor ones crafting heroes whose relationship to the world mirrors the modern one that he sees in Chandler's work. Ford, then, can be seen as extenuating the strains already heard in the genre; instead of showing the alienated hero to the reader and allowing the reader to identify with him while remaining comfortably aware of the conventions of genre, he places the reader squarely into the chaos in which the hero finds himself.

The Ultimate Good Luck does conjure recollections of earlier plots—those of Hammett, Chandler, and Ross Macdonald—as the events whose causes are only suggested swirl about the characters: it is never clear whether Sonny has actually hidden the missing drugs, as he claims, or if the police really did keep a portion of what they confiscated. Memorable scenes are staged, but their significance to the central events are never explained, nor is the reader prepared to encounter them. For instance, Bernhardt takes Quinn, after he has been visited by a drug dealer, to see the body of another murdered dealer. The lawyer explains that the man was killed by the police for having sex in a car and not paying a sufficient bribe, but the explanation does not ring true:

"Did *I* have him killed?" Quinn said.
"No."
"Did Deats?"
"The police," Bernhardt insisted and looked at him seriously. It was a warning.
(96)

The mysterious Deats's role in the plot is never fully explained. Near the novel's conclusion Susan Zago claims that he works for her husband, but her ¬redibility is already in doubt, and the fact that she has him murdered suggests that Deats's relationship to the husband is tenuous so that she could safely carry out the murder. Bernhardt's murder, too, is never accounted for. He is machine-gunned by a Mexican in peasant garb, and his death is not anticipated, nor is it explained. The man who kills him appears to be in the employ of Susan Zago, but she never tells Quinn anything about the murder; she merely notes its having taken place. Finally, with the death of Bernhardt and no further mention of Señor Zago, Quinn's only chance of getting Sonny released lies with Susan Zago's gang. Muñoz, who is apparently her lover, tells Quinn that he can have Sonny released because his brother is a guard, his motivation five thousand dollars and nothing more. No other reason is given, and when a gun battle ensues over a chance comment made in Spanish, no explanation will appear. Much like Chandler's *The Big Sleep*, when the event that precipitates a number of murders is not motivated by logic but by the insanity of General Sternwood's younger daughter, much of the violence in *The Ultimate Good Luck* appears to come unexpectedly from Susan Zago's lust. But whereas Chandler always provides a concrete explanation in his work, Ford does not, leaving his audience as well as his characters wondering what has happened.

The second connection between *The Ultimate Good Luck* and the detective genre comes with the characters who populate the work, each of whom carries a pedigree from previous works.

Quinn's antagonists are immediately identifiable as such. The mobster Señor Zago, holding court in a Spartan office in his isolated villa, looks like a "a kraut butcher." His businessman's demeanor and blue-collar appearance link him to figures of American mobsters in the canon of detective fiction—likewise his henchman, Deats, a sadistic dandy who tokes a joint as he calmly menaces Quinn. Susan Zago, the mobster's American wife, is beautiful and treacherous, her treachery the result of her egotism: she fancies herself a painter, and all of her paintings show her own face. She has been having an affair with the lawyer whom Quinn hires to engineer Sonny's escape from prison and, apparently, with the young leader of a group of casual revolutionaries. There is a suggestion that she has ordered Bernhardt's murder and shows little remorse when discussing him later: "She seemed amused, as if Bernhardt had been a child she was tired of" (188-89).

Quinn's allies likewise assume familiar guises. Quinn's girlfriend, for instance, is beautiful and cool-headed. Bernhardt functions in a somewhat specialized role—that of the liaison between society and the loner-hero. Such figures regularly appear in the genre. Generally, they appear as police detectives who hold equal measures of respect for and frustration with the hero who operates beyond the bounds of regulation. Although the most widely known figure of this type is Dr. Watson, the figure also appears in the American detective novel with, for instance, Lieutenant Dundy in *The Maltese Falcon,* and reappears in various incarnations throughout Chandler's work and up to Parker's. One of the most vivid manifestations is the economist Meyer in MacDonald's work. His is an especially good example as he is not a member of the constabulary (as the figure generally is), and as an economist he helps McGee navigate the shoals of a society that functions via monetary systems. In this regard he is much more like Bernhardt, who himself guides Quinn along the legal system's meandering path, and who attempts to show him the nature of Mexican society.

These novels pivot on the figure of the hero. Harry Quinn is, at first glance, quintessentially such a figure. A loner and Vietnam veteran, he tries to keep his world as self-contained as possible. Referring to the tattoo he has, the words "Good Conduct," he thinks: "All the colleges he'd ever been in didn't teach him what he'd learned in two years out of the world, that once strangers you couldn't see started shooting guns at you and trying to set you on fire way up in the sky, plans didn't take you too far. And the only thing smart you could do was try to stay efficient and keep your private shit together. . . . Good conduct was what kept you in the picture, kept ground underneath you instead of on top, and that was the only basic concept you could count on" (37).

After his return he drifts about, taking a number of blue-collar jobs that enable him to maintain a solitary existence. He works as a fitter's helper on the offshore oil rigs where he is able to escape from the life he shares with Rae in their apartment, afraid because "he saw how much he was losing control *with* her, and he couldn't handle it" (45). The other jobs he holds also remove him from direct human contact—except when such contact involves conflict. They move to California, and Quinn begins repossessing cars from the sailors and marines stationed nearby, staking out their apartments and trailers in a black turtleneck and jeans until he is ambushed by two sailors, strangled unconscious, and kicked senseless in the desert. Before journeying to Mexico he works as game warden in Michigan, hunting for poachers at night, where he enjoys "the high-density sensation of solo work at night. It made you feel out of time and out of real space and located closer to yourself, as if located was the illusion, the thing he'd missed since he'd come back, the ultimate good luck" (77).

The picture of Quinn that emerges in the novel's flashbacks is one of a typical American hero dating back to the novels of James Fenimore Cooper: the loner hero who exists at the fringes of society, living the brutal life of the frontier that calls upon strength and resourcefulness. He places himself in situations that invite conflict, but this conflict enables him to flex his resolve and frees him from the constraints of a universal morality, allowing him to establish his own code of behavior.

While Quinn appears to be a typical hero in his attitude and lifestyle, he deviates from the pattern in one very curious way—he doesn't actually *do* very much. His mission in Mexico is to facilitate Sonny's release from the prison. To accomplish this he employs the Mexican lawyer Bernhardt, with his knowledge of the penal system, to engineer the system of bribes required. And with Bernhardt's employment, Quinn's work is over—he spends the bulk of the novel being shuttled about by Bernhardt on various trips to the prison as the events of Sonny's release unfold along with the complications arising from the belief that he has stolen a portion of the drugs he was carrying. In fact, until his death quite late in the novel, the lawyer absolutely directs Quinn's actions. An instance of their relationship is apparent in a segment of dialogue regarding Deats, the American thug who is moving about the perimeter of the plot. In the employ of the novel's leading underworld figure, he has already threatened Sonny in prison and Quinn in his bungalow. Quinn asks Bernhardt:

"What's happened with Deats?"
"Nothing," Bernhardt said.
"But it's getting done right?"
"Yes. But it is best to be very cautious now," Bernhardt said. "Mr. Deats is not a mystery. But he is a problem to be solved. And we must take pains." (93)

Here, Bernhardt is the one who holds understanding and directs the action while Quinn is left to question and merely follow him. This passage provides a glimpse into Ford's technique of thwarting the reader's expectations. He at once calls attention to the fact that events are swirling around the protagonist and demonstrates how little control he has over these events. Bernhardt's cryptic answer underscores Quinn's helplessness by suggesting that he has direct knowledge and hence a greater degree of control over the situation than does the purported hero. The explosion of a terrorist bomb further underscores Quinn's failings as a hero. When it goes off, killing several tourists, Quinn runs toward the blast's aftermath, leaving Rae behind. She confronts him afterward: "Then you're just a stupid fuck, aren't you? . . . It's the oldest trick they know. Set a bomb and three minutes later set another one, and you get the police and all the other stupid assholes. . . . Didn't they teach you anything in the marines?" (118). In this case Rae, who has no special training, proves to be the more capable of the two in the crisis. Immediately after this event, the reader again sees that Quinn is perhaps the least aware figure in the novel. Relating the apparently random event to Bernhardt in the latter's office, Quinn notices the lawyer's gun lying on his desk:

"Do you need that in here?"
Bernhardt smiled. He leaned his head a fraction toward the wall behind and opened his hands. "Ladrinos steal the paintings from the Palacio de Bellas Artes to hold for ransom." He made a wry face. "The bomb is diversion. But violence is promiscuous." (122)

Of course, it is no fault of Quinn's that he is a stranger to his environment, but such does not negate the fact that he is fairly ineffectual as a protagonist. Indeed, the only point at which Quinn does act comes in the novel's final pages when, driven to a secret location by Susan Zago—another instance of Quinn's being pulled about by various forces and characters—he anticipates a revolutionary's pulling his gun, kills him, and skillfully avoids being shot in the ensuing gun battle in which all others perish. Ford crafts this scene to show that Quinn has finally controlled his circumstances to a greater degree than those around him. The man he is about to shoot, Susan Zago's lover, has snagged his own gun on a lantern he is carrying. When Quinn draws upon him and orders him to freeze, she beseeches Quinn, "He's just a baby . . . . He isn't doing this right, please. You haven't given him a chance" (194). Only here does Quinn become aligned with the mysterious force of chance or luck in the world; he becomes an agent of fortune, while others remain at its mercy.

Of the individual's inefficiency of interaction with the world Quinn is quite aware. He attempts to counter it with his ideal of "good conduct." At the same time he understands it to be at the center of human existence. Quinn states that "the essence of the modern predicament" is that "the guy who had it in for you was the guy you'd never seen. The one you loved was the one you couldn't be understood by. The one you paid to trust was the one you were sure would cut and run. The best you could think was maybe you'd get lucky, and come out with some skin left on" (35). All of the characters are in the same predicament. Sonny is helpless in prison and is dependent on the efforts of those outside to free him, indeed, to ensure his very survival. Sonny's last appearance is marked by his having lost an ear, apparently from an effort to force him into revealing the whereabouts of the missing drugs. Quinn implores him to stop holding out, but Sonny, apparently dazed by what has happened to him, is unable. He is murdered soon after this.

Sonny's case is significant for the effect it has upon the reader, who is unable to determine whether he deserves his situation. He is trapped between the government and the drug syndicate. Arrested for muling drugs to the United States, he is accused of stealing half of the drugs and letting himself be arrested to cover his theft. When confronted by Quinn, he denies any involvement, and the truth of the matter is never revealed. This ambiguity destabilizes the reader's interpretation of both Sonny and Quinn. If Sonny is cheating the employers and using Quinn to escape from the prison, *and* Quinn suspects such, then Quinn is in effect allowing himself to be manipulated in a manner most unbecoming to a dynamic hero. But if Sonny is innocent, then Quinn is helping to redeem an injustice. But the truth of Sonny's situation is never revealed, and the reader is forced to abjure any judgment.

Rae, too, is left without agency. While she does initiate the process of

Sonny's escape before the novel begins, she does little except what Quinn tells her. In flashbacks, the narrative shows how she moves about the country, always following the direction of various boyfriends, until the last one abandons her at the dogtrack, where she meets Quinn.

Even Bernhardt is more a catalyst for the events' occurrence than the motivator of the events. While he guides Quinn through his meetings with Sonny and, later, Señor Zago, all of his machinations remain behind the scenes. The reader finds out that much has been going on. Bernhardt seems to have some familiarity with the murder of the low-level drug smuggler whose body he takes Quinn to see in the night. He has had, at some point, an affair with Susan Zago, and seems to be aligned in some way with Señor Zago—a situation that certainly places him at the mercy of circumstance. And he seems to have some conduct with revolutionary factions in the area. But overriding all is the fact that he seems to have no inclination of his impending murder and is able to do nothing to avoid it. The word *seems* must be used at this point because Ford never satisfyingly ties his story together in the dénouement.

While the argument might be made that such expository lapses point to Ford's failure to account fully for the tradition's demands, several other non sequiturs appear, unconnected to the central plot and suggesting an overriding scheme within the novel to undercut the reader's expectations.

The most glaring of these events is the terrorist bombing that occurs midway through the novel; the bomb, concealed in a Baskin-Robbins, blows to pieces a middle-American family that has stopped outside. Not only does the bomb itself turn out to be wholly unrelated to the plot (it has been set to divert attention from an incidental crime), but in its aftermath, when the Mexican soldiers begin rounding up citizens indiscriminately, we see again the randomness of the novel's world.

The novel is sprinkled with events that thwart the audience's expectations. Early on, Quinn meets a down-on-her-luck American girl who strikes up a conversation with him. They spend the evening and the night together, and she disappears, contributing nothing to the novel except the opportunity for Ford to present an incident in which expectations are thwarted.

Expectation, Reality, and Alienation in *The Ultimate Good Luck*   65

During their evening together, they attend a boxing match at which one of the fighter's eyes is knocked out of its socket. Quinn knows "[i]t was just a pug's trick, he had seen it worked before. It looked plenty bad, but it wasn't as bad as it looked. A good corner could put the eye back, and two stitches would hold it in" (7). Despite this being a known circumstance, all the participants fail to follow decorum: the audience does not know how to respond, the injured boxer walks about the ring in a daze, the referee attempts to cradle the eye but can't seem to manage this, and finally the other boxer inexplicably punches his opponent in the face, at which point the crowd goes berserk. Here, what should have been a choreographed performance turns instead into chaos, just as the experience of reading the novel will for the audience.

While the sinister Mr. Deats circles around the plot's periphery like a shark circling divers in murky water, he actually appears only once, when he and a silent associate question Quinn in his rented bungalow. During this well-developed scene, the two force Quinn into a prone position and place a scorpion on his chest. Ford works the reader here—with Quinn trying to remember just which type of scorpion is the most deadly and his muscles "organizing themselves into a unit, waiting for the scorpion to hit him"(53)—in a scene reminiscent of innumerable B-grade suspense tales. But all proves for naught; the scorpion is dead, meant only to frighten the hero, and Quinn finishes the scene far less courageous than ridiculous.

There is much in the novel's background filigree to suggest that Ford is crafting a world in which elements of the familiar mingle with the terrible or absurd. During Quinn's encounter with Deats, the television is broadcasting a game show. Ford juxtaposes Quinn's interrogation and his efforts to escape the scorpion with a vivid description of the show, even going so far as to describe the differing camera angles. The vividness of his description points to a desire to call forth the images of a world familiar to the reader even as Ford is building suspense through the threat of incipient violence. This is a technique that he will employ at several points. The site of the bomb blast is a Baskin-Robbins, and the family of middle-American tourists, the father, mother, and teenage daughter, are described in detail as well. Ford summons another popular icon when he describes a Pepsi truck that has crashed. As two Mexicans stand next to the burning truck swilling spilled bottles of cola, Quinn drives past, noting "a brand new cab-over Mercedes with PEPSI stenciled backward in red script across the blunt nose. When he got beyond the cab he could see in the mirror the driver inside, his face sprouting blood and jammed up into the windshield" (70). At another point Quinn reads an American paper while riding back to his room, and it is here that Ford wryly demonstrates the absurdity of the novel's world:

All the stories in the American news were published in the wrong syntax. U.S. TEAM WINS ISRAELI RIFLE SILVER. Below it was a photo of some American marksmen holding rifles and smiling in yarmulkes and nylon jackets. Another said ASSOCIATION OF TWINS INTERNATIONAL MEETS, and above it was a photo of some fat twins. There was a story about a grandmother in South Dakota stabbing a lion to death with a button hook inside her travel camper. The story didn't say how the lion had come inside the camper or why there was a lion around at all. Mexicans would understand it. Americans lived in an ocean-to-ocean freak show, and there was a good reason to be here where things were simple instead of up there where things were bent wrong. (48-49)

Things are immediately proven to be not so simple when Quinn is confronted by Deats in the next scene.

At its furthest extension, employing this technique of interjecting into the banal the malignant, *The Ultimate Good Luck*'s narration exhibits a violent and perverse sexuality that affects the reader in much the same way as Bosch's *Garden of Earthly Delights* affects the viewer. In both cases the work pulls the audience between the familiar and the aberrant to create an unsettling vision. When Ford employs this technique, he is not doing so to titillate the reader, but to demonstrate how quickly the familiar environment can change for the individual, how little control each person actually maintains over his or her world. The teenage daughter of the American tourists is described so as to focus exclusively on her sexuality: "she had on pink terrycloth short-shorts that bound in her crotch"; "The daughter was eyeing the soldiers in the band kiosk who were looking at her and smiling and whispering"; "His daughter had noticed Rae and was looking at her curiously, twitching her hip from side to side as if they were sharing something evil" (112-13). In the explosion's aftermath, Quinn, running over, notices first "the American girl's pink hot pants. They weren't on her now but were wadded into the muffling system of the taxi that had been blown over" (116). He next finds her under her father's body, "odd-shaped and missing most of the part of her where her shorts had been" (116). Because Ford never provides a picture of a fully developed individual, one doesn't experience empathy for her, but only horror that her sexuality, her essence in this case, has been corrupted absolutely.

The epicenter of this condition is the jail where Sonny is being held, to which we are introduced in a lengthy passage:

> There were plenty of edifying stories about the Oaxaca prisión. As many as there were parts of the body to get interested in. . . . There was the one about the American jockey . . . [who] came down eventually with a burning that made his testicles swell up and burst before a doctor could get inside. There was . . . the kid from Beloit with an earache who died in two hours when whatever it was in his ear made connection with his brain. People committed suicide with crochet needles. The *mayores* in the "F" barracks beheaded their boyfriends and left them in their beds for days. But the story that interested Quinn was the Austrian woman whose husband . . . was an appliance-store owner and wasn't healthy, and his wife flew from Vienna and visited him every day. And every day the matrons in the women's precinct submitted her to the most intimate personal searches. And after a while, Sonny said, the woman began to come twice a day, in the morning and during siesta, when the matrons had more time, and then more often, until eventually the matrons got bored and wouldn't search her unless she paid them. (14-15)

The degradation of helpless individuals continues even outside the prison. Driving into the prison, Quinn witnesses an army checkpoint where soldiers "watched from under the plank hut while the searchers cruised through the Indian passengers, pointing at bundles and yelling to make the women raise their dresses while the men stood awkwardly with their arms up" (19). Waiting further back in the line is a red Dodge van in which are "three rows of American college girls all talking at once and looking out the dusty windows at the front of the line. . . . Quinn . . . wondered which ones would have to pull down their jeans for the soldiers" (20). Leaving the prison, Quinn sees "the red travel van . . . parked beside the station hut with all its windows broken and its seats pulled out.

None of the girls was around anymore. They were Americans, but there was nothing he could do for them, and it gave him a cold bone feeling to wonder where they were and what they were getting to look at next" (34).

The helplessness that Quinn feels, the same to which many of the characters succumb, is identical to the feeling that Ford instills in the reader who anticipates the familiar patterns of the detective/adventure genre. All involved with the novel, characters and readers alike, surrender the sense of agency and become, in essence, foreigners navigating through a strange land. This state is one that is explained to Quinn early in the novel by the girl he encounters: "You lack a frame of reference that allows you to take the right mental picture" (12). For Quinn, the disenfranchised Vietnam veteran, and for Rae, who has drifted around the United States, the condition is not endemic to Mexico, but exists in America as well. The clearest articulation of this feeling of displacement comes when Quinn describes how he "had had a sense when he joined the marines that the country he was skying out of was a known locale, with a character that was exact and coordinate and that maintained a certain patterned feel. A thing you could get back with if you had a reason. But that patterned feel had gotten disrupted somehow, as though everything whole had separated a little inch, and he had dropped back in between things, to being on the periphery without a peripheral perspective" (36).

This feeling of Quinn's is one shared by many in a culture whose raison d'etre is change and progress, and Ford is attempting to instill that feeling into readers of his work. By adapting the familiar pattern of the detective/adventure novel, he gives his work a disjointed feeling, one that continually knocks the reader about even as it demonstrates how the characters are knocked about by their fictional world. In building this portrayal, he joins with those who have also seen ours as a mutable and frequently malignant world. The novel itself, then, is for the reader equivalent to the modern world Quinn recognizes as hostile to the individual, a world which is itself "the tissue of everyone's loneliness" (86).

We think of the key, each in his prison

Thinking of the key, each confirms a prison
—T. S. Eliot, *The Wasteland*

To be is just as great as to perceive or tell.
—Walt Whitman, preface to *Leaves of Grass*

The Confessions
of an Ex-Suicide

Relenting and
Recovering in Richard
Ford's *The Sportswriter*

Edward Dupuy

Richard Ford is onto something. In his third novel, *The Sportswriter*, he has created a new character in the American literary landscape: a happy man. Frank Bascombe may not seem to fit the mold for what is often considered happiness. He is, after all, a man of losses, a man with a long list of titles beginning with "ex"—ex-fiction writer, ex-husband, ex-lover, ex-professor, ex-father to his oldest son, Ralph. Frank's losses could embitter him, for loss and happiness are terms not commonly conjoined. Nevertheless, Ford's deft portraiture avoids bitterness and irony. Bruce Weber, writing for *The New York Times Magazine,* noted that "*The Sportswriter* surprised many critics with its overarching lack of irony. In the narrator's commodious acceptance of the world's unexpected turns, it was a departure from the alienated, often nihilistic spirit that has pervaded much of America's fiction in this decade" (59).[1] Ford's characterization of Frank asks for some apposition of happiness and loss. The terms are not mutually exclusive, but neither is their relation causal: loss does not cause happiness, and happiness does not prepare one for loss. Ford does unite the terms, however, not only by means of his unironic tone and lambent style,[2] but through the first-person narrative.

Frank is the teller of his own tale. Although no longer a writer of fiction, he nevertheless narrates the events of his own life. This "double reflex" of the novel—a man who says he has given up fiction, yet who tells us, in a work of fiction, that he has given it up and who nevertheless recounts his story—points to the importance of telling for Ford.[3] Ford sees writing as telling. In an essay written for *Esquire* in 1983, he relates his first encounters with the "three kings" of American literature: Hemingway, Faulkner, and Fitzgerald. Although his reading of all three eventually came to bear on his own writing, it was Faulkner who first awakened in him the power and efficacy of language. He came to see that

> language somehow became paramount for its own sake. . . . When I read *Absalom, Absalom!* . . . everything came *in* to me. . . . Somehow the literal sense of all I did and didn't understand lay in the caress of those words—all of it, absolutely commensurate with life—suddenly seemed a pleasure, not a task. . . . Before, I don't believe I'd known what made literature necessary. . . . In other words, the singular value of written words, and their benefit to lived life, had not been impressed on me. That is, until I read *Absalom, Absalom!*, which, among other things, sets out to testify by act to the efficacy of telling, and to recommend language for its powers of consolation against whatever's ailing you. (581)[4]

In part, Frank's telling of his own tale makes possible his consolation, his unique reconciliation of loss and happiness. In other words, *The Sportswriter*, like *Absalom, Absalom!*, portrays the efficacy of language, and though language could not, in the end, console Quentin Compson (he couldn't tell the whole story), it does offer Frank a handle on what's "ailing" him. Frank's act of telling becomes a confession. It not only discloses and acknowledges the events of his life but also reconciles him to those events. Thus, unlike his counterpart in Faulkner's novel, Frank does not become a suicide. He becomes, instead, what Walker Percy, in *Lost in the Cosmos*, calls "an ex-suicide" (78).

For Percy, the ex-suicide is the person for whom "[t]o be or not to be becomes a true choice, where before you were stuck with *to be*" (77). He continues:

> Consider the alternatives. Suppose you elect suicide. Very well. You exit. Then what? What happens after you exit? Nothing much. Very little, indeed. After a ripple or two, the water closes over your head as if you had never existed. . . . Now, in

Relenting and Recovering in *The Sportswriter*

the light of this alternative, consider the other alternative. You can elect suicide, but you decide not to. What happens? All at once, you are dispensed. Why not live, instead of dying? You are free to do so. You are like a prisoner released from the cell of his life. . . . Suddenly you feel like a castaway on an island. You can't believe your good fortune. You feel for broken bones. You are in one piece, sole survivor of a foundered ship whose captain and crew had worried themselves into a fatal funk. (77)

The ex-suicide washes up on an island where he is able to see things for the first time. He contemplates the mystery of his existence. He is different from the "non-suicide," his fellow islanders, who worry about the very things the passengers on the sunken ship have worried over. "Since [the ex-suicide] has the option of being dead," Percy writes, "he has nothing to lose by being alive" (79).

Although Ford himself prefers to see *The Sportswriter* as a "book about getting on" (Bonetti 84), reviewers have called Frank Bascombe a survivor.[5] As such, he is a see-er. Like Percy's ex-suicide, he appreciates the mysteries of the everyday. At the time Frank tells us the essentials of his life—"My name is Frank Bascombe. I am a sportswriter" (3)—that is, at the beginning of the novel, he is trying to get on despite two profound shipwrecks, Ralph's death and his divorce from X. These are two events of his life he would change if he could. Since he cannot, he simply tries to avoid regret and prevent ruin: "[F]or your life to be worth anything you must sooner or later face the possibility of terrible, searing regret. Though you must also manage to avoid it or your life will be ruined.

"I believe I have done these two things. Faced down regret. Avoided ruin. And I am still here to tell about it" (4). Thus begins the telling of his tale and the efficacy of that telling.

One way Frank has avoided regret and ruin is by cultivating an appreciation for the everyday. Like the ex-suicide, he looks, perhaps for the first time, to the world around him for mystery. He tells us, "Stop searching. Face the earth where you can. Literally speaking, it's all you have to go on" (53). Or, at another place, he says: "If you seek a beautiful peninsula, look around you" (113). This attitude is evident in the opening scene of the novel, when Frank meets X at Ralph's gravesite on Good Friday. Since he doesn't "know how to mourn and neither does X" (11), he has brought with him a poem to read. "It is a poem," he says, "about letting the everyday make you happy—insects, shadows, the color of a woman's hair" (19). He tells us that he believes quite strongly in the power of the everyday and tells X, who is skeptical, that he thinks "we're all released to the rest of our lives" (19). Is he not hinting at the freedom and dispensation of the ex-suicide?

This line of conversation fades, however, as do many in the novel, and Frank expresses his like for X's new hair, part of the everyday. She ends up telling him that he is "very adaptable" (21). Like the ex-suicides, then, Frank takes refuge in the simple things around him. He looks for mystery wherever he stands. I do not mean to imply that Frank is a shallow optimist; what he sees, really, is the ever-present possibility for choice,[6] part of his adaptability: "Choices are what we all need," he says (7). Since reading the poem over Ralph's grave does not seem to be helpful, Frank chooses to stop. He does not press the issue. In typical fashion, he tells us: "It is possible that reading a poem over a little boy who never cared about poems is not a good idea" (19). For Frank, possibilities abound.

Another reason Frank can be considered an ex-suicide rests in his relenting nature. As the word suggests, Frank yields—he becomes pliant or flexible—to the vicissitudes of life. As Weber put it in the passage cited earlier, he displays a "commodious acceptance of the world's unexpected turns." He is about as far from Thomas Sutpen, Jay Gatsby, and Captain Ahab as a character can get. Frank does not try to subdue and steer his life; rather, he muses over its inviolable temporality. Things change, and the more he can adapt himself to change, the better is he able to get on. Frank tells us: "[T]hings change in ways none of us can expect, no matter how damn much we know or how smart and good-intentioned each of us is or thinks he is. Who'd know that Ralph would die? Who'd know that certainty would grow rare as diamonds? . . . None of our lives is really ordinary; nothing humdrum in our delights or our disasters. Everything is as problematic as geometry when it's affairs of the heart in question. A life can simply change the way a day changes—sunny to rain, like the song says. But it can also change again" (107). Frank relents time and again to the delights and disasters of life. No doubt, much of his relenting comes from Ford's own view of life. Ford says he thinks people might

Relenting and Recovering in *The Sportswriter*

think *The Sportswriter* is sad, but he sees it as sad only in the way everybody's life is sad at some point or another (Bonetti 84). Frank gets on because he relents to life's inherent sadness. He is wounded, but woundedness does not preclude happiness.

But Frank relents in other ways, too, and, again, this relenting seems to be related to Ford's own views—this time, his views of reading and writing. I do not wish to suggest here that Frank is a simple organ, a convenient mouthpiece, for Ford's own literary theory, that Frank is really a veiled Ford, as Eugene Gant was a thinly veiled Thomas Wolfe. After all, Frank quit writing fiction; Ford still writes. Frank is divorced; Ford is married. Frank has children; Ford is childless. Nevertheless, it is Ford who gives Frank choices and possibilities. Ford says this about the relation between the writer and the characters he creates: "You have options. They don't have any options" (Bonetti 96). It is inevitable, then, that without being strictly autobiographical, both Frank and the novel itself exhibit much of Ford's own experience as a writer and reader.

In his essay about the "three kings" of American literature, Ford maintains that he finally had to relent in order to understand Faulkner. He says: "[T]hough Faulkner could seem difficult, really he was not if you relented as I did" (586). As we have seen, the power of words, language for its own sake, is central to Ford's notion of telling. Here, Ford suggests the power of words for the reader. As the teller captures the efficacy of language, so the reader relents to its power. Telling and reading are really the opposite sides of the same coin—language. In Ford's view, readers must surrender themselves, give in, to the text. Reading to satisfy a system or to justify an abstraction is not real reading; it is antithetical to relenting. Relenting demands personal involvement on the part of the reader, not detached analysis.

Frank is a man who sees the world as a text to be read. Since he claims no system—no myth—to order his reading, he relents to the text of the world just as Ford relented to the text of Faulkner. Unlike Quentin Compson, Frank does not feel compelled to figure out the text, to get a firm grasp on it. He does not feel the "rage to explain," for example, so characteristic of writers in the South.[7] Rather, he luxuriates, when he can, in the wonder of the text itself. He can—and must—leave some things unread, unexplained, and incomprehensible. For Frank, this relenting to the text not only makes him an ex-suicide but also preserves the mystery inherent in the everyday, necessary for the ex-suicide to maintain his status as such.

Frank's relenting nature underlies his reasons for leaving Berkshire College. The college was full of unrelenting teachers. He tells us: "[W]hat finally sent me at a run out of town after dark and at the end of term . . . was that . . . the place was all anti-mystery types right to the core—men and women both—all expert in the arts of explaining, explicating and dissecting, and by these means promoting permanence. . . .

"Real mystery—the very reason to read (and certainly write) any book—was to them a thing to dismantle, distill and mine out into rubble they could tyrannize into sorry but more permanent explanations" (222-23).

For Frank, the teaching profession attempts to undermine the very nature of life itself. Since he sees life as a mysterious text to read, a text full of change, he cannot tolerate the closed readings his colleagues impart to literature. Frank sees their efforts to explain literature, which endures, as inevitably confusing literature with life and thus creating the illusion that life itself endures, is permanent. Teachers become unrelenting to the mysterious text that is the world. They dupe themselves into believing that they can leave nothing unread. Hence, Frank sees that his colleagues wish to live a life of perpetual youth with literature as their passport. In so doing, they depart from truth and deceive their students. The truth is, he tells us, "Some things can't be explained. They just are. . . . Literature's consolations are always temporary, while life is quick to begin again" (223). Life is forever a text which cannot be fully read, and to get on in life, one must finally relent.

Frank's relenting nature carries over into his relationships as well. If the world is a text to be read, then so, too, are the people who live in it. And people, like the world, cannot be fully read, cannot be fully explained. After Ralph's death, during Frank's worst days of dreaminess, a condition he defines as "a state of suspended recognition, and a response to too much useless and complicated factuality" (42)—a word Ford uses for alienation—Frank tells us he "must've slept with eighteen different

Relenting and Recovering in *The Sportswriter*

women" (128). Feeling suspended from the world and from himself, Frank tried to reenter the world through those women. The unifying element of all those relationships was the attempt both Frank and his partners made at full self-disclosure. Full disclosure is something similar to giving a closed reading of a text. It is an attempt to explain everything about oneself, with the hope that such disclosure might, for a time at least, end the terrible suspension of dreaminess. Frank describes the encounters in general terms: "All at once I was longing with all my worth to be part of that life, longing to enter completely into that little existence of hers as a full (if brief) participant, share her secret illusions, hopes. 'I love you,' I've heard myself say more than once to a Becky, Sharon, Susie or Marge I hadn't know longer than *four hours and fifteen minutes*! And being absolutely certain I did; and, to prove it, loosing a barrage of pryings, human-interest questions—demands, in other words, to know as many of the whys and whos and whats of her life as I could" (129).

The problem with full disclosure, however, is that it reduces everything to facts—the antithesis of mystery. As Frank says, "[W]hat I was after was illusion complete and on a short-term, closed-end basis." He was, he tells us, "trying to be within [himself] by being as nearly as possible *within* somebody else. . . . And it doesn't work." Frank realizes he should have relented in his relationships. He should have let "the plain, elementary rapture a woman . . . could confer, no questions asked" please him (130). Full disclosure doesn't work because people, like life, cannot be fully analyzed, cannot be fully read. In Frank's view, to believe otherwise is to traffic in deception.[8]

By the time he meets Vicki Arcenault, then, Frank has learned much. His relationship with her is different because he has "relinquished a great deal. I've stopped worrying about being completely *within* someone else since you can't be anyway—a pleasant unquestioning mystery has been the result" (132). But Frank has not learned his lesson thoroughly. During his trip to Detroit with Vicki, he reverts to a search for full disclosure. He goes through her purse while she is sleeping. In her wallet, he finds a picture of a man he thinks is her ex-husband, Everett. Vicki wakes up, and after a brief altercation she makes an oblique reference to her dead stepbrother, the actual man in the picture. Frank then realizes that he has misread the "text." In his search for full disclosure he has not only got himself caught, but he has trapped himself into a misreading of the signs. His attempt at achieving full disclosure, his struggle to explicate the text, has made him strive for the very permanence for which he vilified his colleagues at Berkshire. He has created a deceptive structure, but he has only deceived himself. Frank does long for a permanent relationship, but not one based solely on analytic factuality. And though he feels ashamed of his self-delusion, he has nevertheless rediscovered the truth about the temporality of life, that "So much of life can't be foreseen" (139). He feels a "swirling dreaminess" return (139), a dreaminess that will abate only with relenting. As he tries to go to sleep, he tells us, "for a moment I find it is really quite easy and agreeable not to know what's next" (141). What is next is an abominable interview with Herb Wallagher, a spring snowstorm, and an early return to Haddam, where Frank finds Walter Luckett waiting for him. None of these events was expected.

Walter Luckett is, of course, what Frank Bascombe would be were Frank not the great relenter. Ford's bringing the two characters together points, among other things, to the difference between yielding and unyielding to texts—both of the self and the world. Walter cannot relent. He cannot come to terms, literally (his short-lived attempt at writing a novel manifests this point), with what has befallen him. Walter must know. He is shaken by his wife's leaving him, and he is compelled to understand his brief homosexual encounter. Like Quentin Compson, Walter embodies the "rage to explain." During their midnight meeting, when Frank has just returned from Detroit, Walter says, "I don't know what you'd want to say about either of us," referring to him and his male partner that night at the Americana Hotel (187). Walter has to say something. Frank's response is completely in keeping with his relenting nature: "Nothing might be enough" (187). In Frank's estimation there is not much to tell, just the "bedrock and provable facts" (188). There is no mystery to Walter's affair. Although Frank would rather not hear it, Walter nevertheless tells his story.

Because Walter's tale is steeped in factuality, he cannot really relent to the consoling power of language. Although his telling does console him

Relenting and Recovering in *The Sportswriter*

in some measure—after the telling, he says, "I do feel better, thanks to you. . . . I feel like some new opportunity is just about to present itself" (193)—Walter has not relented completely. He still feels compelled to explain himself. In fact, he had planned to make himself the central character of the novel he began to write on Easter morning. Walter wanted to explicate his own life. In his suicide note to Frank he wrote: *"It's a novel about me, with my own ideas and personal concepts and beliefs built into it. It's hard to think of your own life's themes. You'd think anyone could do it. But I'm finding it very, very hard. Pretty close to impossible"* (349).

In his zeal to tell about himself, Walter stumbled onto one of the fundamental mysteries of life—the relation between language and reality. Since he relents to neither, Walter finds himself without choices. As Frank explains to X: "Walter gave himself up to the here and now, but got stranded. Then I think he got excited, and all he knew how to do was sentimentalize his life, which made him regret everything" (334). In giving himself up to the "here and now," Walter had finally come upon the mystery he so desperately needed. Instead of luxuriating or wondering at that mystery, however, he felt compelled to dismantle and explicate it— he had to attempt full disclosure. Unable to experience the mystery while at the same time telling about it—a tool "real" writers possess—Walter felt trapped. He saw that his telling would only destroy the mystery. Thus, he tells Frank, "I admire you all the more now for the work you've done" (349). In Frank's early days as a "real" writer, he was able to experience the mystery and tell it at the same time—that is, Frank was able to relent to both language and reality. When he was no longer able to relent to language, when he lost the consoling power of language, Frank opted for reality—for the everyday mysteries inherent in the world about him. He gave up the "rage to explain" so that he could still have choices—"it is no loss to mankind when one writer decides to call it a day" (47).[9] Walter, of course, found himself with only one choice; he exited.

Although Frank and Walter did not really know one another well, Walter's suicide affects Frank more than he is willing to admit. Since death is the only real closure that the world provides, it remains for Frank a part of the text he would rather leave unread. It is too factual for him; there is not enough mystery about it. Hence, he tries to avoid it at all costs. After he hears of Walter's suicide, he proposes to Vicki just as she has realized that their "love" will not get them "all the way to death" (294). He calls up Selma Jassim, whom he has not seen for years, from a phone booth near "Ground Zero Burg" (300), an appropriate objective correlative for his state of mind. In a roundabout way, he even proposes to Selma. As they speak Frank is wounded by an errant grocery cart, and after their talk he is attended by Debra, a modern Samaritan. Although Debra consoles him with a root-beer float, Frank cannot, in the end, escape the task that has been set before him. He knows it will wound him; nevertheless, he must confront the empty fact of Walter's death.

When he returns to Haddam, Frank sees new text to read. His once neutral suburbia is no longer "unprepossessing and unexpectant" (39) but is a lie of "Life-forever" (319); he sees it as trying to attain the permanence of a closed reading—unattached, aloof. But the cold fact of Walter's death has penetrated the lie. Frank says: "Death is not a compatible presence hereabouts, and everything is in connivance—forces municipal and private—to say it isn't so; it's only a misreading, a wrong rumor to be forgotten. . . . This is not the place to die and be noticed, though it isn't a bad place to live, all things considered" (319). The text of suburbia is a text designed to foster a misreading of life. It promises permanence, just as the explications of the Berkshire professors did, but, as we have seen, life is not permanent. Surburbia lies because it is inconsistent; it tries to provide closure while at the same time excluding the ultimate closure—death. Although death is an intruder in the suburbs, life can still be found there.

Of course, in his quest for mystery, Frank himself has tried to avoid the ultimate closure. Death and its cohort, grief, are far too factual for his mystery-laden world. They close off too many possibilities. Nevertheless, the fact of death remains, and Walter's suicide has reminded him not only of that factuality but of Ralph's death as well. Frank grieves doubly— once for Ralph and once for Walter. His grief thrusts him into the unwanted world of facts. On the train to New York, after he has finally read Walter's suicide note—the text, the permanent explication of death— Frank laments: "What I have is awful, mealy factual death, which once you start to think of it, won't go away and inhabits your life like a dead skunk

Relenting and Recovering in *The Sportswriter*

under the porch" (351). As Frank sees it, death shuts off possibilities, especially the possibility to relent. Frank has been able to get on this far because he has yielded to whatever was before him. But he cannot relent to death. If he does, then it "won't go away." The only real way to relent to death, Frank realizes, would be to die, and to die would be to destroy all mystery. Death must remain that part of the world, that part of the text, that remains unread. Besides, if he were to yield to death, Frank would have to abandon his status as an ex-suicide and become a suicide, like Walter. Frank prefers life. He puts his faith in its changeableness and mystery—not in death's permanence and factuality. He ventures to New York, the city of flux, and he is not disappointed. At the eleventh hour on the day of resurrection, life recovers him. Frank lives to confess his tale.

Richard Ford is a most uncommon southern writer—which is to say that, for the most part, his work seems to have little in common with most twentieth century southern writing. On the surface, his southern credentials are convincing enough: he was born in 1944 in Jackson, Mississippi, and grew up there. As a child he lived next door to the Jefferson Davis School and across the street from the house where Eudora Welty had lived as a child thirty-five years before. But Ford left the South at eighteen and lived elsewhere for nearly a quarter-century, and only one of his works—he has written five novels, a volume of stories, and a collection of three novellas—has been set in the South. That novel, *A Piece of My Heart* (1976), takes place largely on an island in the Mississippi River between Mississippi and Arkansas, and in it are touches of Faulkner and also perhaps Cormac McCarthy. Each of the following works is set in a different place: *The Ultimate Good Luck* (1981) in Mexico, *The Sportswriter* (1986) and *Independence Day* (1995) largely in the Northeast and upper Midwest, the highly praised collection of stories *Rock Springs* (1987), as well as *Wildlife* (1990), largely in Montana, and *Women with Men* (1997) in the Northwest and in France. And for reasons other than location, Ford's best work, *The Sportswriter*, seems to have very little in common with the traditional southern novel. Neither does his sequel to *The Sportswriter*, the Pulitzer Prize-winning *Independence Day*, nor does his other work of the 1990s.

Nor does Ford, in his choice of residence or his remarks on writing, demonstrate any particular alle-

Post-Faulkner, Post-Southern?

Fred Hobson

giance to geographical place, southern or otherwise. Bruce Weber, writing in the *New York Times Magazine,* has called him "possibl[y] America's most peripatetic fiction writer" (50), and Ford, who lived in Michigan, New Jersey, Mexico, and Montana, among other places, before returning to "the sticks of Mississippi" (as he puts it), and who now lives in New Orleans, acknowledges that he finds it hard to stay put residentially or artistically. "I try to exhaust my own interest in a place," he has said. "Then I'll just move on, write about someplace else where I kind of notice again how people accommodate themselves to where they live" (Weber 63). Place he defines as "wherever we can find dominion over our subject and make it convincing" (Bonetti 71). It is a postmodern definition of place.

If, then, a devotion to place—generally, a particular place—defines the southern writer, one would have to conclude that Ford is no southern writer at all. But he is, very much so, as I hope to demonstrate, although a writer who suggests that the accepted definition of a southern writer has perhaps been too narrow. It is doubtless true that *most* southern writers, for reasons growing out of the regional location and experience, have been more devoted to place and to history than most nonsouthern ones—but not all southern writers. "We were not a family," Ford has said, "for whom history had much to offer" ("My Mother, in Memory" 44), and he could have said the same thing for place. Ford knew that his mother had been born in a dirt-floor cabin in Arkansas—and that there was Indian blood in his maternal grandmother's family—but he had no idea of his mother's *father's* birthplace or national origin. Ford's father was a country boy who quit school in the seventh grade, worked for a time as a produce stocker for a grocery store, and later became a starch salesman, traveling through the Deep South. Ford's parents lived partly on the road in the early years of their marriage, and moved to Jackson shortly before their only child was born. The young Richard Ford traveled with his father on sales trips through Mississippi, Arkansas, and Louisiana; he also, in his early teens, had a few minor scrapes with the law. Ford's father died when he was sixteen, and two years later, after spending summers with his grandfather who managed a hotel in Little Rock, Ford went off to Michigan State University to study hotel administration.

Such is hardly the biography of a Southern Agrarian: Ford belongs

Post-Faulkner, Post-Southern?

quite literally to a different *class* of writers. He did not come to literature because of family tradition or interests—as a teenager he cared far more for cars and bird hunting than for books—but rather because, at Michigan State, he discovered Faulkner, particularly *Absalom, Absalom!* Reading in his room in East Lansing about Thomas Sutpen is hardly the same as that other transplanted Mississippian, Quentin Compson, talking about Sutpen in his college rooms in Cambridge, but Sutpen's story and the way Faulkner told it fascinated him. It was reading Faulkner, Ford later said, as much as anything else that made him determine to become a writer ("The Three Kings" 581).

If at first (after brief attempts at law school and teaching) Ford attempted to write fiction like Faulkner's—as reviewers noted when *A Piece of My Heart* appeared—he also was looking to Hemingway, and that first novel, in fact, betrays more of Hemingway's influence than Faulkner's. The setting on the Mississippi is reminiscent of Faulkner's "Old Man," and a sure touch with plain white southerners, a certain mythic sense, a narrative complexity, and occasionally the style are Faulknerian. But the dominant style, the pace of the story, the tough-guy tone, and, between chapters, the short semiautobiographical segments recalling childhood (as in *In Our Time*) more nearly resemble Hemingway. The story involves two men who come, for differing reasons, from distant locations—Robard Hewes from California for the love of a woman, Sam Newel from Chicago because he's falling apart—to the remote island in the Mississippi, and one of the men, Newel, is more than a little autobiographical: a native Mississippian, studying law in the North, whose father, a traveling starch salesman (the possibilities in that are endless for fiction) in Louisiana, Arkansas, and Mississippi, had suffered a heart attack and needed company on the road.

A Piece of My Heart is a violent book, and so are *The Ultimate Good Luck*—another Hemingway-like effort which deals with the Mexican drug trade—and *Rock Springs,* stories influenced by Hemingway, Sherwood Anderson, and possibly Ford's friend Raymond Carver. In these three works Ford seemed to have staked out his territory—backwoods country, unsentimental tone, and low-life characters, some running from the law, others running for other reasons. Those who called this minimalist fiction were, in the main, on target: Ford's characters live from day to day, seeming to have few goals save sex, freedom from the law, peace of mind, and enough money to get by. It was also a fiction in which Ford seemed to have put his southern origins behind him for good; except for a character or two who talk like Flannery O'Connor characters, there is almost nothing in this body of work to remind us that the author comes from the American South.

But Ford's ability to change places is matched only by his ability to change voices and literary modes, and his novel *The Sportswriter* is as different from his earlier work as it is possible for a work by the same author to be. In this novel Ford leaves behind backwoods and low life for eastern suburbs and educated professionals, and no one could call *The Sportswriter* minimalist fiction. It is extravagant fiction, and also very wise. But no one called it southern fiction either, and seemingly for good reason. It takes place largely in New Jersey, partly in Michigan, and—for its last nine pages—in a very unsouthern part of southern Florida. *The Sportswriter* is a superb novel, suggestive and richly allusive, but one which seems to have very little to do with Dixie. Ford might be a southerner by birth, but if one searches for the postsouthern, post-Christian southern novel, this appears at first glance to be it.

Ford's narrator-protagonist Frank Bascombe had been born in the South, but that seems to have been largely an accident of geography. Now thirty-eight and prosperous, he doesn't put much stock in those things that are supposed to concern southerners—history, place, religion, family, community, race, or southern mythology. An ex-novelist and currently a writer for a slick sports magazine that sounds like *Sports Illustrated*, he has lived in suburban Haddam, New Jersey, within commuting distance of New York, since he sold movie rights to a novel some years before. He lives, it is clear, in John Cheever country, not William Faulkner or even Walker Percy country. His primary concerns as we meet him are coming to terms with the grief he has felt over the death of his nine-year-old son, Ralph, and the breakup of his marriage not long after his son's death. As the novel begins, after meeting his former wife at their son's grave Good Friday morning—which also happens to be Ralph's birthday—Frank takes off for Detroit to interview a paralyzed famous ex-football player.

He is accompanied by his new girlfriend, Vicki Arcenault. He will return the next day, having had a disastrous interview and having concluded that things won't work out with Vicki. He will nonetheless have Easter dinner with Vicki's family, learn of the suicide that afternoon of a fellow member of the Divorced Men's Club, and take the train later that night into New York to his magazine's midtown offices.

Frank, as I have said, has little regard for the past, and little apparent interest in it. "All we really want," he says early in the novel, "is to get to the point where the past can explain nothing about us and we can get on with life. Whose history can ever reveal very much? In my view Americans put too much emphasis on their pasts as a way of defining themselves, which can be death-dealing" (24). And again, "*I* am a proponent of . . . forgetting. Forgetting dreams, grievances, old flaws in character—mine and others'. To me there is no hope unless we can forget what's said and gone before, and forgive it" (144).

Frank, then, loves to live in the present, in the material world, the consumer world, and Ford the novelist approaches that world as unapologetically as Frank, refusing to be judgmental, declining even to be ironic, at least in his remarks on that world (although not in other particulars). The question of irony, or lack of it, in dealing with mass culture in *The Sportswriter* is one that must be considered, one that goes to the heart of the novel. One might assume, as several reviewers did, that Ford *is* being ironic in dealing with the excesses of American commercial culture: how, one might ask, could a writer of Ford's keen eye and discrimination fail to be? But I am not so sure. Ford is indeed a discriminating writer, but he is also a writer who would object less to the excesses of popular culture than to a particular view—call it elitist or privileged—that would pass judgment on that culture. It is precisely this resistance to easy irony, a resistance to the *temptation* to be ironic in dealing with popular culture, that distinguishes Ford from numerous other contemporary writers; for if an ironic vision is generally assumed to be a literary virtue, such a transcendence of accessible irony—or, perhaps, a deeper irony that turns on itself, ironizing the ironists—may be even more desirable. As concerns Frank Bascombe, Ford's hero is given to looking through mail-order catalogs: "I loved the idea of merchandise, and I loved those ordinary good

American faces pictured there, people wearing their asbestos welding aprons, holding their cane fishing rods" (196). He is indeed drawn to what others would call bad taste—the Arcenaults' house with its life-sized crucifix in Sherri-Lyn Woods, the Arcenaults' poodle named Elvis—and views it all with fascination, without a hint of condescension, and, again, almost without irony. Frank is a good man but not a religious one—in many ways, a spiritual man but not a religious one. He finds his answers to life's puzzles in a palmist. He is at home in the world of things, and he knows in part why he is drawn to things, to mail-order catalogs: "In me it fostered an odd assurance that some things outside my life were okay still" (196).[1] And for the same reason he looks at Johnny Carson, or at the NBA Knicks and Cavaliers on television, *even* the Knicks and the Cavaliers, who were very bad in 1984. The game engages him, distracts him, keeps him from facing the abyss.

Frank Bascombe is a man who assures us not only that the past means nothing to him, but that family, at least ancestral family, counts for nothing. "Does it seem strange that I do not have a long and storied family history?" he asks. "Or a list of problems and hatreds to brood about—a bill of particular grievances and nostalgias that pretend to explain or trouble everything?" (29). "The stamp of our parents on us and of the past in general is, to my mind, overworked, since at some point we are whole and by ourselves upon the earth, and there is nothing that can change that for better or worse" (24). In his own case, Frank was "born into an ordinary, modern existence in 1945, an only child to decent parents of no irregular point of view, no particular sense of their *place* [Ford's italics] in history's continuum, just two people afloat on the world and expectant like most others in time, without a daunting conviction about their own consequence" (24). His father, Frank goes on to say, played golf a lot and died when Frank was fourteen. Frank was sent off to military school on the Mississippi Gulf Coast and went home on holidays "to my mother's bungalow in Biloxi, and occasionally I saw her brother Ted" (27) who took him on trips to Mobile and Pensacola but was not close to him. His mother remarried and moved to Skokie, Illinois, to live with her second husband, and after that, while Frank was at the University of Michigan, his mother treated him "like a nephew she didn't know very well, and

88   Post-Faulkner, Post-Southern?

who worried her, even though she liked me" (28). She then got cancer and died.

Such a family is hardly the Compsons or the Gants or the Fairchilds, or even the families of any number of contemporary southern writers. Frank has no conscious ancestral past, no family burden, not only no grandfathers but no brothers and sisters, no cousins—no cousins, that is, until the end of the story when he happens to run into some in Florida: "Since coming here the surprise is that I have had the chance to touch base with honest-to-goodness relatives, some cousins of my father's who wrote me . . . to say that a Great-Uncle Eulice had died in California, and that they would like to see me if I was ever in Florida. Of course, I didn't know them and doubt I had ever heard their names. But I'm glad that I have now, as they are genuine salt of the earth" (370). His cousin, Buster Bascombe, tells Frank about his father, and Frank realizes, "I hardly remember my father, and so it is all news to me, news even that *anyone* knew him" (371).

This, then, is our unburdened southerner. And not only do family and past mean nothing to him, the South and his identity as southerner, he insists, mean nothing to him either. The South of his remembrance—and this is Mississippi, remember—isn't mysterious, isn't violent, isn't savage, isn't racially benighted, isn't Gothic or grotesque, isn't even *interesting*. In fact, it is not the South that fascinates Frank but—and this will be a shock to those steeped in American regional distinctiveness or lack of it—it is the Middle West that is fascinating, and what Frank constructs is not a southern mystique but a kind of midwestern one. It is the American heartland, then, the much maligned Midwest, the target of much of Walker Percy's satire—to the traditional southern imagination, the tasteless, standardized, materialistic, and just plain boring Midwest—that this ex-southerner is drawn to. It is not the mind of the South he explores, but the mind of the Middle West: it is a practical, matter-of-fact, things-in-order kind of place, a land which finds reality in things, not in ideas—a land populated, Frank discovers, with Barbs and Marges and Sues, where there is available "anything-you-want-within-sensible-limits." In Detroit he reflects, "I have read that with enough time American civilization will make the midwest of any place, New York included. And from here that seems not at all bad. Here is a great place to be in love; to get a land-grant education; to own a mortgage; to see a game under the lights" (115). Even the midwestern accent—sharpened vowels, the dropped definite articles—fascinates Frank. And he approaches everything midwestern, as he approaches the suburban, middle-class culture of New Jersey, without distancing himself, without condescension.

Here we have, then, the southern expatriate for the eighties, with no interest in past, place, family, religion, community, guilt, and burdens of history, family or regional or otherwise. Or do we? It should be obvious by this point that, indeed, we do not—that the more Frank protests he is not interested in the past, in family, in place, and in the South, the more we are convinced that he is; and so, despite his own lack of storied past, distinguished family, and fixed place, is his creator, Ford. Frank's great interest in the *absence* of past, of historical burden, of family heritage, of fixed place, of community suggests a southern mind that is fascinated by these things. A true disregard of place, of history, would require an unconsciousness of it, and Frank has anything but that. Even the midwestern mind, as he defines it, is made up of qualities that are, conspicuously, *not* southern. Frank's is hardly the case of that other Mississippian in the Northeast three-quarters of a century before, Quentin Compson at Harvard, saying of the South, "I dont hate it. I dont. I dont" (Faulkner 378), but it is Frank Bascombe—who resembles in so many ways his creator—saying, "I'm not at all interested in the South. I'm not. I'm not." One recalls, more than incidentally, that Quentin's mother's maiden name was also Bascomb, a fact that would not have been lost on Ford, who, as we have seen, knew Faulkner's work very well. Frank Bascombe, then, is, quite literally, a cousin of Quentin Compson—though a distant one, in another place far removed from Mississippi.[2] In any case—to return to my larger argument—if we read *The Sportswriter* closely we find that Frank, and Ford, are very much interested in the South, in matters that are at the heart of the southern experience, and also that the narrative voice is a particular kind of southern voice, and that Ford is very much, as we shall see, within a particular southern literary tradition.

But, first, to return to place: Despite having no tie to a postage stamp of soil in northern Mississippi or a plantation in the Delta or a farm in Tennessee—and despite being the creation of an author who professes

Post-Faulkner, Post-Southern?

little faith in traditional ideas of place—Frank Bascombe nonetheless is keenly attuned to place. Although he calls himself "a man with no place to go in particular" (338), wherever he goes—and he is indeed on the move—he has a great desire, nearly a compulsion, to link with place, whether the place is suburban New Jersey or Detroit: a great sensitivity to where things are, what happened there, and what they meant.[3] We see this in particular in his detailed description of Haddam, the New Jersey commuter town in which he has lived for fourteen years—not the Haddam in Connecticut of Wallace Stevens's poem "Thirteen Ways of Looking at a Blackbird," although Ford's Haddam resembles Stevens's in certain ways: Frank is indeed one of the "thin men of Haddam" of Stevens's poem, one of the overly cerebral men, and Ford's novel, like the poem, is about ways of seeing, ways of perceiving.[4]

Just as Ford does not disregard place, neither does he neglect family and religion, as might appear to be the case. Family, in fact, is at the center of the novel, although a new kind of family. Frank and his former wife, known only as X, are divorced but still are linked, both through their grief over the death of their son Ralph and in their love for their two remaining children. Frank, who lives in the house they once had shared, sometimes comes to X's house, sits outside in his car, and waits to see what he can see. Further, at the end of the novel, he decides—in a setting not given to such discoveries in most southern novels, and a scene that almost parodies the idea of southern family—that to have an ancestral history, an extended family, even if an unfamiliar one, is not such a bad thing after all. After visiting his newfound relatives, the Buster Bascombes, in Florida, Frank concludes: "And truthfully, when I drive back up Highway 24 just as the light is falling beyond my condo, behind its wide avenue of date palms and lampposts, I am usually (if only momentarily) glad to have a past, even an imputed and remote one. There is something to that. It is not a burden, though I've always thought of it as one. I cannot say that we all need a past in full literary fashion, or that one is much useful in the end. But a small one doesn't hurt, especially if you're already in a life of your own choosing" (371).

One could point to other ways in which Frank is more southern than he professes—in particular, his rage against abstraction or rationalism and his love of mystery. His announced preference for the supernatural, the unknown, in religion—his distaste for "factualists" (204) or rationalists—is not very different from John Crowe Ransom's distaste for rationalism in his book *God without Thunder* (1930), and Frank's protests of those who analyze and categorize, who explain too much ("anti-mystery types right to the core" [222], he calls them), could have been uttered by Donald Davidson in his harangue against sociologists. "Some things can't be explained," Frank says. "They just are" (223).

These and other traditional southern concerns could be explored. So could further elements of parody of things southern. Not only does Ford have his ex-southerner discover his roots in a south Florida stucco bungalow (rather than, say, in Faulkner fashion, in the yellowed ledgers of an old plantation commissary), have him find that the current bearer of family honor is a retired railroad brakeman, "the salt of the earth," named Buster (a far cry from Jason Lycurgus and Quentin MacLachan), have him find religion, as Buster also does, in a palmist (rather than in a thundering Calvinist church or in the Big Woods), have him, at that, find only a "small" past (not one in "full literary fashion"), but Ford, in looking back on Frank's college days, has him describe the novel he had begun when he decided to be a writer, a novel nearly a parody of the usual racially charged, Christ-haunted southern production. It was the story of a young southerner trying to reconcile present with guilty past, being initiated by a series of adventures including "a violent tryst with a Methodist minister's wife who seduces him in an abandoned slave-quarters" (and what else, in one respect, was the postbellum South *but* "abandoned slave-quarters"?). The manuscript, Frank tells us, was "lost in the mail": "I hadn't kept a copy" (36).

Indeed, *The Sportswriter* itself is, among other things, a commentary on the traditional southern novel. It is not accidental that Frank's lone companion in his spacious home in Haddam is "a six-foot-five-inch Negro," an African student at the local seminary and a "stern-faced apologist for limitless faith" (30) who lives in the attic: Frank knows he is there, hears him, and feels a certain comfort in his presence. Other allusions to the southern past or to southern literature present themselves. I have spoken of Frank Bascombe's kinship, however improbable, with Quentin Compson.

Post-Faulkner, Post-Southern?

One must note, in other ways, Ford's sly and clever use of *The Sound and the Fury*. Not only is Ford's protagonist given Quentin's mother's name—and this novel, like Faulkner's, a story of family dissolution—but it begins on Good Friday and takes place on Easter weekend, as *The Sound and the Fury* does, and contains numerous symbols of death and resurrection. Further, Ralph Bascombe's birthday, over Easter weekend, is also the birthday of Faulkner's Benjy—whose original name was Maury, named for his uncle Maury Bascomb.

There is no particular system at work in all this. Rather, there are sly and nearly hidden references to any number of literary works, southern and nonsouthern, in *The Sportswriter*, and I would guess if one asked Ford about them he would say, as Faulkner used to, that he didn't even know they were there, and certainly meant nothing by them. One finds allusions not only to Wallace Stevens but also T. S. Eliot ("The Hollow Men") and Theodore Roethke ("First Meditation") as well. At other times one is reminded of Melville. "My name is Frank Bascombe" (3), the novel begins, echoing the first sentence of *Moby Dick*. "And I am still here to tell about it" (4), Bascombe, like Ishmael the survivor—and a Presbyterian, like Ishmael, whose companion is a giant black man—goes on to say. ("And I only am escaped alone to tell thee" [Melville 536], Melville, quoting Job, begins Ishmael's epilogue.) Indeed, Bascombe's given name is as full of possibilities as his surname. I *am Frank*, he tells us, but in fact he is anything but frank, anything but candid and reliable. This book of "truth-telling" (Koenig 86), as *New York* magazine called it, is in fact, on one level, a book of great prevarication; to be more precise, the narrator is factually reliable but emotionally unreliable. He calls himself a happy man, he insists he is a happy man, but like his ancestor Quentin he protests too much.

One hesitates to carry all this further, and I would not if Ford did not slyly ask for it, but giving his sportswriter the name Frank is doubly curious. For who was America's most notable sportswriter at the time Ford wrote but another Frank, named Deford. And our hero shares a great deal in common with Frank Deford—another with-it, sensitive, attractive man who writes in-depth human interest stories for a slick sports magazine (Deford, at the time, for *Sports Illustrated)*, had also written a best-selling novel (*Everybody's All-American*) for which he sold movie rights, and had endured the death of a child. One finds other suggestions that Ford, heeding in his novel contemporary popular writers as well as canonical ones, has created such a Frank—a Frank, that is, created by (Richard) Ford, Frank *of* Ford, Frank Deford. With any other novelist, I repeat, I might pass up the evidence, resist the temptation, but not with this author, an especially cunning and slippery sort.

Indeed, one could discuss *The Sportswriter* as a particular expression of the postmodern imagination, a novel about writing for writers, a work of literature which is among other things a rejection of "literature," which, as Frank Bascombe tells us, teaches us "lies" (16). (Sportswriting, on the other hand, which teaches us "that there are no transcendent themes in life" (16), is more to be trusted.) But rather than pursue those directions further, I wanted to return to this novel as a particular kind of *southern* novel, to turn to a particular southern literary tradition in which, I believe, it is possible to place *The Sportswriter.* Ford has written something of tradition and literary influences in an essay, "The Three Kings," in *Esquire* in 1983. Two of the three kings, the three writers whose influence he has felt, I have already mentioned—Faulkner and Hemingway. The third is Fitzgerald. But he does not here mention the writer whose work this novel most closely resembles—Walker Percy. For Frank Bascombe in *The Sportswriter* has a *voice* very much like Binx Bolling's in *The Moviegoer,* or, I should say, is a combination of Binx's voice and that of an earlier southern wanderer, Jack Burden in *All the King's Men.*

Frank Bascombe, that is, is another in that line of reflective and somewhat paralyzed well-bred, well-mannered, and well-educated young southern white males who tell their stories in the first person and are moved by the need to connect. (One finds other such examples in Allen Tate's Lacy Buchan in *The Fathers* and Peter Taylor's Phillip Carver in *A Summons to Memphis.*) Like Jack Burden and, especially, Binx, Frank is philosophical in a casual sort of way, a facile sort of way, fond of self-mockery, and given to inventing or appropriating terms to explain himself and his view of the world. Jack Burden, of course, explains his own conduct and that of others in terms of what he calls the Great Sleep and the Great Twitch; Percy, drawing on Kierkegaard and other thinkers, lets Binx talk about everydayness, certification, rotation, repetition, and the "Little Way." Frank has read his Kierkegaard as well—or his Percy. His creed of forgetting—"*I* am a proponent of . . . forgetting. . . . There is no hope unless we can forget" (144)—comes straight from the epigraph to Percy's *The Last Gentleman*, Kierkegaard's "If a man cannot forget, he will never amount to much" (*Either/Or*). And Frank, as well, is in the habit of devising *his* terms— dreaminess, literalism, factualism, relenting—to explain his states of mind and those of others. Dreaminess he defines as "a state of suspended recognition, and a response to too much useless and complicated factuality. Its symptoms can be a long-term interest in the weather, or a sustained soaring feeling, or a bout of the stares that you sometimes can not even know about except in retrospect" (42). Dreaminess results in paralysis, in getting nothing accomplished—operating somewhat like the fugue states of Percy's Will Barrett in *The Last Gentleman* or, even more, like Jack Burden's Great Sleep—and it occurs in Frank's life, as in Jack's, just before the breakup of his marriage. Frank resembles Jack in other ways. He is a writer who cannot write, fleeing from his novel-in-progress just as Jack flees from his dissertation. He tells his story, as Jack does, in a series of flashbacks which bring us finally back to the present. And when his son dies, he responds in Jack Burden fashion. When life becomes too tangled back East, Jack says, "[W]hen you don't like it where you are, you always go west" (Warren 309), and that is precisely what Frank himself does. Immediately after his son's burial, he takes off alone in his car, heading west. Unlike Jack, he can't make it all the way to the West Coast. He turns around and heads back to New Jersey—and dreaminess.

Frank calls himself a literalist, by which he means "a man [who] will enjoy an afternoon watching people while stranded in an airport in Chicago, while a factualist can't stop worrying why his plane was late out of Salt Lake, and gauging whether they'll still serve dinner or just a snack" (132-33). A literalist, then, is more engaged in the moment, more accepting, thinking more concretely. A literalist—that is, Frank—cannot abide "idiotic factualism or the indignity of endless explanation" (206). One wonders if Frank is as much of a literalist as he contends—what else is his story in *The Sportswriter* but an act of explaining, of making himself clear—but in expressing his strong *distaste* for factualism and in embracing literalism he is expressing nothing more than the presumed southern abhorrence of abstraction and preference for the concrete.

It is not only the casual philosophizing, however, that links Frank with Jack Burden and, in particular, Binx Bolling. Nor is it just the similar roles Binx and Frank play, the one—as the title announces—a moviegoer, the other a sportswriter. Both are watchers: one watches movies, the other watches sports. Each is essentially passive. But beyond that, it is the tone, the language, the cadences, the detailed social observation, the attention to southern *types* that links Ford with Percy. The ex-southerner Frank has as keen an eye for varieties of the southern species as Percy's Binx—for instance, in Frank's description of his Vanderbilt-educated internist in New Jersey, Fincher Barksdale, who "is the kind of southerner who will only address you through a web of deep and antic southernness, and who assumes everybody in earshot knows all about his parents and history and wants to hear an update on them at every opportunity. . . . [T]he perfect southerner-in-exile, a slew-footed mainstreet change jingler. . . . At Vandy he was the tallish, bookish Memphian meant for a wider world. . . . At Hopkins he met and married a girl from Goucher who couldn't stand the South and craved the suburbs" (68-69). [5]

All this is not necessarily to say that Ford is Percy for the eighties, Percy for expatriates, a post-Christian Percy, but it is to suggest that Ford, too, is in a tradition, and, at least in *The Sportswriter*, it is not principally the tradition of Faulkner, or of his other kings, Hemingway or Fitzgerald. Rather— as is also the case with a writer such as Josephine Humphreys in *Dreams of Sleep* (1984)—it is essentially the tradition of Percy. There is much more one could say about *The Sportswriter*, particularly how this novel, which is so much like *The Moviegoer* in certain ways, is so very different in others. But I will stop here. Suffice it to say that in *The Sportswriter* Ford, the presumed ex-southerner, has written a book about New Jersey that is very much a book about the South. He has written a southern novel in a southern tradition, a non-Faulkner tradition, in spite of himself. Or perhaps not in spite of himself at all. Rather, cleverly, slyly, he may have written a southern novel that he knew was southern all along. He is modern, indeed postmodern, but he is—to borrow and modify a term from John Crowe Ransom—postmodern with the southern accent.

Post-Faulkner, Post-Southern?

But I did not, as I waited, want to think about only my-self. I realized that was all I had ever really done, and that possibly it was all you could ever do, and that it would make you bitter and lonesome and useless. So I tried to think instead about [her]. "Children" 96

Men with Women

Gender Relations in Richard Ford's *Rock Springs*

Priscilla Leder

In a *New York Times Book Review* article, Vivian Gornick identifies Richard Ford as a creator of the lat-est version of "a certain kind of American story that is characterized by a laconic surface and a tight-lipped speaking voice." Like Hemingway fifty years ago, Ford employs narrators who "[have] been made inarticulate by modern life" (1) to express the isolation and loneli-ness of modern experience. Relationships between men and women serve to dramatize this experience for Ford, as they did for Hemingway. According to Gornick, though Ford has replaced Hemingway's "alle-gorical" women characters with characters who are men's "fellow victims," his depictions of relations be-tween men and women remain limited and unvarying, "irreducible in the writing" (32). In fact, relationships between men and women in Ford vary widely, though they share one central underlying theme: women seem mysteriously self-contained and serene, while men struggle to come to terms with their experience. The stories in *Rock Springs* develop this theme through a range of variations.

Ford's men and women characters are "fellows" in their quest for connection, what Ford calls "affection," and in their capacity for recklessness, especially with drink and/or sex. In dialogue, both men and women can be cryptic, banal, or insightful depending on the situation. Unlike men, however, women do not tell their own stories. The defining point of view in Ford's work, usually a first-person narrator, is always male. In Ford's longer works, with their extensive reflective passages, that point of view dominates the reader's attention. Since the short stories of necessity rely mostly on action and dialogue, the men and women characters command more equal access to the reader's consciousness. Thus, the stories provide the best venue for examining the dynamics of male/female relationships in Ford's fiction.

As Gornick recognizes, that fiction comprehends essential elements of the modern—alienated characters whose inconclusive actions and flat, vernacular language express their meaningless lives. Gornick's references to narrators who have been "*made* inarticulate," and "fellow *victims*" (my emphasis) imply that Ford's characters lack freedom, that they inhabit a world of unchanging despair. However, Ford's particular version of modernity creates a variable world which holds possibilities for characters, and for readers as well. For example, as David Crouse points out in "Resisting Reduction," the inconclusive endings of some of the stories in *Rock Springs* raise questions rather than closing off possibilities, "forc[ing] the reader to reflect" (56). In Ford's flat, vernacular sentences, syntactical innovation unfolds from commonplace phrases, revealing new possibilities in the most ordinary language. Finally, Ford's familiar characters behave and reflect as if they do have choices, especially about their own attitudes. When they struggle with questions of responsibility, they invite readers to consider their own responsibilities.

Relationships between men and women also contain multiple possibilities. Even the one unvarying difference between them—the dominance of the male point of view—is undercut by the men's obvious limitations. Often, male narrators reveal those limitations through their attempts to define not only women characters but also the whole range of experience, including themselves. In contrast, the women characters appear mysterious and powerful in their relative silence. Perhaps because of that silence, the women often seem more self-assured and emotionally autonomous than the men do.

In the stories of *Rock Springs*, men look to women for affection and reassurance, which they often do not find. Rather, they learn the extent of

Gender Relations in *Rock Springs*

their own vulnerability. Only very rarely can they accept that vulnerability as part of their human condition. Sometimes, they defend themselves by asserting power in traditionally male ways, a project which always fails. Most often, they take refuge in words—in "explanations" or in flat, limited verbal formulas. Those formulas typify Ford's particular modernism: on the one hand, their empty futility evokes the meaninglessness of modern existence; on the other, their familiarity engages readers. We can recognize, even laugh at, the banality of a statement like "[Love] was about never being in that place you said you'd never be in," but we also know the uses of such banalities ("Sweethearts" 68). When we can think of nothing else to say, we tell despairing people that "everything will be all right."

Women characters teach men about their vulnerability in different ways. First, mothers indirectly push their sons towards maturity by asserting their own sexuality and desire for freedom. Later, as sex partners, women who seem emotionally self-sufficient bring uncertain men to a sense of themselves and their condition. Men who seek excitement and/or instant status through lawless behavior encounter women who dwell comfortably in places of danger, something the men learn that they cannot do. Other women distance themselves from risky behavior, affirming the importance of responsibility. Interestingly, these responsible women most often provide the affection that men always seek but seldom find.

The variety of these roles reveals the realistic range of Ford's women characters, who seem limited only insofar as they do not tell their own stories. Because Ford's narrators are so often limited themselves, we see through them and their illusions about the women they encounter, which adds to the depth and realism of the women characters. Ultimately, relations between men and women in Ford are "irreducible" only because the women contain the mystery which draws the men towards self-knowledge. The stories in *Rock Springs* reveal the many variations Ford plays on this process of self-discovery.

To give coherence to that process, I shall construct a life history for the Ford protagonist in all his manifestations by considering the stories according to the age and life situation of their main characters. The adolescent protagonists of "Great Falls," "Optimists," and "Communist" confront the mystery of their mothers' sexuality and their fathers' potential for violence by striving for a detachment which will allow them to deal with what they have witnessed. In "Children" the older adolescent narrator moves into the adult world of sexuality and potential violence. Like the protagonist of "Winterkill," he experiences stereotypical male behavior through a peer who is both friend and rival. In "Empire," "Going to the Dogs," and "Rock Springs," the protagonist tests the power of his detachment by trying to manipulate his world and, through encounters with women, learns the limitations of that power. In the most "hopeful" of Ford's stories, "Sweethearts" and "Fireworks," the narrators witness the limitations of stereotypical male behavior in another man, and, through relationships with women, feel reassured of their connection to others.

Absent Mothers

The youngest of Ford's adolescent protagonists, Jackie Russell in "Great Falls" is in his early teens. After warning the reader that "[t]his is not a happy story" (29), the adult Jackie recounts the incident which precipitates his parents' separation: his father finds his mother with another man and threatens the other man with a pistol. The narrator confines himself scrupulously to the perceptions and thoughts of his adolescent self until the very end of the story, thus emphasizing his confusion and his sense of displacement from the shelter of his united family. Throughout the story, his descriptions of the landscape and of the family's solitary house "out of town" (30) emphasize isolation and loneliness.

Despite the isolation, the bleak landscape seems to teem with life when Jackie describes the hunting and fishing "expeditions" he shares with his father, Jack. Though Jackie recounts these in detail, he seems ambivalent about them. "I thought even then," he reflects, "with as little as I knew, that these were opportunities other boys would dream of having but probably never would. And I don't think that I was wrong in that" (30). Jackie undercuts his own statement of appreciation by emphasizing not what *he* feels, but what "other boys would dream." Nowhere in his extensive accounts of catching fish and shooting ducks does he express intrinsic pleasure in the activity.

Jackie's account typifies Ford's ironic treatment of stereotypical male adventure. Though his laconic style often evokes Hemingway's, Ford consistently undermines Hemingway's depiction of hunting and fishing as ritualized, almost sacramental struggles between worthy adversaries. Rather, hunting and fishing expeditions go wrong and/or result in mindless slaughter. Jackie's father does not "know limits," either legal or ecological. He catches a hundred fish in a weekend, and puts out corn and decoys to attract as many as sixty ducks at a time. Then, Jackie recalls: "I would stand and shine a seal-beam car light out onto the pond, and he would stand up beside me and shoot all the ducks that were there, on the water if he could, but flying and getting up as well. . . . [H]e could kill or wound thirty ducks in twenty seconds' time" (31). Jack sells the ducks (which is illegal), then spends the evening drinking in a bar with friends while his son plays pinball and "waste[s] money in the jukebox" (32).

The flat, neutral language with which Jackie describes his adventures with his father suggests his reluctance to identify fully with him. In addition, his account indirectly prepares readers for the discovery of his mother's adultery and diffuses their potential condemnation of her by inviting them to imagine her evenings alone in an isolated house and by revealing that she married Jack, a former air force sergeant, expecting that they would "see the world together" (30). Jackie's mother resembles many of Ford's women characters in that her motives must be surmised; she says little to explain herself. Her conversations with her husband take place off stage, and she is upstairs when her husband and son return home to find a young airman, Woody, standing in her kitchen.

No one contradicts Jack when he acts on the assumption that he has interrupted a tryst. Apparently, he asks his wife to leave, for she packs a suitcase and walks out of the house. His behavior towards Woody reveals that he does "know limits" after all: violence seems his only recourse, yet he cannot carry out the violence or imagine what end it would serve. With his loaded pistol under Woody's chin, he declares, "I don't have any idea what to do with you. I just don't" (40). Jack holds Woody at gunpoint until his wife walks away, then reiterates his bafflement: "I'd like to think of some way to hurt you. . . . I feel helpless about it" (42). Finally, he abandons his assault without resolving it and declares, "I don't want to have to think about you anymore" (43).

Jackie imagines his father as intending to shoot Woody yet afraid of the consequences. "I think he was afraid, afraid he was doing this wrong and could mess all of it up and make matters worse without accomplishing anything" (41). His language reduces the threat by making the shooting sound like an everyday task that must not be "messed up" rather than a choice between life and death. Jackie comprehends his father's frustration and the intensity of his emotions and attempts to diffuse them, even as the young Jackie tries to comfort his father by assuring him that "It'll be all right" (43). His father's paralysis cannot be resolved; it can only be dissipated.

While intense experience overwhelms his father, Jackie's mother "seem[s] so calm," speaking "in just her normal voice" (41). Like other women characters in Ford's stories, she stands untouched and controlled amidst chaos and change, moving away from her son into the mysterious realm of her own sexuality. She never speaks directly to him during the incident which precipitates her departure. Rather, she twice looks at him and shakes her head "as if it was not a good idea to talk now" (40) and twice waves to him from behind a closed window. Both gestures acknowledge the other person while assuming conditions that preclude communication: we wave when distance, noise, or haste make speech impossible. Perhaps she feels it prudent to keep silent in the face of her husband's volatility, but she hardens the distance between herself and her son by twice leaving without him.

Jackie tries to take some responsibility for the resulting estrangement: "Later I would think I should have gone with her, and that things between them might've been different" (42). His wistful conjecture marks his unexpressed sense of abandonment—he ignores the fact that his mother did not ask him to go with her. In fact, she implicitly assigns him to his father with the reminder that "Jackie has to be at school in the morning" (41). In their last conversation, she tells Jackie "I'd like a less domestic life, is all" (47). During that encounter, she begins to emerge for him as a sexual being rather than as a nurturer. After being invited to compliment her, he notices that she looks pretty in a different way, as if "she could be different about things. Even about me" (46).

Though she essentially abandons Jackie, he seems to accept her behavior as he accepts his father's. However, he does not try to imagine what she feels as he tries to imagine what his father feels. Rather, he ponders an unanswered question about her: Woody tells him she has been married and divorced before, but she denies it. This secret embodies her essential mystery—a mystery which distances her from her son and allows her to move serenely through disruptive events.

Unable fully to identify with his father's violence, excluded from the mystery of his mother, Jackie focuses on Woody. He associates Woody with himself, and his fluctuating image of Woody reveals his anxiety and his search for a way to deal with the changes he experiences. When he first sees Woody, he notices "his arms, which were long and pale. They looked like a young man's arms, like my arms" (36). Later, as he and Woody stand outside while the parents talk, he looks again: "They were, I saw, bigger, stronger arms than I had thought" (39). To the narrator, Woody is both young and vulnerable like himself and potentially powerful, as he would like to be. Unlike the violent father, Woody exudes an urbane detachment; Jackie admires him for knowing "about a lot of things, about the life out in the dark, about coming out here, about airports, even about me" (39). The detached urbanity which so impresses Jackie carries with it a kind of isolation. Woody tells the narrator, "'I once passed my brother in the Los Angeles airport and didn't even recognize him'" (39). "Knowing" the world may bring with it the inability to know others.

Through his identification with Woody, Jackie begins to develop the detached reflection which both sustains and limits the Ford protagonist. He thinks of Woody as, like himself, "the one left out somehow, the one who would be lonely soon," and then imagines that Woody, comfortless in his isolation, will have "no one to tell him that it was all right, that they forgave him, that these things happen in the world" (43). In imagining those reassuring formulas, Jackie reveals both their power and their limitation. To offer or to accept such comfort is to take refuge in words and the illusory resolution they provide.

In a series of unanswered and perhaps unanswerable questions, the adult Jackie ponders the incident that ended his parents' marriage and made him feel as if his life had "turned suddenly." He finds resolution in a formula of his own which generalizes and universalizes the behavior which still baffles him: "it is just low-life, some coldness in us all, some helplessness that causes us to misunderstand life when it is pure and plain" (49). For Jackie, as for other Ford protagonists, growing up involves rejecting a possible identity with the potentially violent father and acknowledging the mystery of the mother's sexuality through "explanations" such as this one—formulas which distance him from others even as they allow him to accept and even forgive them.

Like Jackie, the fifteen-year-old narrator of "Optimists" witnesses an incident which leads to his parents' separation and changes him and his life irrevocably. His railroad-worker father returns home early, describing for his wife, his son, and a visiting couple the disturbing accidental death of a hobo. The other man, Boyd, responds with an inexplicably vicious verbal assault on the distraught father, who in turn strikes Boyd a single powerful blow that kills him. The boy, Frank, modifies the incident in his account to the police to make his father seem less culpable, withholding his sense that his father has hit Boyd "to kill him." Though it helps his father, Frank's suppression of his knowledge signals his withdrawal from the man who taught him that "you can hit a man in a lot of ways" (179). He begins to see his father as "a man who made mistakes, as a man who could hurt people, ruin lives, risk their happiness. A man who did not understand enough" (183). The man who can "understand enough" can avoid being caught up in violence—and Frank, like the other young Ford protagonists, learns to aspire to be such a man.

The incident eventually estranges Frank from his mother as much as from his father, perhaps because, like Jackie, he comes to associate his mother's mysterious sexuality with his father's violence. Dorothy in "Optimists" seems calm, "very certain about things then, very precise" (184). Yet the story hints that she may be the cause of the crisis. In puzzling over Boyd's unaccountable antipathy towards him, the father speculates "'Maybe he was in love with you, Dorothy. . . . Maybe that's what the trouble was'" (184). Dorothy's relationship with Boyd, like Jackie's mother's first marriage, remains a mystery.

Her own "explanation" of the incident is equally cryptic. In talking to Frank, she presents it as a stroke of fate, a "coincidence," and offers a story from her childhood. On a "nature tour" with her father's girlfriend, she watched a flock of ducks take off from a frozen creek "'all except for one that stayed on the ice, where its feet were frozen, I guess'" (187). Her account of the incident, like other short narratives related by Ford's women characters, ostensibly explains and reveals but actually confronts the male character, and the reader, with inexplicable sudden death and/or male sexual misconduct. The girlfriend, an Assiniboin whom the mother labels "[j]ust some squaw" (186), supplies the term "coincidence" (187). Like the father's choice of a lover from another culture, the term seems not to fit—we can only guess at what two components "coincided" to bring about the deaths of Boyd or the trapped duck. Unlike the formulas with which men assert their "understanding"—formulas like Jackie's "it is just low-life"—the women's "coincidence" simply acknowledges and even deepens the mystery.

Women possess the mystery of life and death, which eludes the "understanding" men attempt to exert in order to protect themselves from "coincidence" and to cope with its consequences. Both Frank and Jackie seem traumatized by their adolescent encounters with their mothers' mystery, perhaps because their mothers appear to withdraw into it rather than nurturing their sons. (Frank's mother does try to comfort him, but she stares away from him out the window, smoking a cigarette, as she tells the cryptic story of the duck abandoned to "coincidence.") The space between Frank and his mother widens into time: the adult Frank reports that it has been "fifteen years, I think, since I [have] seen her, though I am forty-three years old now, and possibly it was longer" (188).

In both "Great Falls" and "Optimists" the distance between mother and son constitutes a mystery in itself: readers never learn who avoids whom, only that mother and son encounter each other occasionally by chance, through the "coincidence" which moves in and through women. While these chance meetings reinforce some sort of connection (Jackie says, "I can say, at least, that we know each other"), they provide no new understanding (49). In a chance encounter with her son in a grocery store, Frank's mother revives the enigma central to Boyd's death by literally going out of her way to deny any relationship between herself and Boyd. Then, they part in a way that seems like abandonment: she kisses Frank through an open car window and holds him "for a moment that seemed like a long time before she turned away, finally, and left me there alone" (191). She leaves with the man who was with her in the grocery store. Thus, for Frank as for the adult Jackie, who reports seeing his mother "with one man or other," the mother's sexuality continues to draw her away from her son and into some unknown realm.

Les in "Communist," another adolescent protagonist, also undergoes an incident which highlights his mother's sexuality along with male violence. Older than his counterparts at sixteen, he feels not so much abandoned as pushed into male adulthood and confronted with the isolation it can bring. He has already had "a few boxing bouts" and met "some girl-friends from that" (217). When he goes goose hunting with Glen, his widowed mother's boyfriend, he actually fires rather than assisting as Jackie does. The hunt (which may be illegal) seems another example of mindless slaughter, as Glen and Les fire into a huge flock of geese rising from a lake. Unlike Jackie, Les expresses strong emotions about hunting: his awe at the beauty of the rising flock mingles with his sense of power at his ability to destroy them. He thinks, "I could kill as many as the times I could shoot," and a few seconds later he hears a goose fall and land "with an awful sound, a noise a human would make" (227). This tension between male power and compassion intensifies when his mother comes to observe the hunters and geese.

Aileen, the mother, has been critical of hunting and hostile towards Glen, who has reappeared after a long absence. She remarks pointedly that "'[g]eese mate for life. . . . I hope you know that. They're special birds'" (219). When she finally joins the hunters, she admires the beauty of the geese in flight, but she also seems more tolerant of hunting and praises the hunters for the six geese they have killed. Les points out a seventh, wounded goose, swimming near the shore but unable to fly. Inexplicably, Glen refuses to retrieve the goose when Aileen asks him to, and pulls Les back roughly when he tries to do so. Aileen walks away, pronouncing a final condemnation on Glen: "'You don't have a heart, Glen,'

Gender Relations in *Rock Springs*

she said. 'There's nothing to love in you. You're just a son of a bitch, that's all'" (231).

In championing the goose, Aileen rejects the fatalism of the women of "Optimists" and "Great Falls." Rather, she displays responsibility and what Ford calls affection, even though it might be futile (what would they do with the wounded goose?). This opens up a new possibility for the maturing protagonist, one that Les soon has the opportunity to exercise. Glen pulls a handgun and kills the wounded goose, shooting it repeatedly like an enraged assassin. Then he offers the handgun to Les, saying, "'Don't you want to shoot me? . . . I'm ready for it right now.'" His gesture associates the solitary, disabled goose with himself, a Vietnam veteran who drinks "most of the time." As in "Optimists," the wounded bird evokes the man overtaken by anger and violence. Les, though he wants to hit Glen—"hit him as hard in the face as I could, and see him on the ground bleeding and crying and pleading for me to stop"—resists his own anger and opts for his mother's responsibility. Les sees Glen as "scared" of "something soft in himself." Partly because he identifies with Glen, he begins to feel "how sad and remote the world was to me" (232). He takes on the lonely burden of male responsibility, where violence destroys but compassion risks vulnerability.

Later, his mother introduces him to another sort of disturbing responsibility by very seriously and deliberately asking him, "'Do you think I'm still very feminine? I'm thirty-two years old now. You don't know what that means. But do you think I am?'" (234). The question makes Les feel "the way you feel when you are on a trestle all alone and the train is coming, and you know you have to decide." He knows that "that means" he must acknowledge his mother as a sexual being—that she is asking his opinion as a sexual man. He answers affirmatively, but then tries "to think of something else" (235). In this case, the mother's sexuality does not drive her to abandon her son, but it separates them nevertheless.

"Optimists" represents the final example of the process by which the boy loses his nurturing mother. Through that process, he also learns to mistrust the aggressiveness of the traditional male role and to trust the power of language, which both mediates and isolates. In subsequent stories, Ford's protagonists continue to explore both male aggression (which usually fails) and the possibilities of words. In addition, they begin to seek the elusive "affection" and nurturing through relationships with women and male friends rather than with parents.

Indifferent Nymphs

In "Children," seventeen-year-old George experiences male aggression vicariously through his friend Claude, and confronts sexuality in the sixteen-year-old runaway Lucy. Claude's father, a Blackfoot whose rough manner and prison record make him seem "dangerous," has brought Lucy to town and spent the night with her in a motel, then assigned his son to keep her out of sight, bribing him with "shut-up money." Claude initially sees Lucy as a symbol of his own powerlessness in the face of his father's moral carelessness and reacts with childish spite: "'I think we should kill her . . . just to piss him off'" (75). Throughout the day, as the boys take Lucy fishing, Claude alternately exchanges taunts with her, admires her sexually, and tries to show off before her. Later, after he has had sex with her, he becomes protective and proprietary, suggesting that they drive Lucy to the bus station in Great Falls rather than return her to his father, and saying, "'I wish I could marry her. I wish I was old'" (97). Though his attitude towards her changes, Claude always imagines Lucy in the light of his own ego. He remains traditionally male, and his aggressive fishing, like all male adventures in Ford's short stories, ends abruptly when he is cut by a whitefish fin.

Lucy embodies the mythic association between women and nature, both of which invite conquest. George's narration repeatedly describes her green dress with the clichéd epithet "as green as grass" (81). Like nature, she can never be fully explained; her motives, George thinks, are "a mystery" (80). Paradoxically, she seems most mysterious and self-contained when most vulnerable. She responds to Claude's adolescent taunt "'I bet you'd fuck a pig in knickers'" by asking, "'You want me to take my dress off?'" (93) and then takes off all of her clothes. Her naked body, like nature, eludes any formula the boys might apply to her. Looking at her, George thinks: "she was already someone who could be by herself in the world. And neither Claude nor I were anything like that" (94).

In George's experience, he and Claude cannot "be by [themselves] in the world" precisely because they need Lucy to develop and sustain their male identities. Lucy senses this, at one point asking them, "'Are you boys men now?'" (82). Their encounter with her develops their capacity for friendship by forcing them to deal with jealousy and competition, which they do, successfully. Claude's experience with Lucy makes him see himself as someone who could marry and love a woman, and perhaps it tempers his aggression: When he gives her a fish to kill, Lucy throws both the fish and Claude's knife into the creek. Later, he imagines himself loving Lucy as his father cannot. When Claude expresses this, George feels his "own life, exactly at that instant, begin to go by [him]" (98). With Claude, he enters into the inexorable cycle of reproduction, aging, and death, drawn in by Lucy, the light that marks the beginning.

George does not seize his own opportunity to have sex with Lucy and remains relatively passive through most of the day. Rather than act out as Claude does, he engages in the kind of reflection and explanation with which the Ford protagonist typically confronts experience. As Claude and Lucy have sex, he thinks: "She was pushing everything out. She was just an average girl" (95). "Pushing everything out," like many such comments in Ford's works, seems at once apt and cryptic. Does it mean that she is putting fantasies and emotions into action? If so, she behaves much as Claude does, trying on adult behavior. However, Claude and (vicariously) George respond to her, while she initiates action from inside herself, hence her apparent self-possession.

In characterizing Lucy, George at once likens her to himself and his friend, acknowledges her power, and tries to diffuse that power by leveling her into an "average girl." These thoughts fail to satisfy him, perhaps because he recognizes them as attempts to mediate her emotional impact upon him. He tries to think differently, to draw upon the power of language to create empathy: "But I did not, as I waited, want to think about only myself. I realized that was all I had ever really done, and that possibly it was all you could ever do, and that it would make you bitter and lonesome and useless. So I tried to think instead about Lucy" (96). In expressing this desire, George articulates the complex process through which Ford's narrators use language to come to terms with the world. Though language may inevitably serve to distance us from others, may always fail, we continue to imagine that it might also help us to connect, to express affection.

Trying to think about Lucy, George thinks instead about his mother, who has left him and his father and at the time of the story is "gone for good . . . though we didn't know that" (70). There, too, he encounters only mystery, imagining his mother behaving like Lucy, yet thinking such a picture must be "wrong." For George, as for the rest of Ford's adolescent protagonists, the loss of the mother's nurturing is associated with her sexuality. As the oldest of those protagonists, George begins to imagine replacing that loss through his own sexuality, rediscovering his mother in the women he meets. In a process typical of Ford's adult narrators, he seeks self-knowledge through an encounter with a woman who seems to embody the mysterious autonomy he desires for himself.

The thirty-seven-year-old narrator of "Winterkill," Les Snow, resembles the adolescent protagonists, partly because he has been laid off and his life, like theirs, seems a matter of waiting. In addition, he has lost his mother's nurturing because of her sexuality: he has come back to live with her and found her living with a boyfriend with whom he does not get along, though, he assures the reader, "I do not blame him for that" (149). In "Winterkill," as in "Children," two male buddies encounter a woman. Les's friend and neighbor, Troy, and the woman, Nola, seem as marginal as Les himself: Troy is confined to a wheelchair; Nola is widowed, left with only two thousand dollars. All three seek diversion in bars: "Just drunks, you'd think, and be right" (159).

In a scene reminiscent of "Children," Les and Nola have sex in Troy's Checker cab while Troy fishes. Holding Nola, Les thinks of his mother and her boyfriend snuggled warm in bed and tries to warm himself and Nola. Though it may warm them temporarily, their intimacy yields no lasting meaning. "'I'll do this, you know . . . and not even care about it. Just do a thing. It means nothing more than how I feel at this time,'" Nola says (162). Like Lucy, she seems intact in her mystery, acting on her own impulses rather than responding to others. Like the mother, she offers no permanent shelter. Rather, her isolation and mystery evoke a kind of danger, as she tells a story of death and betrayal. She has learned that her fatally sick husband has a mistress, and her wildly emotional response has led immediately to his final heart attack. Though she has loved him, she had begun to anticipate his death and thus seems somehow to have precipitated it.

She seems a danger to Troy and Les as well, not only to their friendship but also through coincidence: while she and Les seek warmth in the cab, Troy hooks what feels like a huge fish, strong enough to pull him out of his chair. At Troy's request, Les wades into the swift, freezing water to retrieve the kill. In a typical Ford twist on male adventure, the "fish" turns out to be a dead deer, and once again, the wounded/dead animal corresponds to the defeated man. Troy looks "as though it was him who had washed up there and was finished" (166). Les's dangerous act brings only pain, as Troy weeps in bitterness at the obvious irony of his catch. Even that intense bitterness seems diminished by nature, as "the river's rushing" (167) drowns out Troy's voice.

As the story comes to an end, the intensity of the characters' experiences—sex, danger, despair—dissipates rather than builds. The three eat together; Troy takes Nola back to the bar; Les walks, thinks, and finally at dawn hears Troy and Nola return and enter Troy's flat. Les concludes "that we had all had a good night finally. Nothing had happened that hadn't turned out all right" (170). As if to complete the symmetry of the events, Les goes out to fish. His act and his pronouncements transform the potentially disruptive events of the previous night into a ritual—a kind of ironic baptism which, perhaps temporarily, sustains the hapless trio. Les, at least, comes to feel "that though my life at that moment seemed to have taken a bad turn and paused, it still meant something to me as a life" (169-170).

The Burning Bush

Les must mediate the potential danger he confronts in order to use it; nevertheless, the danger embodied by Nola provides a passage to a kind of self-acceptance. Vic, the protagonist of "Empire," makes a literal passage on a train from Spokane to Minot the scene for a series of encounters with women who embody danger. In each case, sex with the woman provides a means of confronting the mystery of mortality—an expression of the human need to feel powerful and in control despite our helplessness in the face of death.

As the journey begins, Vic's wife, Marge, completes a game-book quiz which purports to predict how long people will live, asking her husband the questions as she answers them herself. As the reader later learns, the quiz carries an ironic poignancy: a year earlier Marge has become ill as the result of a tumor. Her doctors predict that the tumor is cancerous and that she will "probably die"; however, she recovers completely after surgery. The quiz asks: "'Do you feel protective often, or do you often feel in need of protection?'" (111). Vic answers "both," which turns out to be the best answer, but which leaves open the question explored by the story—when should one be "protective" by trying to escape or shut out the reality of death and danger, and when should one acknowledge them by being open and vulnerable to them?

Vic and Marge are traveling to Minot to provide "protection" in the form of support for Marge's sister, Pauline, who has become distraught at the arrest of her boyfriend and "cut her wrists . . . and bled all over the dog" (116). Though this attempt would never have proved fatal, Vic knows that "[d]eath was not an idle notion to Pauline," who "had taken an overdose once, back in the old wild days" (115). In those wild days Vic felt attracted to Pauline, when her "inflamed look" made him feel "like being in a car going down a hill out of control in the dark" (116). To experience Pauline's sexual power is to participate in her deliberate openness to death and danger—for Vic, to risk a delicious destruction. The more responsible Marge remarks that Pauline "makes life stop when she wants it to," acknowledging the power inherent in her risk-taking, but renounces that power for herself: "'I guess I wouldn't want to be like her,'" and Vic responds, "'You're not like her. . . . You're sympathetic'"(147). Caught up in risk-taking, people like Pauline lose the opportunity for affection—other people fade in the light of the flame of danger.

Vic has only one date with Pauline before meeting and marrying

Marge, but later, during the period of Marge's illness and hospitalization, he again encounters death and danger through Cleo, the wild younger sister of his next-door neighbor. Cleo identifies herself with an entire realm of death and danger—an outlaw motorcycle gang named Satan's Diplomats. Although she presents herself as their victim, her accounts of coercion, threats, and kidnapping carry a certain disturbing relish. For instance, to show Vic the "involuntary" "tattoo of a Satan's head she had on her ass[,] [s]he pulled up her shorts and turned her back to him from across the table, and smiled when she did it" (128). The smile and the provocative gesture belie the distress associated with an "involuntary" tattoo.

Though he listens to Cleo's melodramatic troubles, he balks at talking about his own—his feeling that "[h]e loved Marge, and if she died his life would be over. . . . [H]e'd go out in the woods and hang himself so no one but animals would ever find him" (129). In remaining silent about Marge, Vic allows himself to imagine that sharing brandy and sex with Cleo will help him forget his anxieties and comfort her as well. However, their actual encounter brings no comfort. Rather, it plunges him into an underworld nightmare. Partly inspired by demonic television images from the rock channel Cleo has insisted on leaving on (without the sound), Vic dreams that he has hanged himself only to learn that Marge will survive and "it was too late for him. All was lost and ruined forever" (132). Sex with Cleo constitutes a descent into Hades, not a temporary respite from death and danger. Like the story of Orpheus, Vic's dream ends in the loss of the beloved. In a reverse of the myth, Vic remains in the world of the dead while Marge ascends into the light "smiling out of a sunny window" (132).

In the real-life aftermath of his dream, he receives a phone call threatening Marge's life. The caller, who identifies himself as "the devil," reports that Cleo has died, but Vic thinks he hears her voice in the background. Cleo dwells in the realm of death and danger, remains in the fire (as evident from her wild red hair) without being consumed. In seeking oblivion—"protection" from death with Cleo—Vic has only increased his and Marge's vulnerability. When he realizes this, he takes refuge in the kind of platitude that Ford's narrators often evoke for protection. "Things you do pass away and are gone, and you need only to outlive them for your life to be better, steadily better. This is what you can count on" (136). This combination of stoical acceptance (with its echo of Ecclesiastes) and American optimism ("steadily better") represents the limits of human possibility in the face of death for the Ford protagonist. One must at once accept and remain somehow "cheerful."

Women characters more readily accept death and danger, even dwell within its realm as Cleo seems to do. Having recalled Pauline and Cleo, and thinking of Marge asleep in a roomette as the train rolls on towards Minot, Vic moves yet again into the risk and refuge of a woman's body. Sergeant Doris Benton, one of a group of soldiers on the train, first flirts with Vic and finally takes him back to her roomette for vodka and sex. As a soldier, Sergeant Benton embodies both reactions to death and danger—she protects the country and makes herself vulnerable in order to do so. In addition, she seems allied to a realm of mystery because she is stoned on marijuana during part of her encounter with Vic.

Unable to sleep, Vic joins Doris to escape the boredom of having "nothing to do but stare at a dark, cheerless landscape" (137). But despite the pleasure of the encounter, he wakes and thinks for a moment that "possibly he was dead, that this is how it would feel" (145). Doris affords no escape from the void, for she carries the void within herself: "[Y]ou can do a thing and have it mean nothing but what you feel that minute" (143). Once again, a woman contains the mystery and offers neither escape from it nor a solution to it.

Reunited with Marge, Vic begins to come to terms with the mystery. Out the window of the train, he sees that a "wide fire was burning on the open prairie" (146). The actual peril of the fire recalls the symbolic danger of Pauline's "inflamed look" and Cleo's red hair. Like her sister[s], Marge resonates with death and danger; the sight of the fire drives her to her "remotest thoughts," rather than to thoughts of their own possible danger, which concerns Vic. Unlike the other women, however, Marge reassures and nurtures him. He accepts the peril of death, not only outside the train in the flames but inside, in the form of the scar from Marge's surgery. "This can do it, he thought, this can finish you, this small thing"

(148). He feels "dizzy and insufficient" but "calmed," protected from the heat and light of the fire only by the window shade, conscious yet accepting of its presence all around him.

Vic, in his encounters with women, confronts the death and danger he vainly desires to control. "Lloyd," his comic counterpart in "Going to the Dogs," wants to manipulate the world around him in order to realize the American dream of wealth and success. But two women deer hunters easily manipulate him, teaching him the futility of his dreams of power. After his business schemes have failed and his wife has abandoned him and sold their car, Lloyd imagines stiffing his landlord for the rent and taking the train to Florida. The deer hunters foil his plans: while Bonnie seduces him, Phyllis steals his ticket and money, leaving him to realize that "it was only the beginning of bad luck" (108).

Lloyd represents Orpheus at another phase of the myth—when he is set upon and killed by the Maenads. Bonnie and Phyllis have killed a deer, which death has fragmented into disconnected images, a lolling tongue, melting snow on its entrails. Like dead animals in Ford's stories, the buck represents the hapless man. Unlike such animals, this deer appears as food—the "deer steak" Lloyd covets but never receives. Instead, Bonnie and Phyllis figuratively consume *him*. Dressed in a bathrobe and baking a coffeecake, Lloyd seems feminized, vulnerable to the overtures of strangers.

Ford's Maenads also figure as parodic Dianas, unchaste huntresses with camouflage paste on their faces, heavy women made massive by bulky winter clothing. Phyllis, in particular, affects a harsh style of speech that clashes wonderfully with her Arcadian name. The deer, she reports, "ran like a scalded dog . . . and dropped like a load of shit" (101). Bonnie's speech, though gentler, may be more treacherous; she flatters Lloyd with a compliment that undermines even as it praises: "'You've got arms like a wheelchair athlete" (107). Her compliment gives him the illusion that the spoils of the world are his. "It made me feel reckless, as if I had killed a deer myself and had a lot of ideas to show to the world" (107). (His wife has disparaged his "ideas.") Together, both big women dwarf his aspirations of easy success. Just as women can inhabit the realm of death and danger, they can live more easily in the zone of risk from which Ford's less law-abiding male narrators imagine they can snatch security.

In "Rock Springs," another narrator imagines that he can manipulate his way into the American dream of success. More actively larcenous than Lloyd, Earl Middleton steals a cranberry-colored Mercedes in an effort to move himself, his daughter, Cheryl, and his girlfriend, Edna, to a better life in Florida. When the Mercedes breaks down, Earl walks into a trailer park overshadowed by a huge, mysterious plant to ask for help. In one trailer, a middle-aged "Negro" woman allows him to use her phone. Earl finds the woman attractive and feels intrigued by her almost perpetual smile, which persists even as she tells him of her son's death, her grandson's brain damage, and her own and her husband's displacement. Still smiling, she identifies the plant behind them as a gold mine. Her smiling face, which Earl describes as "shining" at one point, evokes the glittering surface of the gold, but her demeanor suggests that something more complicated lies beneath the superficial shine. She looks at Earl with "a look that seemed to want truth" and says in parting, "I just passed you on to whatever's coming to you" (17), as if she might know his fate.

In a sense, the interaction between shining surface and shadowy depths *is* Earl's fate. In search of his own particular "gold mine," he confuses surface with reality, the illusion of wealth—stolen cars and rubber checks—with genuine prosperity. He also confuses his acts, "which were oftentimes offender's acts, and [his] ideas, which were as good as the gold they mined there where the bright lights were blazing" (17). His ideas, like the gold he has only heard about, create a glossy surface which he believes reflects his true nature. His acts, which have consequences, actually define him.

When Earl, Edna, and Cheryl take a taxi to the nearby town of Rock Springs, they learn of the corruption beneath the brightly lit white surface of the gold plant: the driver complains that the trailers are full of prostitutes and pimps from New York City, "prosperity's fruit" (20), he bitterly declares. The smiling, shining woman might be the pleasant nurturing creature she appears to be—or she might be a prostitute. The discovery of a metaphorical "gold mine" almost always reveals corruption, a failure of moral responsibility.

Gender Relations in *Rock Springs*

Edna suspects the time Earl has spent in the trailer park, asking, "'Did you find somebody over there in the trailers you'd rather stay with?'" (18). Though unfounded, her suspicions aptly express her growing mistrust of the illusion that she fears that Earl prefers to "stay with." Earlier, she has told a story which reveals her own growing sense of moral responsibility. Like other stories told by Ford's women characters, it features unexpected death: Edna has won a monkey from a customer in the bar where she works, and, later, warned that monkeys can be dangerous, she has tied the monkey up in such a way that it strangles accidentally during the night. Though she begins the story as an entertaining anecdote, Edna becomes "gloomy all of a sudden, as if she saw some aspect of the story she had never seen before" (7). She calls the story "shameful" and reproaches Earl for trying to comfort her by absolving her of responsibility. The monkey, even though acquired on a roll of the dice like "easy money," brings with it danger, death, and a responsibility Edna believes she failed to take.

Apprehensive about the consequences of his thefts and lies, she accepts Earl's offer to send her back to Montana. She explains her change of attitude by saying that she no longer likes to go to motels—that the sense of easily purchased freedom and detachment they provide is a "fantasy" she can no longer maintain. Earl, of course, likes motels and readily buys the illusion of security they afford, just as he readily steals the illusion of power and prosperity in the form of expensive cars. In the parking lot of the motel he looks for a car to steal, noting that the owners of one car have "the very same things I would have in my car if I had a car" (26). Just as he identifies with the owners of the car, he invites the reader to identify with him. He asks, "[W]hat would you think a man was doing if you saw him in the middle of the night looking in the windows of cars in the parking lot of the Ramada Inn? . . . Would you think he was anybody like you?" (27). This address to the reader, unique in Ford's short stories, conveys an unusually direct moral admonition—a warning against the "fantasy" of easily purchased happiness and security.

Earl's attempt to connect with the reader has its counterpart in a moment of affection when Edna, having resolved to leave him, says, "None of this is a matter of not loving you, you know that" (25). Ironically, her comforting declaration may come from the same developing sense of responsibility that compels her to leave him. Like Marge in "Empire," Edna has the stability to offer affection because she has renounced the lure of danger in favor of responsibility.

Ties That Bind

Another responsible character, Arlene, the wife of "Sweethearts," comforts her ex-husband, Bobby, even as she rejects his moral irresponsibility. Though she has long been divorced from Bobby and now lives with Russell, the story's narrator, Arlene puts up bail money for Bobby when he is arrested for writing bad checks and then robbing a convenience store. On the morning of the story, Arlene and Russell take Bobby to jail, where he will spend a year. As Bobby struggles with fear, anger, and despair, Arlene both reassures him, saying, "'You're among friends, though, sweetheart,'" and responds angrily to his resentment of her, reminding him that she *wanted* to divorce him (55).

Unlike the women characters who dwell in danger, Arlene's autonomy consists in detaching herself from it even as she accepts its reality. On the way to jail, Bobby throws a pistol into the front seat, saying, "'I thought I might kill Arlene, but I changed my mind'" (62). Russ hides the pistol, but he forgets it until Arlene suggests that they throw it in the river. She tosses the gun out the car window and into the river as casually as a spent cigarette, but Russ defines the gesture as ritual, saying, "Maybe that'll change [Bobby's] luck" (66). For Arlene, avoiding destructive behavior comes naturally, as a part of self-preservation. She explains, "'It's hard to love pain, if you're me.'" Russ, on the other hand, believes that anyone can become a criminal, as his use of the second person demonstrates: "Somehow, and for no apparent reason, your decisions got tipped over and you lost your hold" (68). Avoiding danger requires luck, not getting "tipped over" by circumstances, and constant vigilance, maintaining your hold.

Russell maintains his hold partly by reciting the verbal formulas which sustain so many of Ford's narrators—words which reassure despite their emptiness. He tells himself he knows what love is about. "It was about never being in that place you said you'd never be in." This circular, self-referential formula seems a weak bulwark against the forces of circumstances which can so easily tip anyone over. As Russ continues to ruminate, the last words of the story reveal his most important source of strength. "And [love] was not about being alone. Never that. Never that." Arlene, who can assure Russ that he's still her sweetheart even as she admits, "'We don't know where any of this is going, do we?'" (68) protects him against a future like Bobby's simply by remaining with him.

Lois, the wife in "Fireworks," sustains her husband, Eddie, by trying to encourage him even though he has been unemployed for six months. As in "Sweethearts," her ex-husband—a man who is both rival and counterpart to Eddie—is associated with danger and death. Louie, the ex-husband, shows up at the bar where Lois works. When she calls Eddie to invite him to join them, Lois tells him that Louie has become "'an extraditer,'" someone who "'travels the breadth of the country bringing people back here so they can go to jail.'" Though he isn't in uniform, Louie has the modern trappings of power, "'a gun and a little beeper'" (196). Lois diminishes Louie's success even as she reports it: it's only a "little" beeper, and the man Louie is extraditing has written a forty-seven-dollar bad check.

Over the telephone, Louie tries to engage Eddie in banter: "'You know what an Italian girl puts behind her ears to make herself more attractive?'" (196) and offers to cut him in on what he presents as a profitable sideline in Italian rugs. Eddie rejects these overtures, convinced that Louie is only interested in Lois. As in other stories, stereotypically male behavior marks an uneasy territory between bonding and rivalry. In "Fireworks," however, the potential tragedy of "Children" or "Winterkill" becomes comic because of Louie's buffoonish behavior and Lois's descriptions of him. She tells Eddie that he has grown fat and unattractive and that he has "'a house full of these cheap Italian carpets, and nobody to sell them to'" (209). Even as he resents and feels threatened by Louie, who has asked Lois to go to Florida with him, Eddie regrets hearing about his changed appearance: "It was bad luck if that was the way you looked to the world" (208).

Just as Lois's comments on Louie disparage the threat he represents, her treatment of Eddie helps assuage the fear of failure evoked by Louie's apparent success. As they drive home, observing public and private 4th of

July fireworks, she recalls his mother, a "sweet old lady" who loved fireworks. In a gesture, she draws upon the mother's nurturing power to create a ritual conveying power upon Eddie. Lois dances before the car in the rain, waving a pair of sparklers and "making swirls and patterns and star-falls for him that . . . for a moment, caught the world and stopped it, as though something sudden and perfect had come to earth in a furious glowing for him and for him alone" (214). For a rare moment, Eddie enjoys the full power of women's nurturing.

Thinking about Her

The return of the mother in a blaze of light illustrates the mythic aspects of the women of *Rock Springs*: Lucy, flaming Cleo, the temporary heat of Nola in the cab, all shed a magical radiance. But Ford's mythic touches do not transform his women characters into changeless goddesses; readers can see that men characters create that mythic glow. That glow may illuminate a relationship, like the fire outside the train window in "Empire," or it may blind, like the shining face of the woman in the trailer park. Mythmaking simply forms a part of the difficult process whereby one person tries to think about another.

When George tries to think about Lucy, after first acknowledging that thinking only about yourself is "possibly . . . all you could ever do" (96), he articulates a modern concern. In a world where individuals have become increasingly isolated and autonomous, can one person imagine the experience of another and regard that other as subject rather than object? In *Rock Springs*, Ford repeatedly raises this question. His male protagonists' experiences demonstrate how emotional need can shape one person's perceptions of another, and the language with which they describe those experiences reveals the limitations of their understanding.

Ford's emphasis upon the process of trying to think about the other, along with the variety of his women characters and the many traits they share in common with their men, invites readers to see them as subjects even when the men characters cannot. Finally, their gender seems only the embodiment of otherness—the mystery inherent in the effort to comprehend another person, to think about her. Or even him.

Gender Relations in *Rock Springs*

Several of Richard Ford's works are classic coming-of-age tales in which a teenage boy must witness a parental failure, experience sexual desire and disappointment, pose questions that have no obvious answers, and, like William Faulkner's Sarty or the narrator of James Joyce's "Araby," choose justice over kin or feel his eyes burn with anguish and shame. Ford's male narrators in the short story "Great Falls" (included in *Rock Springs* [1987]) and the novel *Wildlife* (1990) experience loneliness that accompanies self-knowledge gained despite, or perhaps because of, the inscrutableness of others. Although Ford leaves his narrators in isolation at each narrative's end, he reveals the heightened awareness that has projected them into the act of observation. Told in the past tense, each text is narrated by an adult speaker who structures his story carefully, editorializing and revising the incidents that changed the course of his teenage years and shaped his attitudes toward others. Significantly, this mature perspective confirms each speaker's ability to recast an emotionally volatile time as an open-ended story.

Through the scaffolding of each narrator's quest to know himself and his parents, Ford bolsters what on the surface are spare narratives with an underlying philosophical complexity, and his propensity to quote Jean-Paul Sartre outside of the frame of his fictional universes suggests the author's fascination with being, knowing, and nothingness, words that also occur frequently in Ford's fiction. His narrators pose epistemological and existential questions that defy easy answers, finally discovering not only the frailty of human nature

Elinor Ann Walker

but also the frailty of language. Paradoxically, language's instability also provides its magic, its capacity to transform and transcend the ordinary. Ford's narrators in both "Great Falls" and *Wildlife*, in fact, embark upon quests not unlike that of Sartre's own fictional and epistemological seeker, Roquentin, the narrator of *Nausea* who discovers that only art may transform loneliness and transcend existence and time.[1]

Resisting notions that his often-musing narrators liken his fiction to Walker Percy's or other southern works dominated by intellectual male voices, as noted critic Fred Hobson has observed (Hobson [1991] 41ff),[2] Ford prefers to situate his work in the context of a Western literary canon that can lay claim to writers and texts far exceeding the geographical boundaries of the South.[3] To limit certain kinds of characters by a regional frame is to ignore a much vaster sphere of influence, Ford argues. Rather than grouping Faulkner's Quentin Compson, Wolfe's Eugene Gant, Warren's Jack Burden, Percy's Will Barrett and his own Frank Bascombe as "southern male intellectuals" whose thoughts stultify their actions, Ford observes that southerners have no such corner on this market (Walker 133). Ford is much more apt to quote Sartre than Faulkner, as he does in an interview: "To name something is to take it out of the well of the unmediated and bring it up to the level of notice" (Walker 132). It is in this context that his narrators' choices to tell their stories in "Great Falls" and *Wildlife* become significant.

Both narratives depend upon a voice that interrupts time, gliding past the intervening years and back to a season, a day, or even an hour when life as the narrator knew it changed. The texts are in fact quite similar in tone and exposition, and each narrator's self-conscious phrasing indicates his deliberate plan to tell these events as crafted story rather than angst-filled confession. "Great Falls" opens with Jackie's words: "This is not a happy story. I warn you. My father was a man named Jack Russell, and when I was a young boy in my early teens, we lived with my mother in a house to the east of Great Falls, Montana . . ." ("Great Falls " 29). The turning point for Jackie takes place in 1960, when he is fourteen. Joe, *Wildlife*'s narrator, begins, "In the fall of 1960, when I was sixteen and my father was for a time not working, my mother met a man named Warren Miller and fell in love with him" (*Wildlife* 1). Each narrator locates the

Redeeming Loneliness in "Great Falls" and *Wildlife*

memory by place and time and his own age, the past tense removing him from the scene even as he participates as central character.

Furthermore, each son sets the mother at some emotional (or physical) distance from himself and his father, either through the judicious use of "we" or simply by yoking himself with his father: "when I was sixteen and my father was for a time not working," for example. The past tense also hints that this connection between father and son is a temporary link, one determined not so much by kinship as by sheer circumstance: time, place, and action. These syntactical details suggest the rifts that will only widen between the speaker and his parents, so that, by each narrative's end, the "I" has become unquestionably singular.

The disappearing mother further connects these narratives thematically. Both sons witness marital disjunction, usually initiated as an easing of communication between father and mother that develops into a full-blown and profound rupture, often precipitated by the mother's pursuit of another man and followed by her departure. Interestingly, several other of Ford's stories include sons with absent mothers or mothers who have taken up with boyfriends, such as "Children, " "Optimists," and "Communist," all published along with "Great Falls" in *Rock Springs,* as well as the more recent *Jealous,* published in the collection *Women with Men* (1997). This recurrence of fictional circumstance would seem to suggest the author's fascination with familial dissolution, or, perhaps, echoing a metaphysical poetic lesson, the predictability of woman's inconstancy. Some readers might seek to identify the death of Ford's own father in 1960, when the younger Ford was sixteen, as some psychological impetus for exploring themes of abandonment. Ford's own life, however, testifies to his mother's consistent presence in it, as the author himself documents in "My Mother, in Memory" (*Harper's* 44-57). Ford himself has been married to the same woman for thirty years. These facts may undercut attempts to psychoanalyze the author as well as refute unjust charges of sexism on Ford's part. Careful readings of these narratives would also preclude the latter, since the father characters emerge as self-absorbed and somewhat oblivious to the marital problems that precede their wives' departures while their subsequent behavior is revealed as immature at best.

What seems most significant is that in each narrative the sons must deal with *both* parents as frail human beings rather than authority figures possessed of prudence and wisdom. The parents tumble off their pedestals; the sons meanwhile clamber for some purchase on adult ground precisely as that territory becomes defined as mysterious, unpredictable, unreliable. In these works, parents become demythologized when their sons are hardly pubescent (not in itself an uncommon occurrence), and the role reversals that ensue determine each narrator's perspective thereafter. The collapse of parental structure, these texts suggest, is not a phenomenon that necessitates explication; in fact, such circumstances will resist rather than yield to studies thereof. That resistance is what captivates each son. Literally being the only one left out of and with no control over the father-mother relationship, even as he exists as one point of the triangle connecting them, the narrator drifts into his role as outsider before the reader's very eyes. Simultaneously, his parents become ghostlier demarcations of their former selves, now suddenly unknowable. The question that inhabits each narrative is an epistemological one: What can I know when I cannot even know my parents?

"Great Falls" succinctly poses this question. Early paragraphs in the story indicate that Jack and his wife, who is never given a first name at all and in fact is called "Mrs. Russell" only once over the story's course, have long had different ideas about how their lives would proceed. "[My father] had been an air force sergeant and had taken his discharge in Great Falls. And instead of going home to Tacoma, where my mother wanted to go, he had taken a civilian's job with the Air Force, working on planes, which was what he liked to do" (29-30). Jackie's mother married Jack because he was "young and wonderful looking" (30), and because she wanted to escape her present life and see the world, which Jackie assumes they were able to do for a while. "That was the life she wanted, even before she knew much about wanting anything else or about the future" (30). Acknowledging his mother's thwarted or buried desires, Jackie intimates that his mother possessed some internal life that even she was not yet privy to at that age. That internal space seems to grow larger and larger, so that by the time he tells the story, his mother is someone with whom he and his father "lived" (29), almost a stranger.

Redeeming Loneliness in "Great Falls" and *Wildlife*

Jackie more explicitly characterizes his father's passions: hunting and fishing. In so doing, he subtly reveals his father's faults: "It is a true thing that my father did not know limits. . . . [H]e would catch a hundred fish in a weekend, and sometimes more than that. It was all he did from morning until night, and it was never hard for him. . . . It was the same with ducks, the other thing he liked" (30-31). Jackie describes taking these trips with his father and later selling—illegally, of course—the excesses of wild game that he has caught to the Great Northern Hotel. Afterwards, often they would stop for Jack to get a drink, arriving home late. Jackie never wonders what his mother is doing during these weekends or attempts to assess her degree of loneliness. Jack senior emerges as a man who does what he wants, when he wants, and who disregards the rules if they don't suit him. Such descriptions suggest some insensitivity to his wife's needs and desires as well as a nature that defies any external boundaries that don't coincide with his own. Jack is a man of excesses whose passions apparently exclude his wife, at least most of the time.

One night, however, after one of these hunting trips, Jackie and his father depart from routine, a change that instigates an unusual conversation between father and son as well as foreshadows the incident that alters the family dynamic. Jack suggests that they go straight home from the Great Northern and "surprise your mother" (33), cook the remaining ducks on the grill, do "something different" (33). On the way home, Jack adopts a different manner with his son, telling him things that Jackie finds a little odd, such as that his mother had said, " 'Nobody dies of a broken heart' " (33), and asking him questions about himself. " 'What do you worry about, Jackie,' my father said" (34). Pushing his son for an answer, he suggests a few himself: girls, his future sex life, all of which Jackie denies. " 'Well, what then?' my father said. 'What else is there?' 'I worry if you're going to die before I do,' I said, though I hated saying that, 'or if Mother is. That worries me' " (34). Although his father makes a joke out of his response (" 'If I were you, I'd worry that we might not' " [34]), Jackie describes the conversation poignantly: "He smiled at me, and it was not the worried, nervous smile from before, but a smile that meant he was pleased. And I don't remember him ever smiling at me that way again" (34). From his future vantage point, the narrator can cast these moments as fleeting and significant, his younger self as poised unwittingly on the brink of change. He tells the reader that his father then says, " 'I want to respect your privacy' . . . for no reason at all that I understood" (35). The exchange dramatizes Jackie's awareness of his parents' mortality, foreshadows broken hearts and his father's own inscrutable behavior (his sentence uttered "for no reason at all that I understood"), as well as the son's inability to imagine a reason that makes sense at the time. Only in retrospect can this editorializing occur ("And I don't remember him ever smiling at me that way again," for instance), suggesting the narrator's careful reconstruction of the scene and the dialogue.

Meanwhile, the circumstances, departing from the usual routine, surprising the mother, set up the story. The mother will not be expecting them. Father and son will arrive home to find a strange car parked down the road from their house and a young man—not much older than Jackie—in the kitchen. Several confrontations and conversations ensue. The young man, whose name is Woody, and Jackie wait outside while his father and mother talk. When his father comes out of the house, he "looked roughed up, as though he had hurt himself somehow" (39), and soon he pulls a gun from his pocket that he brandishes foolishly in Woody's face, repeatedly asking him, " 'What is the matter with you?' " (40). All four characters end up in the yard, publicly displayed. Jackie observes that no one really thought that his father would shoot Woody, except perhaps his father himself, who "was trying to find out how to" (41). With his mother standing by ineffectually, trying to assure Jack that Woody doesn't love her, Woody unflinching and nonchalant before the father's gesticulations and rapid-fire questions, and Jackie standing by as a spectator, the tableau depicts failed communication on several fronts. Jackie's preoccupation with knowing others has begun as he tries to make sense of the scene.

The verb "to know" dominates many of Jackie's sentences. Woody "*knew* nothing about what was here" (italics mine) (38). While talking to Woody, Jackie finds himself wondering "what Woody *knew* that I didn't. Not about my mother—I didn't *know* anything about that and didn't want to—but about a lot of things, about the life out in the dark, about coming out here, about airports, even about me. He and I were not so far apart in

Redeeming Loneliness in "Great Falls" and *Wildlife*

age, I *knew* that. But Woody was one thing, and I was another" (italics mine) (39). Jackie appears certain of what he does know, and he knows enough to realize just how much is left unknown. Talking to Woody in the yard will not reveal Woody's secrets, or explain "life out in the dark." But Jackie wonders what Woody knows about him, as if now he has to see himself—and indeed the entire realm of his family life—through someone else's eyes. The retrospective narrative voice transforms the teenage Jackie's encounter with Woody into a fundamentally existential moment; Jackie knows he exists and that Woody exists, but he cannot make the common fact of existence pull them into each other's sphere of knowing. In other words, the presence of an "other," while confirming one's own being in the world, does nothing to dissipate isolation. In this encounter, *l'enfer c'est autrui*, as Sartre has written, because Woody's gaze does nothing but alienate Jackie from himself and what he has previously assumed about his world. Jackie's last sentence— "Woody was one thing, and I was another"—asserts the basic separateness that characterizes all human beings, the very notion dramatized moments later by the scene in the yard.

Furthermore, all of the words exchanged in that scene become emptied of meaning. Jack's threats, Woody's response, and Jackie's mother's denial of Woody's love finally effect nothing.

> "Are you in love with her, too? Are you, crazy man? Are you? Do you say you love her? Say you love her! Say you love her so I can blow your fucking brains in the sky."
>
> "All right," Woody said. "No. It's all right."
>
> "He doesn't love me, Jack. For God's sake," my mother said. She seemed so calm. (41)

Woody's contradictory and passive response to his father, his mother's unemotional resignation and imminent departure with Woody, and his father's hollow gesture of violence all conspire, presenting these adults as isolated individuals doomed to utter meaningless phrases. Hell *is* other people, this passage implies, especially when the one supreme isolation-defying instrument, the very thing that sets human beings apart from all other creatures—language—fails.

When language fails, Jackie can only know the circumstances empirically, through hearing and watching, paying attention to the signs that make this place familiar to him: "The wind rose then, and from behind the house I could hear [the dog] bark once from far away, and I could smell the irrigation ditch, hear it hiss in the field. . . . It was nothing Woody knew about, nothing he could hear or smell" (38). Though present in the same surroundings, Jackie and Woody exist in different worlds of knowing. What is "nothing" for Woody assumes significance for Jackie, further assuring each's alienation from the other. Jackie knows these things because, for him, these sensations actually signify something, that is, that this place is his home; for Woody, the same events fail to register, and certainly fail to signify. However, even for Jackie, his awareness of his own being in the world, what the philosopher Martin Heidegger would call *Dasein*, will not be enough. Jackie cannot know others through the signs of the wind blowing, the dog barking, the water hissing; rather he must rely on words, symbols, the very things that his parents and Woody cannot summon effectively.

Woody even lies inexplicably to Jackie, telling him that his mother has been married before. Later, when Jackie asks her if this is true, she says, "'No. . . . Who told you that? That isn't true. I never was. Did Jack say that to you? Did your father say that?'" (47). Jackie never tells her who has made this statement, and his mother's surprisingly defensive response suggests some past of which his father has not approved, but Jackie will never, of course, know the real truth. Likewise, his mother will never know who spoke those words.

Under these circumstances, language is a slippery instrument. In its purest use, language may function semiotically as a symbol connecting an object with a word and, via the word, the person with the object, just as the word "wind" denotes that which is blowing, that Jackie hears and recognizes as "wind," and also connotes other meanings, associations of familiarity, security, knowledge of a place. Drawing upon the writings of American philosopher Charles Peirce, Walker Percy has distilled this semiotic concept into a simple triangular diagram; the speaking person, the word, and the thing the word signifies each make up one point of the figure (Percy, "The Delta Factor" [1984] 40). The picture becomes somewhat more complicated when another person is introduced into the ex-

Redeeming Loneliness in "Great Falls" and *Wildlife*

change; then the word must signify the same thing to both speakers in order for communication to occur. If words lose their meanings or fail to signify, as they have in the conversation that takes place out in the yard in "Great Falls," then language, Jackie discovers, may not be an effective conduit for knowledge.

As the story ends, Jackie continues to frame the memory in terms of some epistemological search; he says that he thought to himself, "my life had turned suddenly, and . . . I might not know exactly how or which way for possibly a long time. Maybe, in fact, I might never know" (49). He goes on to question,

> why wouldn't my father let my mother come back? Why would Woody stand in the cold with me outside my house and risk being killed? Why would he say my mother had been married before, if she hadn't been? And my mother herself— why would she do what she did? In five years my father had gone off to Ely, Nevada, to ride out the oil strike there, and been killed by accident. And in the years since then I have seen my mother from time to time—in one place or another, with one man or other—and I can say, at least, that we know each other. But I have never known the answers to these questions, have never asked anyone their answers. (49)

The adult voice wrestles with the same questions, this passage attests. Despite claiming to know his mother (perhaps meaning here that they are at least acquainted), Jackie suggests that he does not feel comfortable enough with her to talk about these puzzling events. As he has observed about Woody, he "was one thing, and I was another" (39). The story's closing passage only confirms this observation: "Though possibly it—the answer—is simple: it is just low-life, some coldness in us all, some help-lessness that causes us to misunderstand life when it is pure and plain, makes our existence seem like a border between two nothings, and makes us no more or less than animals who meet on the road—watchful, unforgiving, without patience or desire" (49). A "coldness," a "helpless-ness," keeps one person distinct from another, so that two lives cannot re-ally meet, so that "our existence [is] a border between two nothings" (49). In this passage, the speaker synthesizes his epistemological and ex-istential inquiries: we can never know each other, he claims, and, further-more, we exist in the face of nothingness; others may remind us not only of our being but also of our isolation, our existence in the face of what is not, and of our own consciousness that is impossible to explain. Whatever it is that makes us misunderstand each other, the "coldness," the "helplessness," and whenever language fails us, we are no more (or less) than animals, the speaker finally theorizes.

These are the philosophical conclusions that the narrator of "Great Falls" draws, sounding finally much more like Jean-Paul Sartre than a product of Montana.[4] Thematically such a detail is appropriate; the narrator may take the reader by surprise with his existential thoughts. His observation about the human predicament may seem a bleak and unpredictable one, but he has warned the reader from the beginning that this will not be a happy story. Despite such a grim analysis, the narrator's own attempt to make the circumstances yield to language is important, and his Sartrean preoccupation with being and nothingness no accident on Richard Ford's part.

Ford makes the same point in his novel *Wildlife*, which chronicles another narrator's witnessing of familial dissolution: his mother leaving his father for another man, his father's outraged act of arson as a consequence, and then the strange reconciliation between his parents. Also set in Great Falls, the narrative centers around Joe's attempt to know his parents. Like Jackie, he embarks upon an epistemological search, though he acknowledges early in his telling that "[w]hen you are sixteen you do not know what your parents know, or much of what they understand, and less of what's in their hearts" (18). Again, however, Ford provides an adult narrator, one who looks back over his life and relates the details in a certain way. Such a perspective makes the father's words to his son—"When you get older. . . . If you want to know the truth don't listen to what people tell you" (15)—particularly resonant. Language will fail here, too, and here, too, the son will fail to know his parents.

Wildlife, in fact, seems to be an extended exploration of the themes first dramatized in "Great Falls." Just as Jackie suspects that his mother has not been happy with his father's decisions, so Joe speculates about his mother's unfulfilled desires. In *Wildlife*, the Brinsons have moved to Montana because Joe's father, Jerry, had hoped to partake in the area's economic boom. Jerry has been a golf pro, working at small country

Redeeming Loneliness in "Great Falls" and *Wildlife*

clubs mainly in eastern Washington State, though the family has lived in Idaho preceding their move to Montana. Joe thinks perhaps his mother has followed his father simply out of love, but says, "I do not think she ever wanted to come to Montana" (4), where the weather was harsher and the people less friendly. Joe presents his family as outsiders in the town, a fact only exacerbated after his father loses his job at the club and his mother takes a position as a swim instructor at the YWCA. Meanwhile, timber fires rage west of Great Falls, figuratively suggesting the tension smoldering in Joe's own family as his father goes weeks without seeming to look for work. At last a position fighting the fires opens, a chance Jerry enthusiastically takes, despite his wife Jean's vocal opposition of her worries that he knows nothing about fighting fires. Thus Jerry leaves Joe alone with his mother, whose behavior will become increasingly erratic. Almost overnight, in the three days of his father's absence, Joe's assumptions about his family will be questioned; the adult narrator observes: "It should've been a time when I cared about more things—a new girlfriend, or books. . . . But I only cared about my mother and my father then" (25). The "then" punctuates the narrator's perspective, implying that since that time he has learned something about himself and his parents and the boundaries between them.

In her husband's absence, Jean takes up with another man, Warren Miller, who has played golf at the club, entering a dalliance that will set Joe apart from his mother and cause him to see her differently. Seemingly oblivious to her son's feelings, Jean flaunts this relationship, taking Joe with her to Warren's house where she dances drunkenly with him and kisses him. Even after she and Joe go to the car, she returns to Warren's house one last time, leaving Joe cold and watchful in the car, where through the window he can see that "Warren Miller had pulled my mother's green dress up from behind her so that you could see where her stockings were held by white elastic straps, and you could see her white underpants. . . . [H]e was holding my mother outside her underwear and pulling her toward him so hard that he picked her up off the floor and held her against him while he kissed her and she kissed him" (97). Forced into voyeurism, Joe sees his mother as he never should see her: a sexual object whose garters he cannot even call by name, resorting instead to the innocent and descriptive "white elastic straps." Later that same evening, his mother has sex with Warren Miller in her own home, where Joe will see Warren naked in the hall. Again Jean will leave Joe alone while she walks Warren out to his car in the morning's wee hours. Joe waits, *again* looking out the window, forced to watch for something as yet unknown, identifying with a magpie that he catches in the dim light of his flashlight through the window.

Contemplation of this object makes Joe himself like the bird. The bird seemed to be looking at "nothing" (111), and "It wasn't afraid simply because it knew nothing to be afraid of" (112). When it finally flies at the glass, Joe fears that it will crash against the window, but strangely it veers without hitting anything, "leaving me there with my heart pounding and my light shining onto the cold yard at nothing" (112). Confronted with "nothing," Joe likewise becomes invisible, literally and figuratively speaking, as the bird regards the nothingness where he is, glassed in by his own isolation. The repetition of "nothing" recalls the ending of "Great Falls," and Joe's moment in the dark with the bird may be likened to the strange exchange between Jackie and Woody in that story. Only here it is the bird's gaze, not Woody's, that renders the boy aware of what he does not know and of the emptiness that surrounds him and fills him. At first even his mother does not see him when she returns to the house, but, finally catching a glimpse of him in the shadows, she slaps him inexplicably, not once but twice, with each hand. Again he catches sight of her in a way that makes her strange to him, her stomach "and all of that" (114) visible through her open bathrobe. He wishes that "she had her clothes on" (114).

Both Joe and his mother are objectified here; the son can only see his mother as the consummate "other," but her confrontation of him makes him see himself through her eyes to such an extent that he actually apologizes to her, ashamed of having witnessed the scene. As Sartre writes in *Being and Nothingness*, "the Other is the indispensable mediator between myself and me. I am ashamed of myself as I *appear* to the Other. By the mere appearance of the Other, I am put in the position of passing judgment on myself as on an object, for it is an object that I appear to the

Other" (222). Later, in the dark of his room, Joe admits, "I felt like . . . a spy—hollow and not forceful, not able to cause anything" (116). Literally incapacitated by this encounter, forced to see himself through his mother's gaze (and she also is ashamed, though she expresses this emotion through anger), Joe can only ponder the futility of it all: "And I wished for a moment that I was dead . . ." (116). [5] Robbed of his subjectivity and "not able to cause anything," Joe contemplates not existing and the nothingness that threatens to erase his own being.

Faced with what is fleshly and carnal (his mother) and with the emptiness without and within (symbolized by the vacant stare of the bird and Joe's own invisibility), Joe confronts evidence of being and nonbeing, states that defy the use of language to describe or dispel them. Appropriately, Joe offers no explanation of his mother's behavior and describes his own silence in his mother's presence as deliberate. These extremes—his mother's visible nakedness versus his own strange bodily emptiness—render him speechless. He describes her angry countenance, his awareness that she might hit him again, his recognition that he is actually afraid. His mother continues to talk to him, asking him if he wants to leave, telling him that he can tell his father that she's "not up to" (115) making things better. But Joe cannot say a thing, worried that if he speaks his mother will not answer back and that he will then be left with his "own words . . . to live with, forever" (115). This thought reminds the narrator, who now intrudes in his adult voice, that certain words should not be said and are useless under certain circumstances. "And there are words, significant words, you do not want to say, words that account for busted-up lives, words that try to fix something ruined that shouldn't be ruined . . . and that words can't fix anyway" (116). Here, then, is Joe's acknowledgment of language's failure.

Confronted by this same failure when his father comes home from fighting the fires, Joe knows that his father wants to know the truth about his mother and Warren Miller, but he cannot bring himself to tell his father the whole story. After answering several of his father's questions, Joe again lapses into silence, because, he says, "I did not say anything else because even though I could see it all in my mind again . . . I didn't think I knew everything and did not want to pretend I did, or that what I'd seen was the truth" (150-151). Joe makes a distinction here between something that he can see and something that he can know, suggesting that the act of knowing is not based sheerly on empirical evidence but rather on something that defies rational explanation. The "truth" about his parents, their different ways of being unfaithful to each other and the relationship that persists between them, is something that Joe will concede he has never known by the novel's end.

Arguably, the novel's climax centers around Joe's father's own irrational attempt to burn down Warren Miller's house, an act that, like the strange scene that Jackie witnesses in the yard in "Great Falls," becomes very much a public spectacle. A crowd gathers as Warren Miller emerges from the house with another woman who is wearing silver high-heeled shoes that Joe has seen in a closet in Miller's house. After setting the porch on fire, Jerry remains stationary as Warren strides toward him, cursing him and finally hitting him squarely in the face. During all of this commotion, Joe notices more people coming out of their houses and younger boys angling for better views, a fact punctuated by Warren's angry inquiry, "'What do you think all these people think of you? A house-burner like this. In front of his own son. I'd be ashamed'" (167). Jerry replies, "'Maybe they think it was important to me'" (167). But Joe suspects that all of the spectators, including the firemen who have by now arrived, know Warren Miller, whereas "we, my father and I, and my mother, didn't know anyone" (167).[6] Acknowledging that they had only themselves to "answer for us" (167) if things went wrong, Joe presents his family as self-contained, unbelonging, "strangers" (167). Faced with a crowd of people whose stares can only intensify his family's shame, Joe experiences real isolation, another Sartrean moment when the presence of others only certifies one's loneliness.

In the narrator's own words, "not very much happened" (167) after that. Miller tells the firemen that there has been some misunderstanding; a fireman scolds Jerry harshly for starting such a senseless fire in dry weather, reminding him of the smoldering wildfires that Jerry himself has battled. Joe ends up living with his father when his mother moves out.

Warren Miller eventually dies. Joe acknowledges not really having any friends but believing that his life "*was* like other boys' lives" (175). He has to admit, however, that he "did not have a life except for the life at home with [his] father" (175), a fact that he does not find strange "even now" (175), in his adult voice and from his adult perspective. He does include the detail that the wildfires have continued to burn, that they "did not die out easily" but instead "smoldered all winter" (175), that they could not be put out the way that one would think that they could. The narrator only alludes to the fires' symbolic overtones; he resists the explication himself, leaving the image open to his audience's interpretation.

What Joe does do is to admit his wonderment about the world that has enfolded him so tightly. "I wondered . . . if I would ever see the world as *I* had seen it before then, when I did not even know I saw it. . . . [if] that when you faced the worst and went past it what you found there was nothing. Nothing has its own badness, but it does not last forever" (174). The crisis makes him see the world with a keener eye; he suggests that prior to these events he "did not even know" that he saw the world. Pursuant to this new awareness, though, is Joe's suspicion that he has also encountered something that is not so concrete as the world, a "nothing," not a something, in fact. Existence and nothingness seem inextricably bound; to know one is to know the other, Joe suggests. Furthermore, the act of knowing is itself a tricky enterprise. After his parents' eventual reunion, Joe can only admit that "God knows there is still much to it that I myself, their only son, cannot fully claim to understand" (177), and with those words the novel ends. This admission is striking given Joe's own assertion throughout the text that his entire world has consisted of his parents and his close observations of the rifts and reunions between them. Despite his rendering of the story, he finally must accede to something that resists explanation: the unknowableness of the two people who were closest to him in the world.

Joe's conclusion, and the novel's, makes no attempt to explain, to analyze, to interpret; rather, it suggests that the mere telling of the story is enough. His transformation of the events into story does not, Joe must admit, make the events make more sense, but he tells it anyway, as if the act itself assumes some significance and in itself redeems the memory of his isolation. Richard Ford has acknowledged his own fascination with loneliness and what he calls its "cure":

> It's what Emerson in his essay on friendship (interestingly enough) calls the "infinite remoteness" that underlies us all. But . . . [the] predicament is a seminal one; that is, what it inseminates is an attempt to console that remote condition. If loneliness is the disease, then the story is the cure. To be able to tell a story like [*Wildlife*] about your parents is in itself an act of consolation. Even to come to the act of articulating that your parents are unknowable to each other, unknowable to you, is itself an act of acceptance, an act of some optimism, again in that Sartrean sense that to write about the darkest human possibility is itself an act of optimism because it proves that those things can be thought about. (Walker 141)

In both "Great Falls" and *Wildlife*, the events that occur are not spectacular events that require theorizing or explanation. But it is the narrator's way of grappling with his life that transforms it into story material while at the same time allowing the narrator to transcend his past through the self-conscious fashioning of the story. He is at once the present "I" and the future "eye" who sees the events at some distance. It is the adult perspective, in fact, that allows the speaker to frame his search as an epistemological one, and the existential reckoning with the surrounding world accompanies this quest for knowledge about others and the self. In the passage above, Ford provides a lens through which to view his narrators' searches while the texts themselves provoke a Sartrean examination of loneliness and ways of redeeming that state.

In *Nausea*, Sartre's novel that expounds upon many of the same points that he makes in the more complex *Being and Nothingness*, the main character, Roquentin, tells his story through a diary which records his efforts to discover something about himself in relation to other people and objects. His epistemological search is essentially a mental one, revolving around his thoughts rather than events that happen to him. His sensation of nausea derives from the notion that he is simultaneously alienated from his consciousness of himself and yet unable to escape it. Doomed to failing relationships with other people as well, Roquentin becomes more and more repulsed by his own body. Finally, though, he experiences a revelation while wandering by the sea and into a garden, and that is that any attempt to categorize a thing using abstract language is a false attempt to understand its being. Language, in fact, is simply imposed on the world by human beings in an attempt to make the world orderly.

Instead, Roquentin discovers the disorderliness of the world, the characteristics that defy groupings and namings by species and kind. In the famous contemplation of the chestnut tree, Roquentin offers this explanation: "This root . . . existed in such a way that I could not explain it. Knotty, inert, nameless, it fascinated me, filled my eyes, brought me back unceasingly to its own existence. . . . 'This is a root'—it didn't work any more. I saw clearly that you could not pass from its function as a root, as a breathing pump, *to that*, to this hard and compact skin of a sea lion, to this oily, callous, headstrong look. The function explained nothing: it allowed you to understand generally that it was a root, but not *that one* at all" (174). Roquentin himself resorts to metaphor in his description ("breathing pump," "skin of a sea lion"). The irony, of course, is that he still must use language, but here he employs it differently, not to categorize. The root itself brings him back over and over again to its individual properties, its essence that defies generalizations about roots. When he ponders that the root has been called black, he exclaims, "Black? I felt the word deflating, emptied of meaning with extraordinary rapidity" (175). In other words, the thing will defy the word that normally describes it. Confronted by the root's unrelenting existence, Roquentin must instead use words that are not usually associated with the root in order to even approach capturing its being in language.

What Roquentin ultimately realizes is that only art escapes the realm of existence; art objects—a painting, a song, a novel—are unreal and ideal, transcendent of time. As he hears a voice sing, "Some of these days / You'll miss me, honey" (234), he acknowledges that the record can be scratched, even destroyed, but the song will not cease to exist. Such a thought inspires him, not to commit suicide, as he has already contemplated, but to write a novel that would require its reader to "have to guess, behind the printed words, behind the pages, at something that would not exist, that would be above existence" (237). Likewise he has had to guess at the essence of the root, at what lies behind the words that normally would fail to describe it.

Roquentin's search may also clarify Jackie's search in "Great Falls" and Joe's similar quest in *Wildlife*, demonstrating how each narrator's discovery of language's failure will not prevent him from telling his story. Time after time in these two narratives, words themselves are emptied of meaning, as quickly as Roquentin cites the deflation of the word "black." This phenomenon, though, does not obstruct the more complicated effort to create a story that will actually require a probing beyond the words on the page, to get at what the words point to, not just what they say but what they symbolize. To describe that which exists requires metaphor, the deliberate and creative misuse of language that allows the language-user to compare two things that are not usually likened. Significantly, Ford and his narrators do not call attention to moments in their stories that might be named metaphorical or symbolic, as if to suggest that meaning must be derived from language, not dictated by it. Only the repeated patterns of certain words—"knowing," and "nothing," for example—invite what Sartre would call the "guess" at something beyond the printed page.

Sartre is certainly not the only philosopher or intellectual to find some sort of redemption in art. Heidegger praises the poetic voice; Kierkegaard notes the importance of the aesthetic reversal. If one is alienated, to read (observe a painting, hear a song, etc.) about another's alienation may to some extent relieve the alienation. Modernist writers including Ezra Pound and Wallace Stevens find art the only ballast against an unstable world; Stevens goes so far as to replace religion with art. Regardless of its name, whether it is called despair or anguish by philosophers such as Kierkegaard and Heidegger, or simply "the border between two nothings," as the narrator of "Great Falls" pronounces, loneliness spurs its host to contemplate something beyond the self. In fact, some cognizance of loneliness in the face of an unyielding universe of the self, the world, or the other seems to be required for art to perform its transcendent function. In this way, then, loneliness is redeeming even as (or precisely because) it necessitates a redemption from its state.

Despite their realizations of language's potential for failure and the frailty of human beings, the narrators of Richard Ford's "Great Falls" and *Wildlife* decide to reconstruct something that has happened to them, and to tell it in such a way that it becomes a deliberate rendering of a specific

Redeeming Loneliness in "Great Falls" and *Wildlife*

time in their lives, a time that continues to open into the future, as their adult voices testify. By the inclusion of remarks that explicate and interpret the past (or that acknowledge that the past cannot be explained), the narrators expose the artifice of their constructions even as they participate in the narratives' unfolding. This process entails forays into musings beyond the simple facts of what has happened, contemplations of senses and objects that in themselves suggest something other than themselves, as the magpie and the fires do in *Wildlife*. In other words, each narrator transforms a traumatic event into a constructed story: life into art.

Jackie and Joe experience bereavement, disappointment, and betrayal at the hands of their parents, and in both texts, a painful rift between father and mother leaves the son caught between the two, but able to name the unknowableness that characterizes human beings, even those bound by blood. In the ever-widening gap between self and other, these narrators locate the reader, offering some consolation that even that which resists understanding gives way to telling. "If loneliness is the disease, then the story is the cure" (Walker 141), Richard Ford asserts. But loneliness itself is also redemptive, its evocation of nothingness the very state that invites transcendence through art. Language's paradoxical role complicates this endeavor; in fact, each narrator must first realize that there are things that "words cannot fix anyway," as Joe observes, and times when words cannot even be uttered. As Jean-Paul Sartre explains, language is an imperfect tool, but the attempt to use language figuratively, to force meaning from the unwieldy word despite its inherent imperfection, is itself an act of creativity that reaches beyond the mire and blood of existence. It is in this sense that Richard Ford makes these narrators creators of their own worlds, sovereign over their lives if by nothing else than words and their calling to something beyond their presence on the page.

Richard Ford approached the mythology and literary conventions of western fiction from the perspective of a native southerner who has spent most of his life in the South and the East, and, following the publication of *Rock Springs* and *Wildlife*, he has not returned to the western subject. As Russell Martin puts it, in explaining Ford's absence from his 1992 anthology of contemporary western writing, Ford is among those "writers with strong connections to this Western country whose lives and work are now focused elsewhere" (xxii). But why should Ford have decided to write about the West at all? Why, one must ask, should a native southerner, educated in the Midwest and resident more recently at Chicago and Princeton, elect to devote a substantial portion of his creative life to an alien and marginal culture?

As a writer from outside who briefly entered the literary culture of the West, Richard Ford is hardly an anomaly. The audience for cowboy myth in its classic form—in dime novels, popular fiction, film, or television—was created for consumption by a national and, in practical terms, largely an eastern audience.[1] The classic western story, which gradually came to center on male initiation experiences,[2] was adapted for each subsequent generation of readers. In the 1930s and 1940s, the "singing cowboy" (in the person of Gene Autry, Roy Rogers, and Tex Ritter) sentimentalized and softened the cowboy's rugged image. A third generation of cowboys, identifying the cowboy with the gunfighter, appealed to audiences in the 1950s and 1960s concerned with defending American democracy against Cold War enemies. A fourth-generation cowboy myth, popularized in film and country music during the 1970s, introduced the cowboy "drifter" and "outlaw," as defined in songs like Waylon Jennings's "My Heroes Have Always Been Cowboys"(1976). In his outlaw persona, the cowboy projected "a peculiar blend of nostalgia and pessimism" (Savage 90). In the decade after 1975, the outlaw figure was featured in a succession of popular songs, collected on such albums as Willie Nelson's *Red-Headed Stranger* (1975) and *Wanted: The Outlaws* (1976), which repeated "the isolation, violence, and inconsolable sorrow habitually associated with the genre" (Dunne 227). As Michael Dunne notes, one important feature of outlaw mentality is the awareness of a life of lost opportunities. Or as Waylon Jennings sings in "My Heroes Have Always Been Cowboys," the cowboy as a kind of poet *manqué* has wasted his life: "Picking up hookers instead of my pen / I let the words of my youth slip away" (quoted in Dunne 230).

In its more extreme variants, as Bill Malone writes, the outlaw figure verges on dangerous forms of survivalist figuration. Hank Williams, Jr.'s, song "A Country Boy Can Survive," for example, "was virtually a survivalist hymn with its emphasis on rural independence and its underlying hint of violence" (393). Richard Ford's more radical examples of western "independence" similarly echo, in a prescient manner, the militant antigovernment sentiments that reportedly led to the actions of those responsible for the Oklahoma City bombing in 1995. For the most part, however, his protagonists are too demoralized even for resistance. What they do share with the militant extremists is an embittered loss of faith in American society, particularly as it relates to the traditional roles of young white males, who feel increasingly marginalized and have reacted either by dropping out, in acts of passive resistance (as Ford's protagonists do), or by striking back, either in literal or fantasized gestures.

Like the popular media, Ford draws on the figures of the drifter and outlaw—those romantic losers forever unsettled in love and in trouble with the law. At the same time, the social realism of Ford's writing continually undercuts the element of fantasy in western myth and implicitly interrogates the often commercialized and colonizing usages of regional myth. Indeed, by exploring radically different geographical locales for his writing, Ford asserts a powerful artistic independence which frees his

Ford's Postmodern Cowboys

work of parochial attachments to particular "subjects" as such. The more profound aspects of social limitation, forms of human oppression which are not localized or culturally specific, are the focus of his art. At the heart of this form of social oppression is the control of consciousness, through the processing of cultural images and linguistic authority.

In Ford's postmodern western, the social and economic dilemmas of America as a whole are not escaped but only magnified by the desolate, ecologically damaged New West, which as Craig Lesley has written, "contains working people living a hardscrabble existence and trying to stay ahead of the bills and banks" (2). Ford's protagonists live just such lives "on the edge" where economic survival is unsure and social relationships are unstable. As Martin perceptively writes, the American West, more so than other regions of America (but no more so than Ford's native South), is the product of a colonial history as eastern and European financial interests have historically "developed" its resources: "The entire region, perhaps inevitably, became a kind of colony, a place whose wealth was channeled elsewhere and that suffered, therefore, a colony's classic sense of inferiority as well as its gnawing, troubled urge to assert its independence" (xviii). In this colonial economy, human beings are subjected to the same shortsighted economic forces as the environment: both are stripped of value until they are exhausted and then abandoned, and like Earl Middleton in the title story of *Rock Springs*, they are colonials whose injured mental life "leaves something out" (9). Within this society, Ford's postmodern cowboys are utterly out of place; they stumble through life, hoping at best to avoid being hurt or causing harm to others and aspiring only to understand and communicate their anxiety.

In the title story "Rock Springs," Ford presents three characters who are immediately recognizable as victims of a restrictive social environment: a father fleeing imprisonment on a "bad check" charge, his young daughter, and his current girlfriend. En route to Florida in their stolen Mercedes, this hapless family cannot help but suggest and parody the typical western "family vacation," as the three characters comment on the scenery and search for a motel where they may spend the night. Along the way, Ford's protagonist, Earl Middleton, stumbles upon the fabled "gold mine," the object of all generational eschatologies, but finds that its wealth is controlled by corporate owners and that its workers subsist in a grimy boomtown of trailers that only resemble "homes." A potentially more valuable discovery is Earl's chance meeting with an elderly black woman and her grandson. Within her cramped trailer home, the woman seems to have created "[s]omething good and sweet . . . instead of just temporary" (14). Unlike Earl himself, who has refined lying to an art, the black woman appears to speak sincerely of love and family, and in questioning Earl about himself, she "seemed to want truth" (14). Together with her exemplary husband, off working hard in the mine, she has uncomplainingly taken responsibility for a brain-damaged grandchild, apparently abandoned by the child's parents. In this chance encounter, as presumably in all such encounters, Earl is easily seduced by his own conventional paradigm of family happiness, and it is clear that he seizes on this idealized family as a nostalgic reminder of the kind of homey goodness and responsible stability that he associates with "real" families. Yet his idealization of "family" is a gauge of the disruption of his own social existence; it seems a misguided and desperate effort to secure meaning. It is precisely the instability and rootlessness of his life, and his inability to escape his limitations, that makes Earl a figure of particular narrative interest. His "leav[ing] something out," a feature that his girlfriend, Edna, identifies as his chief character trait, admits an absence denied by others; his disorganized flight from authority suggests the limited opportunities of his environment.

Like several stories in *Rock Springs* ("Going to the Dogs" and " Fireworks," for instance), the title of the story "Great Falls" refers allegorically to social breakdown as well as to the literal setting of Great Falls, Montana. The story traces a series of "great falls"—adultery, maternal desertion, premature death of the father, and a son's loneliness—that come to seem inevitable to the westerners who stoically accept and even take pride in their barren lives. When Jackie's father, Jack Russell, retires from his job at an air base in Great Falls, he elects not to return to his "home" in Tacoma, Washington, and one imagines that it is the "placelessness" and dissociation of Great Falls that he finds attractive. Russell's transgressions of the legal system, as he supplements his income by selling illegally procured fish and game to local caterers, resembles the widespread resis-

Ford's Postmodern Cowboys

tance to federal governance of western lands, a part of a regional culture in which federal "law" is connected with a long history of colonial intrusion. It is not surprising, in a way, that when Russell confronts his wife's lover he asks first about Woody's home and if his parents are living, as if to position the younger man in relation to communal boundaries which he himself lacks. Russell's rootlessness and indifference to the law are liberating but also place Russell and his family at risk, as his son, Jackie, comes to understand after his parents' breakup when he says, "We were all of us on our own in this" (48).

Ford connects Jack Russell's rootlessness with the kind of work he performs, first at the air base in Montana and later following the oil-field boom in Ely, Nevada, where he is killed in an accident; his labor is temporary and dissociated from society. Military bases are established or closed according to national priorities (or politics) and mining and drilling operations are even more transient. As Martin notes, "[A]t the close of the twentieth century, the West's frontier legacy of boom and bust still hasn't abated. Immigrants continue to barrel into the region, certain that it harbors those things that their lives have always lacked, and they continue, most of them, to end up disappointed" (xviii).

Jackie's mother is also uncomfortable in the confinement of settled relationships—so much so that when she abandons Jackie, she explains tersely, "'I'd like a less domestic life, is all'" (47). At the end, Jackie can only say of his mother that he has seen her "from time to time—in one place or another, with one man or another—and I can say, at least, that we know each other" (49). The verb "know" in this sentence suggests mere acquaintanceship more than friendship or intimacy, and when Jackie and his mother do meet by accident in a grocery after many years of separation, they have only a few words to say to each other. As Gilles Deleuze and Felix Guattari have written in theorizing "minor literature," an author from a marginal culture must find a point of "underdevelopment" and must develop a patois to express forms of deterritorialization. Paradoxically, a regional writer such as Richard Ford, whose work is embedded in a sense of place (albeit a *shifting* sense of place) may be best situated to utilize the "impossibilities" of marginal culture (by writing outside the dominant language and national culture). His writing does not attempt to reterritorialize itself by reauthorizing traditional referents of place (in the sense that Gabriel García Márquez may attempt through the amassing of local myths, legends, and particulars of place); rather it embraces its deterritorialized condition by exploring the gaps and incongruities of language. In the story "Sweethearts," for example, Ford employs the nuances of provincial speech. On the morning he is to enter prison for a year, Bobby is still anguished by love for his ex-wife, Arlene, who is now married to Russell. Bobby's admission that he had considered murdering Arlene and perhaps killing himself or Russell terrifies his ex-wife, as one might expect, but it is also a kind of archaic assertion of romantic love that seems out of place in his oppressed situation. How can Bobby assert faithful love for Arlene in a society where he cannot even be assured of employment, to say nothing of physical freedom? When Arlene and Russell toss Bobby's pistol into the river after driving him to prison, it is as much a purification—against the displaced conventionality of Bobby's awkward fidelity—as an expression of their fear.

As Deleuze and Guattari have suggested, within marginal literature, all personal relationships are "shadowed" by political facts. "Children" is a story set in the Hi-line section of northern Montana, near the Canadian border, "an empty, lonely place if you are not a wheat farmer (69)." Like the Four Corners region of the Southwest, which Martin describes as "not the absolute end of the earth back then [in the early 1950s], but . . . close enough to make you sort of skittish" (xiii), the Hi-line's very emptiness constrains the lives of its inhabitants. Driven by anger, escapism, or sheer boredom, its young people seem to respond destructively to the mere vacancy of the land. The association of the narrator, George, and his "friend," Claude Phillips, is as arid as the mechanized farming culture of the Hi-line. George comments that he didn't really know Claude or anyone else very well, and he implies a connection between his separateness and the environment: "You did not learn much of other people in that locality" (70). In the culture that the "children" of the story are entering, maturity involves learning to live "on your own" in a frighteningly complete sense. George understands that the young runaway, Lucy, separated from her family across the Canadian border and temporarily paired with Claude's father and later with Claude, "was already someone who could

Ford's Postmodern Cowboys

be by herself in the world" (94)—a fact that seems disturbing because it is so much an accepted part of George's experience. Perhaps because he is trying to come to terms with his own mother's desertion—he notes that her leaving "that part of Montana" was "not unusual" (82)—George finds nothing remarkable in Lucy's promiscuous independence: she seems to him pretty much a "normal girl." The fact that she is "running away" is not unusual and doesn't seem "a bad thing" to George.

It is clear that the conditions of George's childhood, in their dissociation of feelings and experience, have resulted in the creation of a new idiom. When Lucy says that she "loves" George and Claude and claims that she would rather spend the night with them than with Claude's father, George understands it as "just talk": "I knew that wasn't what she meant. It was just a thing to say, and nothing was wrong with it at all" (90). Nor do Claude's actions—his disrespect and hatred for his father and his casual affair with Lucy, whom his father puts under his "protection"—trouble George, who sees that "nothing you did when you were young matters at all" (98). In fact, little that one does as an adult matters to the larger world, "a place that seemed not even to exist, an empty place you could stay in for a long time and never find a thing you admired or loved or hoped to keep" (98).

The quest that all of Richard Ford's adult protagonists undertake has everything to do with this definition of experience as "an empty place." While they seem cowboys—transient laborers with few loyalties or social ties—it is evident that Ford's protagonists are at least shadowed by the absent virtues that George lists: a full place where you *can* find attachment, things you *can* admire and love and hope to keep. In their failure to obtain such a place or to find something to admire or love, Ford's characters construct a unique patois which may be based on absence and failure rather than success. Narrators such as Les Snow in "Winterkill" and "Communist" or Frank Brinson in "Optimists" carve their own right way to act and speak, appropriate to their own experience.

In representing the impossibility of these lives, Ford draws on the nuances of regional working-class speech as it creates unexpected meanings from familiar words. Expressions such as "you could trust me to . . .," "that's a sure fact," or "I had known him to . . ." cite but simultaneously undermine conventional meanings of "trust," "fact," and "know." Presumably the difference between a simple "fact" and a "sure fact" is a context in which "fact" is not "sure," a linguistic distinction which reflects precisely the uncertainty of regional culture. It is urgent for Ford's characters to express their tentativeness of experience in carefully drafted speech, but what they invariably discover is that the stories of their lives are inconclusive or even inconsequential. It means a great deal, however, to arrive at the conviction that nothing matters.

In "The Language of African Literature" (chapter 1 of *Decolonising the Mind*), Ngugi wa Thiong'o writes of the centrality of language to cultural identity: "The choice of language and the use to which language is put is central to a people's definition of themselves in relation to their natural and social environment, indeed in relation to the entire universe" (4). The imperialist domination of African languages and cultures resulted in a colonial alienation of African identity, for the repression of language closes off communication between self and others, between self and nature, and indeed "between me and my own self" (15). Particularly ironic is the fact that so many African writers, under the mental control of imperialist nations, participated in the devaluation of their own local cultures and in the exaltation of European languages and cultural models. One of the worst effects of this process was the exclusion "of the participation of the peasantry and the working class" from the cultural debate (26).

It is not coincidental that Richard Ford, like so many regional writers before him, should focus on a region's particular oral language. Like Faulkner, O'Connor, Wright, Welty, and Morrison, Ford understands that the writer's work is one of the recovery or at least the utilization of repressed speech, particularly the orality of marginalized social groups. Like his predecessors, Ford creates art out of excluded forms of orality. Indeed, Ford himself, as a writer whose works have achieved critical approval, appears to stoically accept the possibility that his work might at any time fall out of favor, or that he might not continue writing at all. As he told Kay Bonetti, "[I]f next year I decided I didn't want to write another book, or if I couldn't write another book, it wouldn't be the worst thing in the world to happen to the world or to literature or to me; it would just be something else that happened" (84). In this, Ford admits that his literary world, and experience in general, is largely beyond his control. The outside world is filled with potential harm, largely as a result of the fact that art is so little understood and "employed," so that Ford's narrative focuses on language as a way to admit and confront the emptiness of experience. While Ford's comments on his role as an artist are characteristically "cool" and indifferent, he is deeply engaged in opposing internal colonialism and reversing its effects. His meticulous uses of regional and working-class orality are inseparable from a political consciousness of the repression of local cultures within an assimilationist model of American democracy (a model meticulously analyzed in Sacvan Bercovitch's recent book, *The Rites of Assent*). Ford's comments on the precision with which he renders regional and class speech betray a serious artist compelled by both technical and ethical concerns.

Richard Ford admitted that, as an individual, he found the "voice" of *Rock Springs* similar to his own (Bonetti 95). In the expression of a provincial working-class culture, Ford brings to postmodern writing the voice of the aggrieved, excluded provincial, forever denied significance within the national culture. Ford's own self-conception as a writer involves a belief that language affords "consolation" against the kind of anxiety produced in an unreflexive, colonized use of language. In the interview with Bonetti, Ford stated that Faulkner "treated me with and to language which was about things that made the world more orderly to me." On the next page, Ford suggested that literature "*can* be consoling. It *can* say "the thing not before said. . . . We think we know what love is; we think we know what passion is; we think we know what hatred is. We know, in fact, a lot about those things. And literature's opportunity is to say about those concepts what hasn't been said yet, so that we know more about them, so that we'll find a way to take some solace in them" (80). For this writer from a fractured and excluded culture, immediate experience is always inarticulate and inherently painful, but presumably, experience *does* become more "orderly" as the myths we live within are better understood.

In any provincial culture, the cultural mythologies have been created or at least largely shaped from the outside by hegemonic cultures. In his western fiction, the mythology of individual opportunity which the national culture has for long associated with the western frontier occupies

Ford in several stories. "Empire," for example, is a fable of the duplicity of personal freedom. Riding the Great Northern line between Spokane, Washington, and Minot, North Dakota, Victor Sims enjoys the pleasant illusion of detachment that he associates with train travel: observing others from his compartment without being observed, crossing a near wild landscape without personal risk. Sims believes that he need exercise no control over events in his life, but that, paradoxically, his life is continually getting better: "Things you do pass away and are gone, and you need only to outlive them for your life to be better, steadily better" (136). Several ominous events in the story suggest that this philosophy is not reliable: Sims's seduction of Cleo, a neighbor's sister, leads to a phone call from Cleo's biker friend, Loser, who threatens Sims's wife. Like some repressed voice of conscience, Loser charges that Sims has been an "asshole" who has betrayed his wife and "doesn't deserve her." A similar suggestion of consequences is implied by the wildfire that threatens the lives of all the train passengers.

It is in the context of what Ngugi calls cultural alienation that Sims's benign fatalism "makes sense." When a culture has been denied the opportunity for coherent significance, all expression must be accidental and purposeless. For example, Sims's brief tryst with Doris Benton is only one episode in a lifetime of disengagement, suggested at the beginning of the story by his answers to his wife's personality quiz (for every question, he answers "None of the above"). Even his marriage to Marge is largely accidental, for he had been almost equally attracted to Marge's sister, Pauline. Indeed, when he first met Marge, he at first thought she *was* Pauline, whom he had once dated. Both Marge and Pauline presumably attracted Sims because of their "imagination for wildness" (116), a quality which involves all of them in accidental and bizarre relationships—such as the pairing of the neurotic and superstitious Sims with the unsentimental, mechanical Sergeant Benton. Like George in "Children," Sims does not feel that "things you do" have any lasting impact; his actions matter so little that he invents stories about his past, including the falsehood that he had served in Vietnam during the war. If Sergeant Benton catches him in this lie, which he regrets only because he is caught, she is equally unconcerned. For her part, Marge shares Victor's attraction to a deceptive freedom. Even as she watches farmers in the distance battling the flames, their farms destroyed by the wildfire, she remarks: "'The world's on fire. . . . But it doesn't hurt anything'" (147). With her sense of "how happy I am" and his feeling of being "alone in a wide empire, removed and afloat, calmed, as if life was far away now" (147-48), Marge and Victor travel within a discourse of illusory freedom, chance events, and inconsequential preoccupation.

In one of the finest stories in *Rock Springs*, "Winterkill," the adult Les Snow describes his and Troy Burnham's meeting with Nola Foster. All three characters are victims of a harsh, unforgiving economic system, and their condition is intimately connected with internal colonialism and with their status at the bottom of that system. At the beginning of the story, Les is represented as an individual alienated from all society— "alone, where I didn't mind being at all" (168). Les's conception of "trust" is oddly mechanized, based on "predictability" rather than social obligation. If one could *predict* that Les will act in a certain manner, one could "trust" him to act that way. By his own code, Les is faithful toward his friend, Troy, whose paralysis below the waist leaves him physically impotent, but, as we learn at the end of the story, Les is simultaneously attractive to Nola (herself a wanderer who spends her days in barrooms in the company of various men). For his part, Les finds it difficult to enter a long-term relationship since he is frequently out of work and waiting for better times which may require geographic removal. Yet the economic system is only part of a quiescent culture in which Les's posture is that of "waiting." Ford peoples his fiction with characters who are, in more than a literal sense, "out of work" and "waiting" for their luck to change. The question of their survival is posed well by Frank Bascombe near the conclusion of *The Sportswriter*: "Where do sportswriters go when the day is, in every way, done, and the possibilities so limited that neither good nor bad seems a threat?" (339).

Understandably, the best Les Snow can imagine is a life in which harm "stays away" and in which he hurts no one, rather than a system in which he "acts." When the freezing river yields a dead fawn, one of the unprotected creatures that die in the course of the winter, Les takes the "winterkill" as further evidence of the world's ubiquitous danger. For Les at the end of the story, Troy and Nola, whom he leaves together undisturbed, appear as two further examples of winterkill—damaged individuals who can only find momentary comfort in one another, but who are unable to change their condition.

Frank Brinson is another character in *Rock Springs* who finds that the cultural myths of individualism and economic opportunity associated with the West are particularly unreliable. In the story "Optimists," Frank's father, Roy, a switch-engine fireman on the Great Northern Railway, believes that his union has created a "workingman's paradise" until he finds his job threatened by layoffs. By late 1959, the railroads have begun to cut workers: "everyone knew, including my father, that they would—all of them—eventually lose their jobs, though no one knew exactly when, or who would go first, or, clearly, what the future would be" (172-73). Under this pressure, at the end of a horrifying night when he sees a hobo cut to pieces by a train and bleed to death on the tracks, Roy Brinson snaps. After he is insulted by Boyd Mitchell in his own home, Roy lands a single punch which kills his abusive neighbor. He spends five months in prison for manslaughter, but his entire life unravels afterward.

From this episode, Roy's son, Frank, concludes that, as he says, "situations have possibilities in them, and we have only to be present to be involved" (181)—a strikingly agentless analysis of social repression. As Frank comments: "The most important things of your life can change so suddenly, so unrecoverably, that you can forget even the most important of them and their connections, you are so taken up by the chanciness of all that's happened and by all that could and will happen next" (187). Frank's reaction to the catastrophe is impassive, just as, in cowboy music, there is a conventional lack of protest to the "loneliness, social alienation, poverty and the strain of arduous physical labor" (Dunne 227). Yet protest of a sort is implied—at least from the perspective of the narrative if not from that of Frank—in the very act of recording the cowboy's voice.

If Ford's text registers the distress of the working-class culture he narrates, it is practically impossible for Ford's western characters to articulate their own resentment. As Ngugi puts it, "It is the final triumph of a system of domination when the dominated start singing its virtues" (20). Just how out of place cultural criticism is in the American West is illustrated by the story "Communist," in which Glen Baxter fantasizes a net-work of communists in Montana and suggests an impending social revolution. Ford, however, undermines Baxter's rhetoric by showing that his personal crises have driven him outside society and that his political radicalism is a measure of his control rather than his independence. Baxter, currently an unemployed young man living with Les Snow's mother, competes with her for Les's approval. If Aileen hopes for a middle-class future for her son, Baxter attempts to inculcate his radical ideals and, at a deeper level, to pass on his heritage of futility and stoic acceptance to the boy. While Glen Baxter seems to have been only a minor influence on Les, he, in fact, turns out to be a formative substitute for Les's father. The entire point of Les's retelling Baxter's story twenty-five years later is that Les hopes to better understand his own situation by rehearsing that of his exemplar. Despite his mother's opposition, Baxter's influence has been lasting.

By contrast, Aileen's authority has been slight. Les feels that he doesn't know his mother very well and in fact feels more comfortable when she is absent. At the time he tells the story, Les is forty-one and admits that his last real communication with his mother occurred when he was sixteen. In the last paragraph, in what is also the last line of the collection *Rock Springs*, Les speaks of the separation from his mother with sad resignation, suggesting that he has accepted the loneliness and fragmentation of his social environment: "I am forty-one years old now, and I think about that time without regret, though my mother and I never talked in that way again, and I have not heard her voice now in a long, long time" (235).

Stories such as "Communist" explore the role of the male code of stoic acceptance within a colonized western culture. Paternal and maternal ideals compete for Les's approval, since Baxter's passion for hunting reiterates the boxing lessons that Les received from his father before his death. His father had trained him to stay on his opponent until he falls(226)—an implicit irony since Les's father soon "falls" himself and his place in his wife's bed is taken by the younger, fitter man, Glen Baxter. Baxter, in his turn, imparts a similarly fatalistic male code to Les. When, for example, Baxter returns from months of drifting following his sister's funeral in Florida, his "story" seems to Aileen Snow unreliable, and Les, who better comprehends his incoherent desperation, comments that "[a] light can go out in the heart" (232). Baxter has crossed the line at which it no longer matters whether his life can be imagined coherently: he can poach while claiming he is not poaching, he can live with one companion or another, he has lost whatever protection language affords. In an episode in which Baxter and Aileen argue over leaving a wounded goose to die on the freezing lake, he attempts to pass on a stoic masculine code that accepts the harshness of the outside world and that insists on the limits of pity. Aileen understands perfectly well what Baxter is attempting to teach, and her fury over his leaving a suffering bird on the lake is more deep-seated: although her vision of life is never developed in the story, it is clear that she is uncomfortable in the "half-wild" country in which she lives and that she opposes the male code of killing and fighting. She even has hopes of Les's attending college—the ultimate apostasy, apparently, for the cowboy hero.

While the West, with its store of cowboy myth and frontier ideology, is especially well suited to Ford's purposes, a similar absence of social discourse is apparent in all of Richard Ford's works, including those set in suburban New Jersey (*The Sportswriter* and *Independence Day*, the American South (*A Piece of My Heart*), and expatriate Mexican society (*The Ultimate Good Luck*). The mountain West offers a convenient symbolic landscape for expressing the rootlessness of an increasing number of Americans, for in the West, pursuing quintessential myths of freedom and opportunity, Americans have typically preferred to "pick up stakes" and "move on" rather than confront communal problems. Yet the cowboy and frontier myths encode cultural values and mask social problems shared by the nation as a whole.

Like Ford's protagonists in *Rock Springs* and *Wildlife*, Harry Quinn and Rae in *The Ultimate Good Luck* lead transient and rootless lives, and they are essentially early sketches for the outlaws who appear later in his fiction. Rae, who appears at the beginning of the novel traveling in the company of a bronco rider and car thief named Frank Oliver "figured out that what she was doing was simply craziness and nobody in his right mind would be doing it, but it was all she could bear to think about longer than a minute" (41). Against the backdrop of the seventies drug culture in the expatriate American community in Oaxaca, Mexico, Quinn is also something of a colonial amnesiac, a figure who attempts to follow a merely personal code (that includes loyalty to "buddies") that leaves out any collective vision, as, for example, in his respect for the use of weapons without regard for their social damage. When Quinn's attorney, Bernhardt, toward whom he feels some sense of attachment, is shot to pieces by a campesino, and the entire magazine is unloaded into his body (stopping only "when there wasn't enough left to shoot at"), Quinn remarks laconically: "It was skilled work, something Bernhardt wouldn't have expected" (155).

Like Ford's western characters, Quinn learns from experience to suspect all settled relationships or institutions, and his rule is to avoid human connection altogether. At one point Quinn recalls a childhood experiment of placing a frog in a pan of water over a gas flame. As he gradually increases the heat, the frog sits calmly in the water until it realizes the danger, but it is now helpless to move, staring "out past the time when it could move even if it needed to." The lesson for Quinn is that human beings are in the same position: the frog is "an illustration of how people let certain things they're used to go on so long that they don't know that the things they're used to are killing them" (152). His solution is to remain mobile and in apparent control of his life.

The Sportswriter and its sequel *Independence Day* focus on the character of Frank Bascombe, a divorced suburbanite who resembles Ford's western protagonists in his reflections on the illusory myths of individualist society. At the beginning of *The Sportswriter*, Frank compares his own experience with the myth of the American Dream as he reflects on "the good life" he had expected with his wife and three children: "Just exactly what that good life was—the one I expected—I cannot tell you now exactly, though I wouldn't say it has not come to pass, only that much has come in between" (3). In contrast with Ford's western characters, to some degree Frank's social isolation is masked by a more benevolent suburban environment (he, after all, continues in the same job, lives in the same house and neighborhood, and retains some of the same acquaintances), but Ford's artistic purposes in the New Jersey novels are not essentially different from those in his western fiction. The middle-class enclaves of central New Jersey are represented as equally desolate and shallow, equally lacking in communal attachments. In its unique patois of sports-talk, the suburban male community expresses an absence similar to that of Ford's western figures. It may be, however, that the western material allows a more blatant representation of alienation. Like the physical environment of the West, which must weather greater extremes of climate and geography, the social environment subjects human beings to unusual stresses of isolation and trauma.

Perhaps because of the severity of their conditions, many of Richard Ford's western characters are shown to vividly imagine their now lost families and childhood communities. As he records an ambiguous definition of "family" and the tentativeness of all social relationships, Ford's language employs the colonial tropes of emptiness and impossibility: the ways in which parents fail their children, the loneliness of adults "out in the world" without families, the "chanciness" of all social ties.

Like Earl Middleton, moving furtively in the parking lot of a Ramada Inn in Rock Springs, Wyoming, Ford's protagonists often have a sense of déjà vu as they observe the apparently purposeful lives and ordered communities of others. Like Earl, peering into the windows of "a Pontiac with Ohio tags"—an imperial sort of family car loaded for a western vacation—they experience the colonial's startled admission into the presence of the colonizer. As Earl puts it: "It all looked familiar to me, the very same things I would have in my car if I had a car. Nothing seemed surprising, nothing different. Though I had a funny sensation at that moment" (26). Earl's "funny sensation" is associated with the unfamiliar and uncomfortable knowledge that he is being observed; however much he tries to escape notice of the controlling legal and social systems, he is always within the jurisdiction of cultural hegemony.

Like all of Richard Ford's postmodern cowboys, Earl Middleton wants mostly to be left alone, to find "solace" from the pain of his alienation, "to put things like this out of your mind and not be bothered by them." As Earl reflects at the end of "Rock Springs," what he wants out of life is not more freedom and opportunity but less adversity and grief, not more of the American Dream but less: "Fewer troubles, fewer memories of trouble" (26).

Richard Ford's Frank Bascombe is the star and impresario of his own postmodern story to ward off cynicism and attain "normalcy" in an undramatic life where "[e]verything is as problematic as geometry" (*Sportswriter* 107). In *The Sportswriter*, Frank is thirty-eight, divorced, and living in Haddam, New Jersey, a kind of John Cheever exurbia within easy commuting distance of New York City. The town has no special "placeness" or enduring historical legacy per se, and, like Walker Percy's own Covington, Louisiana, is an "interstice" beside the throughway. Frank's former wife and their two children live separate lives in separate houses in this tidy, relatively peril-free town.

With *Independence Day* Frank is now forty-four. He is a more than modestly successful Haddam realtor and an owner of two rental homes and a hot dog-birch beer stand just outside of town. His ex-wife, Ann Dykstra, is now married to Charley O'Dell, an affable old Yalie who is an architect and lives in a swanky home with a great sashaying porch in indelibly Yankee Deep River, Connecticut. As in *The Sportswriter*, Frank philosophizes about the world and the human condition and solipsizes his way through truculent prospective home buyers and feckless lovers. Through hackneyed conversations with his ex-wife, Frank discovers that his son, Paul, has become remote and taciturn and is seeing a psychiatrist in New Haven. Frank has a rather cryptic relationship with his son and worries over the boy's mental "irregularities" and the sorts of disarming responses to the Rorschach tests he may be giving his psychiatrist. He plans a sort of "let's get to know each

Isolation and Alienation in the Frank Bascombe Novels

William G. Chernecky

other better" whirlwind trip around Connecticut and Massachusetts to the Basketball Hall of Fame in Springfield, and eventually to Cooperstown, for some dad and lad quality time at the Baseball Hall of Fame. But Paul is no athlete, nor is he even interested in the techniques or legacies of sports. Frank tries to find any sort of connective passageway between himself and his son, but Paul remains aloof and enigmatic, a participant in only the contrived life of his mind. For Paul, the excursions to the halls of fame are like a forced march that he phlegmatically endures. While in baseball history country, Paul jumps into the 75 mph "Dyno-Express" batting cage and tells his father, "Gimme the cocksucking bat" (*Independence* 360). Paul is seriously hit in the eye by a fastball and ends up in an Oneonta, New York, hospital. Frank is deflated and forlorn from this whirlwind escapade with his son, and they both return to their homes in Deep River and Haddam.

Riding along the plotlines of both Bascombe novels is an intricate montage of cultural images that Frank turns like a kaleidoscope of contemporary America. He has a camera eye that takes in the glittering multitude of images/signs that Americans are obliged to encounter—motels, merchandise catalogs, airports, theme rest stops on turnpikes, clothing, yuppy families on bicycles, "signs that say HERE!," miracle mile main streets, fast food restaurants, and ticky-tack subdivisions with bucolic titles like "Hedgrow Place" and "The Thistles." Many of these self-conscious images call particular attention to their "imageness" and remind Frank how derivative, mechanical, and concocted they are. As he whisks down the New Jersey and southern New England roads, Frank reflects on the possibilities of any authentic meanings down the long aisles of the social supermarket. These cultural accoutrements create a structure of feeling for him, a pattern of impulses, tones, and restraints and shade his experience of America at or beneath the threshold of awareness.

In both novels, Frank Bascombe looks for the "figure in the carpet" beyond the overt content of people and things around him. He wants to plumb the mysteries beyond cultural entities that are overlooked by other characters he considers to be the "literalists" of the world—surface surfers who Frank claims are without subtexts. These unreflective characters rarely suspect any philosophical corollaries to experiences and more often unquestionably accept the world as a whole. But Frank thinks about other characters/events in terms that alternate between breathless understatement and a chilling recognition of the greater social implications they offer him.

Frank Bascombe is quick to disassemble events and characters for their subliminal meanings. He extracts ulterior meanings and often collates events to private philosophical themes so that people and events are nearly parodies of themselves. Towards the end of *The Sportswriter*, for example, Frank arrives at the Haddam city hall complex to identify the body of his acquaintance-friend Walter Luckett. From inside the building's glass doors Frank watches a family cycle down the street:

> Two cyclists glide across my view. A man ahead, a woman behind; a child in a child's secure-seat strapped snug to Papa. All three are white-helmeted. Red pennants wag on spars in the dusk. All three are on their way home from an informal prayer get-together somewhere down some street, at some Danish-modern Unitarian hug-a-friend church where cider's on tap and *damn* and *hell* are permissible—life on the continual upswing week after week. (It is the effect of a seminary in your town.) Now they're headed homeward, fresh and nuclear, their frail magneto lights whispering a gangway to old darkness. Here come the Jamiesons. Mark, Pat and baby Jeff. Here comes life. All clear. Nothing can stop us now. But they are wrong, wrong these Jamiesons. I should tell them. Life-forever is a lie of the suburbs—its worst lie—and a fact worth knowing before you get caught in its fragrant silly dream. Just ask Walter Luckett. He'd tell you, if he could. (319)

Frank handles this scene by flattening people into objects on the landscape. He makes many of the novels' other characters into interesting objects. External events are formulated in his own private tensions because of his process of internalization. For the narrator, people and events become less events experienced and more objects of speculation. But Frank's ability to abstract patterns from people and events only adds to his solipsistic worldview and inevitably alienates him from the world around him. Frank Bascombe's limited points of view emphasize the isolation of his individual consciousness. Bascombe's solipsism that involves judgment of behavior and perception distances him from the primary things that offer meaning and purpose to life.

Readers discover early in *The Sportswriter* that Frank's propensity for analysis helps create his carefully articulated view of how the world operates. He categorizes people and events and offers all sorts of conclusions about the motives of characters' actions. Contrary to his own maxim that others are ultimately unknowable to ourselves, he constantly objectifies other characters. But this makes Frank less a participant in the ebb and flow of life around him and more a spectator and analyst—like the sportswriter he is. According to his own solipsistic philosophy, the world is populated by literalists and factualists, or as Frank affixes the distinction, "A literalist is a man who will enjoy an afternoon watching people while stranded in an airport in Chicago, while a factualist can't stop wondering why his plane was late out of Salt Lake, and gauging whether they'll still serve dinner or just a snack" (132-33). Oddly enough, Frank dislikes those who analyze, categorize, and dissect the mysteries of life with the scalpel of rationalism. But while Frank claims that "[s]ome things can't be explained. They just are" (*Sportswriter* 223), he continuously applies his own solipsistic ratiocination to people and events, objectifying them down to their psychological parts. This uncanny proclivity to analyze and then compartmentalize tends to formulate barriers between Frank and other characters. Ostensibly, he's got their scores and knows the cut of their jibs.

Dialogue is not a particularly striking means of understanding Frank's world. In *The Sportswriter*, crucial data is not gleaned through Frank's conversations, but dialogue gives readers a passing glance at how Richard Ford's figures generally comport themselves, their general temperaments, and their levels of diction. Usually after any potentially interesting conversation, Frank conveys his philosophical insights about the other character's psychological motives. For Frank, the "oral" process of dialogue, like the nature of language itself, is too elusive for true meaning. Frank customarily speaks at other characters, not with others. What is paramount to Frank is not what other characters tell him, but what he thinks they tell him. "People never tell the truth anyway" (76), he says, and he himself confesses to possessing "a number of different voices, a voice that wanted to be persuasive, to promote good effects, to express love and be sincere, and make other people happy—even if what I was saying was a total lie and as distant from the truth as Athens is from Nome" (64).

With *Independence Day*, however, Frank has mellowed. He is less reflex-ively judgmental, and his solipsism is less lunging and jagged. Two rental homes, Frank's birch beer stand, and his realty job with the Lauren-Schwindell Agency have ensconced him in Haddam's "tree-softened" streets, pursuing an elusive sense of "normal life." He coaches a T-ball team, attends the Realty Roundtable, dresses as a clown for parades to "spruce up the public perception of realtors as being, if not a bunch of crooks, at least a bunch of phonies and losers" (*Independence* 116). He fishes at the Red Man Club and takes part in the annual Parade of Homes. Language and words are more an ally in *Independence Day* than in *The Sportswriter*. For Frank, words now have an amelioratory affect and flush out the mind's avalanche of criss-crossing emotions and articulate bridges to others.

If *The Sportswriter* can be roughly regarded as a novel involving the nar-rator's alienation and "separateness" from the flux of people and events, *Independence Day* is very much a work of contrition and amelioration. The sequel is not just Frank's stoic obligation to trudge through his Existence Period, but also an effort at ever-modulating engagement with others. Language, or as Frank calls it, "words," is the only practical medium to bridge and heal the chasms between people. He discovers that words en-list people in the collective world around them. Bascombe realizes that language is the most immediate and direct extension of our senses that puts people in touch with the extended senses of others. Frank's conver-sations with his ex-wife, Ann, and with his stepbrother, Irv Ornstein, are perhaps the most meaningful. Words not only put him in immediate phys-ical proximity with others, but language is the most direct medium with which to convey and initiate a kind of spiritual kinship with others. Frank comes to understand that conversation unites place and time and offers a sampling of its inchoate qualities of tonal, textural, and harmonic sub-tleties between speakers. His talks with Irv Ornstein become a soothing tonic as Frank follows conversation's vivid sense of doubleness shared by the realities of the voice, the story, and the listener.

Although Frank Bascombe makes individual progress in terms of his relationships with others, when the Bascombe novels are viewed in a larger cultural context they clearly demonstrate how Americans have retreated to purely personal preoccupations. Having little hope of improving their lives in ways that matter, people have convinced themselves that what matters is psychic self-improvement: Getting in touch with their feelings, eating health food, jogging, learning how "to relate," and overcoming the fears of pleasure are all important. These pursuits are elevated to a program and wrapped in the rhetoric of authenticity and awareness. They signify a retreat from what is truly important in American life and a repudiation of the recent past. Frank lives for the short term, for what's around the corner. He has a longing for but no sense of historical continuity—the feeling of belonging to a succession of generations originating in the past and stretching into the future. It is no wonder readers find Frank all alone at the beginning of *The Sportswriter*, saying, like a specter still eclipsed by darkness, "My name is Frank Bascombe. I am a sportswriter" (3). Even *Independence Day* ends with Frank all alone in the 4th of July Haddam crowd, another applauseless person clapping for the stars of the parade that passes him by.

A kind of therapeutic sensibility is especially evident throughout *Independence Day*. Beleaguered by depression, anxiety, a host of shadowy discontents, and a feeling of inner emptiness, the new "psychological" man of the late twentieth century pursues neither self-aggrandizement nor spiritual transcendence. Therapy to achieve some measure of peace of mind is the successor to rugged individualism and religion. As cultural critic Christopher Lasch claims: "Therapy constitutes an antireligion, not always to be sure because it adheres to rational explanation or scientific methods of healing, as its practitioners would have us believe, but because modern society 'has no future' and therefore gives no thought to anything beyond its immediate needs" (*Culture of Narcissism* 13).

Dr. Stopler of New Haven, Paul's enigmatic psychiatrist, informs Ann how little modern science knows of the mind's confusing machinations, but he believes that distressed family relations are precursors to childhood mental illness. Quite to the contrary, Frank wonders why mental health means the overthrow of inhibitions and the immediate gratification of every impulse.

Progress in the twilight of the twentieth century no longer carries the valence it once did in previous generations, particularly with nineteenth-century Americans. Progress was once interpreted as humanity positively thinking out its destiny. But Frank Bascombe reflects the notion that much of what constitutes progress is quintessentially change. In preparation for their anticipated trek in *Independence Day* to the halls of fame, Frank has forwarded to his son the unusual fatherly offerings of the Declaration of Independence and "Self-Reliance" and claims that: "I believe his instincts are sound and he will help himself if he can, and that independence is, in fact, what he lacks—independence from whatever holds him captive: memory, history, bad events he struggles with, can't control, but feels he should" (16). Frank acknowledges that he cannot be Paul's therapist, only his father. But his relatively short exposures to Paul are only glancing, and he avoids any heavily laden sessions where he ends up quizzing or fighting Paul and maybe offering inappropriate advice. Instead of the seemingly rapid and canned answers Dr. Stopler offers Ann about Paul, Frank delivers Emerson as a practical schematic for his son's future actions.

In the very first paragraph of *Independence Day* Frank lets readers know that the "psychological man" is alive and at work in Haddam when he notes, "The marriage enrichment class (4 to 6) has let out at the high school, its members sleepy-eyed and dazed, bound for bed again" (3). But instead of listening to head-shrinking counselors and psychiatrists whose legacies abound in contemporary America, Frank totes around highlighted and underlined copies of Tocqueville and Emerson for his son. When Frank discovers that Paul has no idea of who John Adams was, he also realizes that while the two speak in words to one another, there is no shared, underlining cultural context to buoy those words.

Cultural literacy places greater value on national than on local information. But so many of the Pauls of the Nintendo generation have a narrow radius of interest. For the Pauls, there is little in the way of understanding the present in light of the past. Frank offers the tableau of John Adams, James Fenimore Cooper, and Emerson, but they are just old dead guys to his son. Paul Bascombe's lack of any sense of collective memory causes Frank to realize that collective memory is largely responsible for formulating national identity. It is America thinking about the present and contemplating its future out loud—America talking about itself. Paul's stunning lack of knowledge about America puts him beyond the pale of collective memory into a private and remote world all his own.

In the course of Frank's father-son jaunt, he realizes that some of the lurking chasms between the two are more than an "age thing." What separates Paul from his father is not just a generation gap. While approaching greater Hartford on I-91, Frank claims that "History's lessons are subtle lessons, inviting us to remember and forget selectively, and therefore are much better than psychiatry's, where you're forced to remember everything" (*Independence* 259). He believes Paul's problems may ultimately reside in his inability to integrate his disheveled past with his "hectic present" so the two can be conjoined in a "commonsense way and make him free and independent" (*Independence* 259). Frank mentions John Adams and how the patriot believed joining the disparate colonies into some cohesive order where they could be "independent together" was tantamount to orchestrating thirteen clocks to all strike simultaneously. Paul's rather nonplussed response—"Who's John Adams?"—causes Frank to think that beyond age and dress, which separate the generations, problems with the cultural fabric of continuity have parted the generations. Frank sees that the cultural and historical echoes of the past have not been passed to Generation X. What were once communally shared items of knowledge such as who John Adams was or the reasons for celebrating Independence Day are no longer conveniently understood by the Pauls of the next generation.

Ford's Frank Bascombe novels reflect the contemporary American cultural climate where people no longer yearn for personal salvation, let alone any return to some earlier epoch, but for the sense, the ephemeral illusion, of personal well-being, good health, and psychic security. Reagan and Bush and Dukakis and Republicans and Democrats all disappoint Frank, and no new heroes are on the horizon. Idealism is on the wane. The American political arena offers no possible respite from the tribulations and angst of conventional life. Frank tells his sometime-girlfriend, Sally Caldwell, that he has no compulsion to go to Pago Pago to join any particular cause. Instead, he is trying to establish his postdivorce, post-blowup identity, not submerge his identity into any sort of larger cause. In American society in an age of diminishing expectations, Frank turns to secularized salvation. Religion holds no mysterious guideposts to life's spiritual treasures. On their Sunday morning stroll to the Baseball Hall of Fame, Frank and Paul pass the well-dressed worshipful as they file into Cooperstown's churches. Frank claims that "Paul and I, on the other hand, fit in well with the pilgrim feel of things temporal—nonworshipful, nonpious . . ." (*Independence* 340).

Frank peeks at Tocqueville's *Democracy in America* and later into Emerson's "Self-Reliance" which point to an earlier type of American individualist—"the American Adam" of the "Imperial Self" celebrated in nineteenth-century American literature and philosophy. In fact, during his trek outside Trenton en route to his girlfriend Sally Caldwell's South Mantoloking beachfront house, he passes the De Tocqueville Academy and considers sending Paul there if he ever decides to live with him again. After he reaches Sally's she later claims to have left "de Tocqueville out for you since you're taking a trip and also reading history in the middle of the night" (*Independence* 161). Frank even rests on Sally's bed with a worn copy of *Democracy in America* and reads "How Democratic Institutions and Manners Tend to Raise Rents and Shorten the Terms of Leases." He thumbs further back and finds "What Causes Almost All Americans to Follow Industrial Callings." Then he finally zeroes in on "Why So Many Ambitious Men and So Little Lofty Ambitions Are to Be Found in the United States" (*Independence* 154). Frank thinks he can find some insights into this segment and reads: "The first thing that strikes a traveler to the United States is the innumerable multitudes of those who seek to emerge from their original condition; and the second is the rarity of lofty ambition to be observed in the midst of universally ambitious stir of society. No Americans are devoid of a yearning desire to rise but hardly any appear to entertain hopes of great magnitude or to pursue lofty aims . . ." (154).

The inherent concerns of the social and the individual man interested not only Emerson and Tocqueville, among other nineteenth-century philosophers and commentators, but also those Americans interested in the human potential movement in the seventies. According to Peter Marin in "The New Narcissism," Americans in the seventies became reacquainted with the old maxim of the American Adam, which asserts that "the individual will is all powerful and totally determines one's fate" (48). But the drawback of this narcissistic focus upon the self is that it also intensifies " the isolation of the self." This thread of thought is part of a timeless American tradition of social examination. Marin claims that Americans in the late twentieth century have never arrived at some accommodating middle ground between public responsibility and developing the potential of the self. In his *America's Coming-of-Age*, Van Wyck Brooks criticized the transcendentalists for not exploring "the genial middle ground of human tradition" (38).

The "American Adam," like his transcendental descendants, attempted to ignore his own past and formulate what Emerson called " an original relation to the universe." Nineteenth-century orators and writers reiterated in various permutations Jefferson's theory that the wide earth belongs to the living. The severance of ties with the Old World, the destruction of primogeniture, and the more ephemeral bonds between family members led American philosophers to conclude that their countrymen could relinquish the troublesome ties with the past. They accepted Tocqueville's general thesis that their whole destiny is in their hands. Tocqueville believed that America's unique social conditions dissolved ties that bonded one generation to its predecessors. "The woof of time is every instant broken and the track of generation effaced. Those who went before are soon forgotten; of those who will come after, no one has any idea: the interest of man is confined to those in close propinquity to himself" (qtd. in Lasch 9).

Frank Bascombe is cut off from any reasonably predictable future by his divorce and the move of his children into their new home with Charley O'Dell in Deep River, Connecticut. While en route to gather his son for their whirlwind July 4th weekend to the basketball and baseball halls of fame, he considers having his girlfriend, Sally Caldwell, join them with an overnight bag. Frank imagines that the three of them would look like some living models of America's social casualties, castaways of the "new-dimensional family modality" (*Independence* 187). Trundled off together in a tidy but fractured social package would be a "divorced father, plus son living in another state and undergoing mental sturm und drang, plus father's widowed girlfriend, for whom he feels considerable affection and ambiguity, and whom he may marry or else never see again. Paul would view it as right for our times" (*Independence* 187). Frank's irretrievable claims to any endearing history are like his recollections of "the distant South" that was once his homeland. Somewhere along Mississippi's Gulf Coast is Frank's spiritual home, while Haddam offers no mystic chords to the past. It is only a reasonably appointed town, a place, a turnpike stop that is "damned easy to cozy up to " (*Independence* 93). In terms of history and home, Frank offers the stoic philosophy that is a kind of notion to live by in twentieth-century America. "Best just to swallow back your tear, get accustomed to the minor sentimentals and shove off to whatever's next, not whatever was. Place means nothing" (*Independence* 152). He claims that unlike spiritual homes, "[p]laces never cooperate by revering you back when you need it. In fact, they almost always let you down . . ." (*Independence* 151-52).

Like most Americans in the twilight of the twentieth century, Frank perceives his family legacy and history in general as a mystifying force, not a vehicle that enlightens the here and now. His parents are enigmas who are cursorily known but never near to being understood, and he claims that when he thinks of them they arrive in a series of fractured recollections "in some revisionist's way. " Frank believes that if he were able to pursue his history, "it would no doubt explain my whole life to now" (*Independence* 163). But like Nietzsche's "last man," he is devoured in the vortex of the brief shining moment of the now, largely disconnected with his past and poised to react to the next big event, the next new spectacle in the future, what he calls "joining life's rough timbers end to end" (*Independence* 107).

Dealing with realty's loose ends, visiting a here-and-now girlfriend, and picking up his troubled son for a whirlwind escapade around southern New England and upstate New York—all on the July 4th weekend—form the essential plotlines of *Independence Day*. The notions of personal independence and collective responsibility play in the shadows of Independence Day itself.

The 4th of July is perhaps the nation's only holiday that commingles the historical concept of national binding unity with personal freedoms. But in some ways this concept is anachronistic. The connectives between collective memory, national identity, and personal freedoms are tenuous, if not at odds with one another. Frank knows this from reading Tocqueville. Frank Bascombe fully recognizes that his past is key to understanding himself today, but scavenging through the past is a droll and dubious task for most Americans. He realizes that most people reckon themselves only in the visible here and now and the predictably near future. He claims that his former wife, Ann, and occasional girlfriend, Sally Caldwell, live their lives as amnesia victims. As literalists, they do not hobnob with the shadowy goblins of their history. Like most Americans, who they are is a pragmatic function of their socioeconomic footing in the great American crowd.

For whatever the historical past may mean for Americans, Frank cannot find any collective consciousness among the long-haul trucks and idling buses, the trash receptacles and people lining up for Roy Rogers burgers, Giants novelty items, or comical condoms at the Vince Lombardi Rest Area on the New Jersey Turnpike. While en route on the turnpike and through the circuitry of Connecticut roads, Frank is caught in a conundrum about personal independence in the face of the American mob where the July 4th troupers are "as chaotic as a department store at Christmas" (*Independence* 178).

While Frank claims he may someday grapple with his own past and articulate his family legacy in the distant South on paper, his journey to the basketball and baseball halls of fame is an effort to tap into America's collective past. Both places are shrines to the two sports, museum-arenas of sepia-tinted memories. For Frank, who we are as a people is tantamount to who we have been over the passage of time. His feelings run along the lines of T. S. Eliot's thoughts in "Tradition and the Individual Talent" (1917) where the poet claims that "the historical sense involves a perception, not only of the pastness of the past, but of its presence . . ." (qtd. in Hyman 61-62).

The general intellectual spirit that articulated the Declaration of Independence was more likely to allude to the burden of history than to any possible uses of the past (Kammen 35). The July 4th signers in Philadelphia generally believed that the primary concern of the youthful and effervescent new country should be the present and future rather than the past (Kammen 42). The transcendentalists reiterated this philosophy in various forms, starting with Emerson's essay "Nature" in 1836. In his 1838 divinity school address, Emerson informed the new ministers that memory and soul were in direct conflict, and he preferred aligning himself with the latter. But Frank totes a green copy of Emerson's "Self-Reliance" as a sort of chapbook, reference guide, or even portable moral compass from which he postures rhetorically to Paul from Emerson's own postures.

In language fashioned in the pedantic-parable style, Emerson conveys in "Self-Reliance" man's relationship with the past:

> If, therefore, a man claims to know and speak of God, and carries you backward to the phraseology of some old mouldered nation in another country, in another world, believe him not. Is the acorn better than the oak which is its fullness and completion? Is the parent better than the child into whom he has cast his ripened being? Whence, then, this worship of the past? The centuries are conspirators against the sanity and authority of the soul. Time and space are but physiological colors which the eye makes, but the soul is light; where it is, is day; whence it was, is night; and history is an impertinence and an injury, if it be anything more than a cheerful apologue or parable of my being and becoming. (1151)

Frank is torn between the composite history that he admits has made him who he is and his cautious regard for his future in the Existence Period. He is a late-twentieth-century American, while the rugged individualism of the transcendentalists is fashioned for so very few today. Frank takes wary little steps and wants to test life's waters for the full agenda of precipitating effects and ramifications for all his future actions. He believes bold, genuinely individualistic steps into the future are the subjects for teeth-gnashing Existence Period melodramas. This deliberation on past and future has made him Janus-faced. He is so confused over the matter that he claims: "You have, on the one hand, such an obsessively detailed and minute view of yourself from your prior existence, and on the other hand, an equally specific view of yourself *later on*, that it becomes almost impossible not to see yourself as a puny human oxymoron, and damn near impossible sometimes to recognize who your self is at all" (*Independence* 248).

Emerson's "Self-Reliance" is more outrageously bold experimentation with Existence Period consequences than a practical series of maxims to live by. Like most modern Americans, Frank is willing to hold on dearly to the here and now and take deliberate short, safe steps into the near future. "I'd rather not be delving into the past now," he thinks resignedly while speaking to his ex-wife in Deep River, "but into the future or at least the present, where I'm most at home" (*Independence* 252). Frank vacillates about his interests in dredging the past and determines that nostalgia just isn't what it used to be for him.

One of Emerson's pivotal points in "Self-Reliance" is the notion that people need to be philosophically organic and move from "being" into what he calls "becoming." This suggests that any single point in our lives is ephemeral because we are obliged to continue moving toward goals of individuality and actual self-reliance. Hence, being is part of the flux of life toward the preordained goal of becoming; while becoming only ends in became—death. Being is tantamount to becoming and the present progressive form of both verbs suggests that by being we are fundamentally becoming. Emerson claims we are always becoming; no "finally arrived" or "you've become" category is affixed to the equation. But while Frank knows "Self-Reliance" and can handily quote at will a pithy theorem for living, he twists the philosopher's "being-becoming" concept to his own solipsistic view of the world.

While he sits with his ex-wife on the great porch of Charley O'Dell's compound, Ann raises the subject of Frank's tipsy call to her from the Vince Lombardi turnpike stop. In the flush of great expectations for the father-son holiday, he regrets parting with Sally Caldwell in such an off-balanced way, and, perhaps under the influence of the wine consumed just hours before, Frank evidently offered his ex-wife his philosophy of life through Emerson. Instead of Emerson's being-becoming theorem, Frank formulated the life axiom of "being-seeming." "Ann has already explained to me how yesterday was much worse than I knew, worse than she explained last night when she said I thought 'be' and 'seem' were the same concept" (*Independence* 244). Ann takes umbrage with Frank's rampant philosophizing about their lost marriage and spotlights his inability to objectively examine events because he combines his memories with his

Isolation and Alienation in the Bascombe Novels

own rosy solipsistic views. "You started it!" she insists. "You started it last night, about being and seeming, as if you were the world's expert on being. You just wanted something else, that's all. Something beyond what there is" (*Independence* 254). At this point, Frank only wants to cut his losses with Ann and gather Paul from the intimidating lawns and Charley's great blue house for I-91 and the Basketball Hall of Fame. As a temporary peace offering, he acquiesces to Ann's criticisms and says, "I'm sorry I drove you crazy when we were married. If I'd known I was going to, I wouldn't ever have married you. You're probably right, I rely on how I make things seem. It's my problem" (*Independence* 255).

Frank's acknowledgment of his "be-seeming" theory is troublesome for two primary reasons. On the one hand, "be-seeming" is at direct odds with Emerson's "Self-Reliance," his current self-help reference guide. Frank Bascombe has ostensibly rejected Emerson's "being-becoming" axiom. The concept of "becoming," of organically moving to self-guided perfection, is superfluous or perhaps inappropriate for Frank's life view. This suggests the lack of any agenda of quintessential goals of self-reliance and personal independence, or that these goals articulated by Emerson are not germane to Frank's life.

Secondly, Frank's rather off-the-cuff and tipsy revelation that being is tantamount to seeming is the nexus of his philosophical solipsism. What is paramount to Frank is that "being" has no ability to be objective in and of itself. When his son is hit with a 75 mph fastball at the Dyno-Express in Cooperstown, the ramifications are clear and odious: "There is no *seeming* now. All is *is*" (*Independence* 369). While Emerson's being-becoming involves critical self-examination, Frank's be-seeming mandates anxious scrutiny, which only tends to regulate information signaled to others and the interpretation of the received signals. This formulates an ironic chasm from the mundane routines of everyday life; Frank Bascombe's philosophy is essentially predisposed to the presentation of the self as a commodity.

Frank Bascombe's "be-seeming" theory is quintessentially a role theory. It creates an ironic gap from the activities of routine life because of the theory's inchoate self-critical detachment. How one seems to others is the objective correlative. Social interaction degenerates into little more than role playing at times for Frank where an ironic distance is interposed, thus creating a gap of "seeming" between the person and event and the event itself. In this manner, Frank tends to make himself vulnerable to the social pressures surrounding so many events. Because of Frank's credos for the Existence Period, he refuses to take seriously some of the routines he is obliged to perform, and this protects him from personal injury. By attempting to demystify his daily life, he telegraphs to himself and others the general impression that he has risen beyond an event or task through his "knowingness" in "seeing," but he trudges through the tasks and performs the expected motions and does what is expected of him.

Instead of his old flash assessments of literalists and factualists, Frank has formulated a more complex, abiding, and less incendiary philosophy of life he calls the Existence Period. This is less a metaphysical understanding of the world than a daunted way of assessing and coping with life's teeth-gnashing contingencies, or as Frank claims offhandedly, it is a preventative strategy: "'You shouldn't get trapped by situations that don't make you happy'" (*Independence* 295).

Frank's stoic Existence Period philosophy gradually accrued after a series of personal disasters, particularly his son Ralph's death from Reye's disease, his divorce, the departure of his children to Deep River, and a series of stillborn relationships. The key to this thinking, as Frank conveys some of the dynamics of his theory, is not to throw himself wholeheartedly into any particular enterprise where the probabilities of unpleasant melodramas outweigh potential emotional gains. The philosophy entails a stoic aloofness because "it is one of the themes of the Existence Period that interest can mingle with uninterest in this way, intimacy with transience, caring with obdurate uncaring" (*Independence* 76). This sort of "adaptable strategy for meeting life's contingencies other than head-on" causes girlfriend Sally Caldwell to tell Frank that he is too noncommittal and "disengaged" for her liking (*Independence* 10). He guardedly looks after "Number One, which seemed a good aspiration as [he] entered a part of life when [he'd] decided to expect less, hope for modest improvements and be willing to split the difference" (*Independence* 112).

There are hardly any of Ariadne's threads in Carl Becker's *Declaration of Independence*, Emerson's "Self-Reliance," or even Tocqueville's assessment

Isolation and Alienation in the Bascombe Novels

of rugged frontier independence in the Existence Period logic. These texts that Frank totes around during his "split-the-breeze" tour are elusive for most contemporary Americans who live amid the atomizing individualism of modern life. For Frank and contemporary America and his "beseeming" logic, where self-esteem is validated by others, the country is peopled with very few Emersonian-styled rugged individualists who view the nation as a wilderness shaped to their own designs. Frank's Existence Period theory causes more problems than it attempts to alleviate. This is the sort of private worldview that contemporary cultural anthropologists criticize in a society of diminishing expectations and a preoccupation with the self. In an afterword written years after the initial publication of *The Culture of Narcissism: American Life in an Age of Diminishing Expectations*, Christopher Lasch added: "People responded to others as if their actions were being recorded and simultaneously transmitted to an unseen audience or stored up for close scrutiny at some later time. The prevailing social conditions thus brought out narcissistic personality traits that were present, in varying degrees, in everyone—a certain protective shallowness, a fear of binding commitments, a willingness to pull up roots whenever the need arose, a desire to keep one's options open, a dislike of depending on anyone, an incapacity for loyalty and gratitude" (239).

Alexis de Tocqueville's *Democracy in America* is no paean to the twin Jacksonian virtues of equalitarianism and majority rule. What perhaps strikes Frank's interest in the text is Tocqueville's rejection of any equation between equality, with its leveling doctrines that permeated most areas of national life in the 1830s, and freedom. Tocqueville questioned whether this new country's liberties, those older concerns for individual differences and freedom, could long flourish amid the new interests of equality and democracy. For as conditions became more equalitarian, Americans' personal liberties and freedom were sacrificed for a unique quality of sameness (Heffner 11). This penchant for belonging to a national majority caused Tocqueville to believe that "every citizen, being assimilated to all the rest, is *lost in the crowd*, and nothing stands conspicuous but the great and imposing image of the people at large" (qtd. in Heffner 11).

What rings again and again in Tocqueville's reporting is the issue that Americans have subordinated their interests in the various liberties and freedoms of the individual to an uncanny concern and fear of the majority, that vast and imposing reflection of the citizenry at large. It appeared to Tocqueville that instead of equality and democracy working in tandem with liberty and freedom, the majority hoisted the tyranny of equalitarianism over the heads of men. Americans seemed to take more pride in their sameness than in any sense of individuality or personal independence. According to Tocqueville's observations in 1832, America reflected virtually no independence of mind or any real personal freedom of discussion.

Frank questions whether his choices in life actually constitute his exercise of untrammeled personal freedom or whether he has independence in any real sense of the term. He realizes that freedom and independence are not nearly the same matters. On the one hand he knows he can shift for himself on a daily basis and travel in his car to virtually anywhere he wants. "An important truth about my day-to-day affairs is that I maintain a good share of flexibility, such that my personal time and whereabouts are often not of the essence" (*Independence* 176). Frank claims he could theoretically rob a convenience store in Trenton, then fly away to Caribou, Alberta, and walk naked into the muskeg and no one would really notice him at all for days. But he realizes that the choices and vagaries of personal freedom have little to do with true independence (particularly vis-à-vis Emerson). The latter entails living a personally tailored life according to one's precepts and philosophies while still being a part of society. The independent man is cognizant both of the concerns of the great crowd and of the primacy of exercising his individuality in the flux of society. Frank brings this to a peak in *Independence Day* when he claims:

So, if I didn't appear tomorrow to get my son, or if I showed up with Sally as a provocative late sign-up to my team, if I showed up with the fat lady from the circus or a box of spitting cobras, as little as possible would be made of it by all concerned, partly in order that everybody retain as much of their own personal freedom and flexibility as possible, and partly because I just wouldn't be noticed that much *per se*. (This reflects my own wishes, of course—the unhurried nature of my single life in the grip of the Existence Period—though it may also imply that laissez-faire is not precisely the same as independence.) (176-77)

Unlike the crowds on the New Jersey turnpike who viciously jockey for road positions and "relax" at the burger stands and ogle the slick-cheap

Isolation and Alienation in the Bascombe Novels

novelties, Frank is a cogent observer of human nature. He knows that un-trammeled freedom, or laissez-faire independence, has little in common with the self-reliant human being. But Frank has dug himself a philo-sophical niche somewhere within sight of both the American Adam, or "the first man," and the contemporary American, "the last man." The modern American over-the-counter interpretation of freedom is little more than simply the absence of restraint (Fukuyama 148). The "first man" concept of Locke and Hobbes was transformed by the American Founding Fathers and "domesticated" for the American landscape and sensibilities. According to this ethos, the American Adam subordinated his desire for public recognition and the drive for simple material com-fort, the "things of the world," and instead sought a common under-standing with other citizens that their rights should "stake out a sphere of individual choice where the power of the state is strictly limited" (Fukuyama 159). For the transcendalists, there was something particu-larly contemptible about an individual who could not raise his sights above and beyond his own narrow self-interests and physical needs. The American Adam transcended his physical needs and prurient concerns and recognized the noble passions of patriotism, generosity, courage, and public-spiritedness. American liberal democracy was "a moral agent whose specific dignity is related to his inner freedom from physical or natural determination" (Fukuyama 161). It is this moral dimension and the inner struggle to attain personal independence or self-reliance that was for the Founding Fathers the catalyst of democratic liberalism. Each citizen is free and cognizant of his own self-worth and recognizes his fel-low citizens for those same qualities.

While Frank aspires to the great psychic potentials of the American Adam, he lives in a culture that is largely dominated by "the last men." These new democratic men are prideful recognition seekers who fuel their own contrived notions of self through comfortable self-preserva-tion. Nietzsche claimed that the last man has lost track of any historical consciousness and is adrift in a culture of desire and reason. He is clever at discovering new methods to satisfy a host of petty wants through the calculation of long-term self-interest. The outside world is only important in the ways that it may impinge upon his day-to-day life. While content with his own immediate happiness or short-term psychic self-satisfaction, the last man is unable to feel any sense of shame in himself for being unable to rise above those wants (Fukuyama 301).

For the last men, history holds no specific gravity. For them, history only teaches that people pursued horizons beyond number in the past—civilizations, religions, ethical codes, and value systems—and that their horizons were the only ones possible. The last man knows that these horizons were the only horizons, not any metaphoric solid ground but a mirage that vanishes upon approach and gives way to another horizon beyond the last. Perhaps that is why the last men of contemporary America are the *last*: they have been jaded by their fleeting glances into the past and largely "disabused of the possibility of direct experience of values" (Fukuyama 306).

Frank Bascombe realizes that achieving personal independence and the ability to exercise self-reliance is a task that now involves great personal cost and consequences. In a nation like contemporary America, the duties and responsibilities of citizenship are minimal. But the relative "smallness" of the private person when compared to the largeness of the country makes such persons feel they are no longer their own master at all, but weak and powerless in the face of events beyond their control. While Nietzsche's greatest fear was that the American way of life would ultimately become victorious, Tocqueville was simply resigned to its inevitability and content that it would spread.

Frank Bascombe is fully aware that the 4th of July crowds are primarily concerned with their physical security and material plenty, precisely what the politicians he dislikes so much promise their electorates. But Frank also knows that Americans could be content in their material happiness and short-term psychic satisfaction but at the same time *dis*satisfied with themselves awash in the crowd. And so with his Existence Period philosophy and its stoic outlook, Frank scans the American horizon and quietly collects his past losses, saying to his audience, "Best just to swallow back your tear, get accustomed to the minor sentimentals and shove off to whatever's next, not whatever was" (*Independence* 152).

This interview was conducted on July 25, 1997, in the relaxed atmosphere of Ford's townhouse on Bourbon Street in New Orleans, a residence that in its rich and eclectic appointments reflects Ford's nomadic existence over the last two decades. Ford had recently returned from a three-month stay in Berlin, where *Independence Day* had been translated into German. *Women with Men* had been published earlier that summer, and so I decided to open the conversation with a series of questions about that book.

A Conversation with Richard Ford

Huey Guagliardo

HG: Let's begin by talking about your most recent work, *Women with Men*, a collection of novellas. I'm interested in why you chose this form, which a reviewer for *Time* referred to as "the orphan of contemporary fiction. Too lengthy for modern magazines and too short for penny-pinching publishers."

RF: I think probably that alone was an inspiration, to try to write in a form which seems to me highly serviceable, a form in which a lot of wonderful literature has been written, and yet that doesn't get a lot of use by American writers. Magazines do dictate much of what is written. I had just finished a long novel, and was not in the mood to go back to writing, serially, short stories. I wanted to write something the long story form perfectly suited, a substantial piece of work that is not a novel but is longer than a short story.

HG: The first two stories of the trilogy were published previously—*The Womanizer* in *Granta* and *Jealous* in *The New Yorker*—and yet the three pieces are woven together beautifully. All explore human loneliness and the complexity of human relationships. All involve marriages that have fallen or are falling apart. The most important link, however, seems to be the characters' inability to bridge the loneliness and connect with one another. One character declares in her suicide note that she will "die knowing nobody." I kept thinking of a famous line from *Cool Hand Luke*: "What we have here is a failure to communicate." In your mind, how do the novellas fit together?

RF: I think they fit together in the way you just described. They are also about varying degrees, varying sorts of human solipsism. The thing that defeats affection in each of these stories is one person's inability really to look outside him- or herself, so much so that the needs, the preferences, the well-being, the sanctity of others are, in effect, completely ignored or misunderstood, causing calamity. All three stories have at the end some calamitous event that is a somewhat hyperbolized version of modern life. In a cautionary value they would basically say what realistic fiction, if not always, at least often says: Pay closer attention to what you're doing or bad things will result. They also make the claim that this is a Western phenomenon, in the broadest sense of West: all of us Anglo-Saxons and Germans and French and so on suffer some sort of solipsism, a way in which we cut ourselves off from people. It is unmistakably, as a theme or set of concerns, a variant on some of the concerns of *Independence Day*.

HG: Do you see the middle story, *Jealous*, which takes place in Montana, as a kind of center panel that bridges together the two longer stories, both set in Paris?

RF: They're published in the order in which they were written. I always meant that there would be two Paris stories and then there was this Montana story which came in between. No, I wouldn't say that the middle story bridged it; that would probably be arguing for a more meticulous structure than I had. I was interested in the stories being, as I said, variants on some principal concerns of mine; and so it would probably be using retrospect too liberally to say that I see it as such. But on the other hand I do believe, as you suggest, that those stories are actually quite well

A Conversation with Ford

united, and how one relates to the other could be something that falls under the aegis of stories not being finished until they go outside the control of the writer.

HG: Were you alluding to Hemingway's story collection *Men Without Women?*

RF: In no way.

HG: You don't think then, that it's possible to view Larry, the young Montana boy in *Jealous,* as a sort of Nick Adams character?

RF: Not to me. Unless all teenage characters going through the first throes and pangs of facing adult life are examples of Nick Adams characters. I don't know how, for instance, Sherwood Anderson's "I Want to Know Why" or Isaac Babel's "The Story of My Dovecot" . . . I don't know how those would be Nick Adams stories. The truth is that I called the book *Women with Men,* and somebody said, "I guess you're bouncing a title off Hemingway's wall." I said, "Why?" And they said that Hemingway wrote a book titled—what is it?—*Men Without Women?* And I said, "Oh, gee, if I knew that I didn't remember it." And they said, "Well, okay, that's fine if you didn't know that, but now you know it; so do you want to run the risk of having people say that you're doing that?" And what I said was, "I don't give a shit. Let them do what they please. I'm not going to sacrifice a good title of my book because of something some guy did seventy or eighty years ago."

HG: I found it interesting that Charley Matthews, the protagonist in *Occidentals,* has written a novel called *The Predicament.* Is writing a process of discovery in that you typically place characters in certain *predicaments* to explore their reactions?

RF: Oh, of course. Absolutely. I think that's what I routinely do. That's why it's important for me to think about a book before I write it, to get in mind a whole series of possible cul-de-sacs or crises that I can anticipate coming to as I write along rather intuitively; because I think that the illumination of character is often accomplished by putting the characters into a situation whose outcome I don't know, and then literally writing out of that tight spot and seeing what happens, seeing what people say and do, how I the writer and you the reader might feel about them once you're on the other side of those predicaments. It's funny, but when I was writing *Occidentals* there was a time when I wanted to call it *The Predicament*. But I didn't want to sacrifice the title *Occidentals*, and it also drew too much ironic and almost tongue-in-cheek attention to that rather subordinated part of Charley's life, his life as a novelist; it kind of made fun of the story all the way to the end by ironizing it, and I didn't want to do that. I wanted it to come out a serious story. I was somewhat shocked when I got to the end at what a dark story it turns out to be. It starts off, as you might agree, in a comic mode and works its way into that darkness, from which it never completely extricates itself.

HG: You have written successfully in all three fictional forms: novel, short story, and novella. Walker Percy said that he chose the novel because he found the short form too limiting. What do you find most appealing about working in the shorter forms?

RF: It gets over in a hurry. Its effects are no more concentrated. I like reading short stories, and I like the thought that I could write one that would make somebody feel the same way that I did when I read all of the thousands of short stories that I have read and loved. But the truth is, I think, I write short stories because they are gratifyingly brief and return a satisfying sense of accomplishment to a rather limited amount of effort.

HG: And the novel? Would you share Percy's view of the novel as being more open to all sorts of possibilities?

RF: Sure, but there is an impulse among many writers to justify what they do. Not that Walker particularly felt this need; I think he felt eminently justified in everything he did in a literary sense, and the books will bear it out. But there is a way in which people say, "Oh, I don't write poems; I would never write poems." Or, "I only write novels. The short story is a lesser form." I just don't like to participate in those kinds of exclusionary logics. The truth of the matter is that I feel that writing essays, memoirs, six-hundred-word "Talk of the Town" pieces for *The New Yorker*, thousand-word op-ed pieces for the *New York Times*, short stories, novels, novellas

A Conversation with Ford

are all the same to me. They are what I do. I'm a writer; that's all I am. So I write, sometimes at this length, sometimes at that. To hang any more notable logic on it wouldn't be faithful to how I feel.

HG: I'd like to know how you regard your role as a writer of fiction and how the reader fits into your conception of that role.

RF: I think to be a novelist, to be a short-story writer—whatever I am—is a high calling, because it's a relationship you establish, through your very best efforts, with a reading public whose welfare you're seeking somehow to ameliorate. I'm sure I came to that role, in part, by thinking about Walker when I first encountered him, back in the seventies, and also from Chekhov. Walker, in a book like *Love in the Ruins*, is particularly interested in having a doctor ministering to a public of some kind. Not that I see that as my role. I don't think that I have that sort of literary/medical value, certainly, but I do think I offer my best efforts, my fondest consolations, and my most important thinking to my readership. And, too, I wouldn't even be a writer had I not been able to imagine finding a readership. Even at the beginning when I gave it precious little thought because it seemed so remote, it was always my intention to write for somebody else to read. Sometimes you hear writers say, "Well, I only do it for myself, or I do it for a very limited audience," or reasons that are basically, it seems to me, exclusive of a wider readership. For me it was always sort of second nature to think that I'd like to have as wide a readership as I could. I don't believe I fully recognized that aspiration until I'd written *The Sportswriter* and was beginning to feel that there were a few people out there whom I didn't personally know who had read books of mine.

HG: *The Sportswriter* has frequently been compared to Percy's *The Moviegoer*. There are some obvious, perhaps superficial, similarities between the two works. Frank Bascombe's narrative voice in *The Sportswriter* reminds many readers of Binx Bolling's voice in *The Moviegoer*. Each character is about to have a birthday . . .

RF: I never thought of that.

HG: Really? In addition, sports seem to function for Frank in the way that movies work for Binx, as a way of avoiding alienation and despair. Twenty years ago you wrote a piece for *The National Review* in which you expressed your admiration for Percy's writing, especially, as you just put it, its "literary/medical value." You also said that you would "rather read a sentence written by Walker Percy than a sentence written by anybody else." Because there are many subtle similarities between the two novels, I can't help but wonder if you were consciously influenced by *The Moviegoer* in writing *The Sportswriter.*

RF: Sure, sure. I hadn't read it in ten years when I started writing *The Sportswriter.* But I would also just say—having said yes, of course, I was quite consciously influenced—there were other books which influenced me as much which are less obvious: *The End of the Road*, by John Barth; *Something Happened*, by Joseph Heller; *A Fan's Notes*, by Frederick Exley. All of them first-person narratives.Wonderful books. They all were as persuasively influencing upon *The Sportswriter* as was *The Moviegoer.*

HG: I would like to explore a few other ways in which your work might be similar to and different from Walker Percy's. Percy's characters often find God by finding one another. This is especially true in *The Moviegoer* and *The Second Coming* where human love becomes a symbol of man's capacity for redemption and reconciliation with a Christian God who both transcends the immanent world and is infused within it. Love, in other words, bridges the gap between immanence and transcendence. In an earlier interview, you talked about your characters being redeemed by affection. Of course, Percy, a Catholic writer, used the word *redemption* in its traditional Christian sense, whereas you seem to have something else in mind. Yet your characters seem to be searching for that same sort of intersubjective relationship, what Frank Bascombe calls "the *silent intimacies* . . . of the fervently understood and sympathized with." In what sense are your characters *redeemed* by love?

RF: This is interesting, I suppose, vis-à-vis Walker, who—I guess he did, he certainly seemed to—believed in an afterlife. It's problematical to me how life on earth, affectionate life on earth, love, can somehow equal the love that God has for us. Maybe it's just in an emblematic way. For me—

and I mean for me insofar as I write characters—facing apocalypse, facing the end of life for which there is no redemption about which I feel confident, what we are charged to do as human beings is to make our lives and the lives of others as liveable, as important, as charged as we possibly can. And so what I'd call *secular redemption* aims to make us, through the agency of affection, intimacy, closeness, complicity, feel like our time spent on earth is not wasted.

HG: Percy also believed in the affirmative power of language and in the "aesthetic reversal of alienation" through literature, arising through the reader's alliance with both the alienated character and the author. You have written about the "efficacy of telling" and about the fact that "precious language" has the potential to provide consolation to someone in despair. Am I correct in assuming that you would agree with Percy's view and with Frank Bascombe's assertion that "words can make most things better"?

RF: I sometimes get painted with a very dark brush for that line, because some people read it to mean a fundamental cynicism about me: that is, you can say anything and make it be true. I suppose the way we cast our dilemmas and affections into language has a lot to do with how we conceive of them, so there is—I don't think of it as cynicism—but there is a way that language colors experience; there's no doubt about that. But I think language is consoling in other ways, is always able to give us pleasure by its sonorities, its poetical qualities, by simply the way it pleasures our ears, and so far as it comes from another, sweetens our view of that other, sweetens our view of the world, a world that can give us literature, that can give us the telling of stories. I think the telling of stories is in and of itself a way of persuading the reader away from whatever is plaguing her or him, and of asking the reader to believe that another and more felicitous order can be put on experience, and that this order has a structure that is, in an almost abstract way, pleasurable, and beautiful to behold. So I don't know how that lines up with what Walker said about those things, but my view, I think, is a great deal more feet-on-the-earth rather than looking on above the horizon line.

HG: Although he believed in the power of language to bring human beings together, Walker Percy often wrote about the exhaustion or devaluation of language in the modern world.

RF: He made a lot of fun of it.

HG: He certainly did. There seems to be evidence in your work that you share Percy's concern about the devaluation of language. I've mentioned what strikes me as an important theme in *Women with Men*, that is, the failure of the characters to connect, the failure of language. The last story, *Occidentals*, especially seems to emphasize the failure of language. There is all of the business about the French translation of Charley's novel. His publisher tells him that "People spend too much time misunderstanding one another." Certainly this is true of Charley and Helen who could use a translator to help them to communicate with one another. Language is a barrier even for two people who speak the same language. When Charley says "I love you," Helen tells him to "Think of some better words." When he can't think of anything better to say, she says they should "Leave words out of it." Would you comment on this notion of the devaluation of language? Is "meaningful language . . . exhausted by routine," as Charley describes his failed marriage to Penny, and as Percy contends?

RF: You sum it up about as well as I could. I don't know that I could improve on that very much.

HG: Well, Percy wrote that "the trick of the novelist, as the Psalmist said, is to sing a new song, use new words." In your *National Review* piece you credit him with doing just that, saying that he does "what great literature would always do if it could: reinvent language moment to moment." In what ways have you tried to reinvent language in your work?

RF: By trying to write sentences the reader does not see through like a clear pane of glass. By trying to imagine language as being a window whose pane and whose surfaces you luxuriate in and, in the process, see beyond. That came to me from all of my reading, much more than from Walker; by the time I wrote that piece on Walker, you know, I'd been to graduate school, been a college professor, done a lot of things. I'd read all of those wonderful people that we now think of as postmodernists in the late sixties and early seventies. I had read a story like Donald Barthelme's "The Indian Uprising," in which a character (referred to only as Miss R) says there is enough satisfaction in "the hard, brown, nut-like word" for "anyone but a damned fool." One idea I came to as a young man was that written language was just a mode of communication to be read in a denotative way. What I came to understand as a more sophisticated reader is that language is a source of pleasure in and of itself—all of its corporeal qualities, its syncopations, moods, sounds, the way things look on the page. So that's what I bring to language that vivifies it, other than simply the use of words out of their usual context in the e. e. cummings sense; but I do it in a novelist's mode, not in the poet's mode, so that my responsibility is, finally, to make a cohesive, linear whole out of something, unlike, say, cummings or Wallace Stevens.

HG: Is your work informed by what Helen Carmichael in *Occidentals* defines as "spirituality"; that is, "a conviction about something good that you can't see"? If so, what would that something good be?

RF: Survival. That you can believe in the efficacy of things you can't predict or see the evidence of, in the faith that if you invent them they will cause you to survive, literally survive. And maybe more: survive with dignity, survive with pleasure, survive with a sense of life's being worthwhile. The scene you mentioned in *Occidentals* when Charley wants to say *love* . . . In *Jealous* there is a very similar scene when Doris sits at the bar talking to Larry and to Barney Bordeaux. She asks Larry about the great themes. She asks, What do you believe in? And she says, you can't say love; you can't say sex. But I believe—meaning me the author here—I believe in the efficacy of love. Those two—at least Charley in *Occidentals*—I set apart from that. I think he is in some ways, because of solipsism, not to be accessed by belief in love. But I believe in that; I believe in the things that draw you sympathetically closer to others, and that the promise of that closeness is a valuable commodity. And other things too—art. For a guy who thinks of himself as almost totally an Aristotelian, I am kind of a Platonist about those things.

HG: *The Sportswriter, Wildlife,* and *Independence Day* are first- person narratives. *A Piece of My Heart* and *The Ultimate Good Luck* are in the limited-omniscient mode. What factors determine your choice of voice? Is it easier for you, as it may be for readers, to identify with Frank Bascombe and with Joe Brinson, the young narrator in *Wildlife?*

RF: I never identify with Frank; I never identify with Joe. I always maintain a rather scrupulous artisan's role toward my narrators. They are always the illusions of characters made up of language, illusions that I myself manufacture, and they are never me, nor do I ever confuse them with being me; thus, while the relationship that the reader shares with the character through the agency of a first-person narrator might seem to be somewhat more streamlined, there is for me, once I establish my hold on that form of narration, no difference between a first-person and a third-person narrative in the actual execution of those novels. Practically speaking, it's all the same when you're writing it; it's just the illusion of address that is different. Finally, once you allow yourself as a writer and can concede on the reader's behalf that the address is working, it doesn't matter which it is. Choosing one over the other is almost a matter of instinctual first principle; which is to say, how I first lay hold of the material. One of the first kinds of decision-making that goes on in my head or in my voice as I'm speaking those lines—and I do always speak lines to myself—however that seems most native to those lines is how I narrate the book. I loved the opening line of *Occidentals* [Ford got up to retrieve a copy of *Women with Men* from a desk on the other side of the room]. There is something about the opening line of *Occidentals* which I had in my head long before I ever really wrote the second line: [reading from story] "Charley Matthews and Helen Carmichael had come to Paris the week before Christmas." Well, that's a line which dictates the point of view, if it is, in effect, going to be about Charley and Helen, which it is. So, it was just a sort of instinctual principle, which became the book's first principle.

HG: Critics often focus on the question of Frank Bascombe's reliability as a narrator in both *The Sportswriter* and *Independence Day.* Do you regard Frank as reliable?

RF: I regard all narrators as works of art. Reliability is for the reader to decide. I mean, I regard him as the thing that all narrators, indeed, all fictional characters, are: they're provocateurs. They say things, and do things, and you as a reader in the sanctity and serenity of your chair can entertain what they say and be moved by or disapprove of or agree with what they say, so that their reliability is actually, really, not much of an ongoing concern because they're not real. They're made up. It matters to me and you, as human beings, whether or not each of us is reliable, but narrators don't have to be. Or maybe another way of saying it is sometimes they are and sometimes they aren't. They don't need to be, or maybe they can't be. There is a great line of Richard Avedon's: "Portraiture never tells the truth." *Characters* don't tell the truth. They hypothesize; they speculate. That's their relationship to their maker, the author; they're speculators about things. They may say things that are useful, and very right, very moving, but their obligation isn't to tell the truth. The *book* may tell a truth by comprising all these other gestures.

HG: You've given your wife, Kristina, a great deal of credit for the creation of Frank Bascombe. She encouraged you to write a novel about a character who is essentially optimistic about life and its possibilities. You've said that you don't identify with Frank, but do you at least share his optimism?

RF: I probably do, because if I don't share it explicitly, I share it implicitly. There's that great line in Sartre which I am always quoting to people which says that "For a writer to write about the darkest possible things is itself an act of optimism, because it proves that those things, whatever they are, can be thought about." To me, no matter how dark the things you're writing about—if you're *Céline*, irrespective—being a writer means making something with language that you give to a readership, which it will entertain into the future; so it is, in a kind of chronological way, optimistic enough to believe that there will be a future in which these books will be read.

HG: Will there be another Frank Bascombe novel in that future, or have we seen the last of Frank? Is there a chance that you will do with Frank what John Updike did with Rabbit Angstrom?

RF: I would write another book about Frank if I could, but it would have to be a book that is at this moment unforeseeable. Which isn't to say that I won't finally foresee it—at the end of *The Sportswriter* I don't think there was any way I could have forecast that I'd write a book in which Frank was a real estate agent. I don't think now that I could forecast what kind of book I would write about Frank, but it would be something more than just what happens next after *Independence Day*. I think a third book about Frank would have to be unique and stand alone and be nonreliant on the other book for its first principle in holding the reader's attention and affection. For me, probably the most difficult part of writing *Independence Day* was not the part to make it a good book, if I can anatomize it in this way; but the most difficult and tiresome and tedious parts were making this book seem like the sequel I wanted it be. I thought to myself that if I could write this novel and have it be just as good about another character, that's what I was after.

HG: Speaking of Updike, I think of you and Updike as the best observers of life in America writing today . . .

RF: That's a nice compliment, but Joan Didion is awfully good, too.

HG: Indeed, she is. Your novels *The Sportswriter* and *Independence Day* depict life in the middle-class suburbs of America, where you yourself once lived. For the most part Frank delights in his suburban existence, but at the same time there is the ominous sense that all is not as ordered as it appears. Frank says in *Independence Day* that "there is a new sense of the wild world being just beyond our perimeter, an untallied apprehension among our residents, one I believe they'll never get used to, one they'll die before accommodating." What are your greatest concerns for America as we stand on the threshold of a new century?

RF: That it will become ungovernable. That our sense of a whole will deteriorate. And I'm not talking about ourselves as simply a nation-state, but that because of our geographic size, because of the inevitability of greater and greater degrees of multiculturalism, because of immigration, because of economic disparity, because of racial strife, racial inequality, the country will basically balkanize along lines which are not now com-

A Conversation with Ford

pletely visible, but other than in terms of the states. Whether we know it or not, there is a great deal of strife going on in the country between those forces which are basically what you might call the old states' rights forces (those conservatives who want, in fact, some in good ways, to conserve a sense of America as a historically comprised nation) and those people—and there are a lot of people—for whom that notion of states' rights, federalism, simply has no meaning, and, moreover, who are not served by that particular way of imagining America. There is a lot of strife between those people. The people on the other side are often immigrants who have not been served well by this society's economy, who are on the low end of the socioeconomic scale. Those forces pull hard in a destructive way. If I had to say what one thing was it's that; that we will lose some sense—not that we will lose some sense of the past—lose some sense that it is worthwhile to keep this country whole along some lines yet to be imagined, because federalism, and states' rights, and conservatism, those movements have interesting things to say for themselves, but one of the things that they don't do is that they don't adapt very well, by definition, to new forces, to new demands, to immigration, to multiculturalism, to the rise of the lower classes that have been isolated by race. That makes me afraid that, basically, we will lack the imagination to go on reinventing America in a wholesome way.

HG: You and Kristina moved to New Orleans about seven years ago after living in at least a dozen states over the years. As a native New Orleanean, I have often puzzled over the passage in *The Sportswriter* where Frank says that "a town like New Orleans defeats itself. It longs for a mystery it doesn't have and never will, if it ever did." What exactly does he mean? Do you share that view?

RF: That's an answering knell to one of Walker's characters in *The Last Gentleman*, who says the place where I was living when I read those books—Ann Arbor—was a *nonplace*. That was me, basically, lobbing a salvo back over Walker's wall. But, yeah, I think that even more profoundly today. I mean that New Orleans steeps itself in its history and obfuscates all of its fundamental urbanness and modern problems by turning its head, by letting there be so many variant views of the city. I actually wrote an essay about this very thing for Canadian Broadcasting over the winter. I mean, New Orleans deludes itself more than any city I've ever lived in, and I've lived in most of the major cities in the U.S. It deludes itself that it's "the city that care forgot," it deludes itself into believing that it's "the Big Easy," it deludes itself into sort of somehow living up to all of its sobriquets. The fact is it's a great big urban complex with a theme park in the middle, and everything else about New Orleans is just like every other city in America. Yeah, but I think, currently, the city is as little deluded as it has ever been, with the casino falling flat, with the murder rate up, and with a pretty good, aggressive mayor running things. I think it's probably about as close to facing facts as I've known it to be certainly in the time I've been here. There isn't in New Orleans a past—in a municipal sense—there isn't a past to look back on in which there was a great period of realism, where people saw what they had here and mounted a campaign based on that. Most of the campaigns that have been mounted in the past have been of the pie-in-the-sky variety. Building the casino was like building the Superdome. The city has had a hard time over the years facing facts.

HG: In *Occidentals*, New Orleans is Helen Carmichael's "favorite American city." Is it yours?

RF: [Laughing] I did that as a nicety to my wife. No, its not my favorite American city, not by a long shot. Chicago is. Probably New Orleans would be second. And maybe if I didn't live here, it would be first.

HG: You gave up writing fiction for a time. As you look back at that period now, would you say that you stopped as a result of frustration brought about by the fact that your first two novels, *A Piece of My Heart* and *The Ultimate Good Luck*, were not commercially successful?

RF: Yeah, using as indices of commercial success whether or not they sold a lot of copies, whether or not they got sold into paperback (and thus kept in print). It was probably generally true that I gave up writing in 1981 because it was a year of extreme personal heartache and stress in my life. My mother was dying, and Kristina and I were somewhat unsettled— not in our married life, but in our geographical life. I was not liking living

A Conversation with Ford

in the suburbs of New Jersey. There was a lot of upheaval in my life, and one of the things that I thought was, "Well, you've published two books, you've had a good shot at this whole enterprise, and you haven't made much of a go of it, so get on with finding something that you can make a go of." And maybe, in a way, I might have begun to see the anxieties, and the contingencies, and the uncertainties of trying to make a writer out of myself as slightly absurd at that moment because so much else in my life was not settled, and so much else in my life was sorrow.

HG: In 1996, *Independence Day* became the first novel ever to win both the Pulitzer Prize and the PEN/Faulkner Award. What has this recognition meant to your life and career?

RF: I'm sure it's changed some things. I have more readers. Probably, the most significant thing that's changed is that—just on the strength of that book's having a good publishing life and then later on winning the Pulitzer Prize—it caused a lot of people to read that book that hadn't read books of mine before. I'm not—and you can get other people to disagree with this—but I don't think of myself as a very competitive person, and I'm not goal-driven in the sense of looking covetously at prizes and things like that. But, at the same time, when those things, just by happenstance, come to you, there are certain little anxieties in your life—there have been in my life—that I wouldn't have even ever admitted that I felt, and didn't think I did feel, that have to do simply with the recognition of myself as a guy who is trying and to some extent succeeding in making at that point a contribution to the world. Some of those anxieties were not resolved but were simply *demarked* from how they had been before. It was as though the world said to me, "Okay, okay, okay, we admit it; you're a writer." But those moments in your life come, and then you just relinquish them; and other people get those kinds of accolades. I went over to the doctor's today and I was looking at a copy of *Newsweek*, and here's this wonderful book, *Cold Mountain*, by Charles Frazier. And here is somebody else coming along for whom it is said, "If there ever was a great American novel, a novel which could be a masterpiece, this is certainly it." So however I felt a year ago when I got that prize, I felt it at that moment; and then I went back to feeling the way I always feel. And I wrote another book, and I'm well on the way to writing another book, so life had a nice high moment, and then it just resolved itself back to my usual practices and habits.

HG: As an English professor, I wonder about your attitude toward teaching and your feelings about the academic environment. Your characters Frank Bascombe and Charley Matthews express their disillusionment with teaching and with academia. You taught writing earlier in your career but quit, I believe, to devote more time to your own writing and because, as you once said, quoting Eudora Welty, you "lacked the instructing turn of mind." Yet you recently returned to the classroom to teach a creative writing course at Northwestern University. What made you decide to teach again? And what are your feelings about teaching and the academy?

RF: To answer a question that you didn't explicitly ask, on the way to answering one that you did, my experience in universities, as an observer of other people, has been that it's life like everywhere else. It's life like at IBM, it's life like at National Cash Register; it's full of the petty grievances, the backbiting and low-horizon anxieties and agonies of every other life; whereas it poses as something of a higher order, so that the discrepancy between how things are and how things purport to be is always quite vivid to me. Which totally excludes, quite frankly speaking, my own experience, which has been—from the times I've taught in my life—actually quite rewarding and sometimes even—exultant. But I'm not typical because I don't come and stay, and I'm sympathetic to those people who do. I think it's harder for them to keep their sense of mission, their sense of dignity, and their sense of importance alive under the onslaught of years, under the onslaught of students, under the pressures of colleagues who are somehow just putting in their time. I went back to teach at Northwestern at the end of a long project—*Independence Day*—and with that comes the belief that maybe I know something new, that maybe I have a renewed vigor for the vocation of writing that I might have exhausted earlier. I always try to go back into the classroom at times when I feel like I'm most enthusiastic to try to talk to young students on the strength of my own experience as a writer. I couldn't do it year after year after year, because I'm relying so much on the wind filling my own sails from my own work, whereas a person who is a true, trained literary scholar has that great canon of literature always to fill his sails.

HG: I recall a letter that Flannery O'Connor wrote in response to a professor's outlandish interpretation of "A Good Man Is Hard to Find." She said, "Too much interpretation is certainly worse than too little, and where feeling for a story is absent, theory will not supply it." Do academics, especially the "anti-mystery types" that Frank Bascombe encountered in his brief stint at the academy, have a tendency to drain the life out of literature?

RF: I don't know. I don't read the things that are written about my books. I just can't. I've tried to, every once in a while, but I just haven't been able to sustain any but a kind of vain and sometimes antagonistic interest. But the only way I came to read literature with any wider sensation at all— other than just the really palpable sensation of the language—was by reading R. P. Blackmur, by reading Harry Levin, by reading *The Nature of Narrative* [by Robert Scholes and Robert Kellogg], by reading all kinds of critics. So I have never found that, as a rule, the true literary criticism, which is broad-based and humanistic in character, eviscerates or denatures literature at all. It's only small minds that denature and eviscerate literature. Everything else, I think, is perfectly fine. A notion embodied in Blackmur's essay "A Critic's Job of Work," in which he talks about what criticism is for and how its varieties can be applied to the text, what value it can hold for the reader, I think, is a substantiable and corroboratable position to hold. I read great critics when I was young, and I've never been sorry. I read William Gass, Frank Kermode . . .

HG: Cleanth Brooks?

RF: Yes, my God, you can't generalize about the pusillanimous quality of criticism with people like—giants like that.

HG: What about your work habits? I think it was O'Connor who said that she wrote for three hours every morning and spent the rest of the day getting over it. Do you try to write every day?

RF: I've been a writer now—it will be thirty years next year—and during that thirty years I routinely go through periods when I don't work. But when I am working on something, which is to say, when I have a task for myself—I'm writing a story, I'm writing a novella, I'm writing an essay, I'm writing a novel—I work at it every day. And if something comes up, like having to go to the doctor or having to attend to some emergency, I feel grudging when I don't work. So I generally—particularly more effectively in the last ten years—have streamlined my life so that when I'm working on something, nothing gets in my way; and I work on what I work on seven days a week, holidays, Thanksgiving, New Year's, same thing, until it's done.

HG: How many hours a day do you put into your writing?

RF: Never fewer than four, usually five or six.

HG: Do you use a word processor?

RF: I do in the stage of writing a story in which I want to get it into type, but I write with a pen. I used to write with a pencil, but finally—much as I like sharpening pencils and niggling around with them—I found that a Bic pen works best; a regular old twenty-nine-cent Bic pen is great.

HG: I believe that you sold the film rights to *A Piece of My Heart*. How did that turn out? Was the film ever produced? Have you sold film rights to other works?

RF: I did do that. I sold the option, anyway, to Paramount, and I went out to Paramount in 1975 and wrote a screenplay for a really wonderful man named Richard Sylbert. My screenplay wasn't any good, and before we could really get worked around to do a revision of it, Sylbert was discharged as the vice-president of production. Dick Sylbert is a three-time Academy Award-winning production designer, and he was the first person in Hollywood history to be brought from what is called below the line, which is to say, from a nondirectorial artistic position to become a studio head. And he lasted a year and a half. He's a great guy—he's a friend of mine to this day—and a supremely talented man, but he was let go before that project could ever come around again to have a serious rewrite. So

A Conversation with Ford

then it languished, and over the years for practically every book I've written there have been options. Only one thing has been made, a movie called *Bright Angel* with Sam Shepard and Dermot Mulroney, which I wrote myself in 1989, and which was not very good either. And now next year, next fall, somebody is going to make a movie out of *The Ultimate Good Luck.*

HG: Has production started yet?

RF: No, but they're in preproduction now. They start filming in November in Mexico.

HG: That's a very cinematic novel.

RF: Yes, it is.

HG: Do you think it's your most cinematic work?

RF: I have to think about that. There are plenty of those stories in *Rock Springs* that are fairly cinematic to me. Probably it [*The Ultimate Good Luck*] is as cinematic as anything I ever wrote, but I don't think much about that as a measurement for a book.

HG: You recently returned from Berlin where *Independence Day* was translated into German. I understand that your popularity in Europe is growing.

RF: I've really had good publishers in Europe; and they have just, in a kind of assiduous, long-term way, been steady in trying to get my books published. And when I go over there—as I do a lot because I like to go—they do as much, seemingly, as they possibly can—and more than I've seen done for almost anybody else—to get my books in front of the public. That translation of *Independence Day* has sold more than fifty thousand copies in hardback, which was quite a lot. But I think one of the things that has made it possible for me to publish books well in Europe is that I didn't go to Europe until I was forty-two, and when I went I still had the kind of wide-eyed awe and enthusiasm of a young man. And so I have been willing to continue going back, and going back, and going back, and I don't know that every American would be as lucky as I have been or would take to it as much as I have. But I have been so romantically enthusiastic about going to Europe that I think the Europeans—the people

I've met, the journalists, the booksellers—they sense how glad I am to get to do this, what a privilege it is, and how lucky I feel like I am to get to do it. And, in a way, they cotton to it, which isn't to say that I have always gone out and sold my books, but I do think that my own enthusiasm for it is winning. Generally, though, Americans of our generation who do go to Europe go with our hat in our hand. The generation before ours was the generation that fought World War II, and they went to Europe with a sense of their own inherited or earned worth which our generation, who watched America plunder through Vietnam and finally retreat, never felt. We always felt like we were guests of another country because we had been such poor guests of so many countries. So, I think, most Americans when they go to Europe now are extremely sensitive to the culture that they are visiting and extremely decorous and try to both represent our country well and to offend the host country as little as possible. It doesn't make us any smarter; we're just quite well-behaved.

HG: You mentioned a new project. Have you started a new novel?

RF: No, I probably won't even think about that until the winter. I don't know what it will be. I've got a few stories that have been lingering around in my mind and proving their worth to me. I finished one this week, and I've got another one that I'd like to write when I go back out west in August. I think maybe with some perseverance, in a couple of years or maybe in another year, I might be able to write what I think of as a suite of stories, ten stories. I'll probably by the end of the summer have three, maybe one more in the fall. I'd like to have five stories finished by January; that would be half of the book. But that's all I'm working on. I've got a couple of essays to write. That's about all. I'm supposed to write a book. I have a long-term contract with Knopf, and it does have a schedule which commits me to writing a novel; but nobody really cares if I do or I don't as long as I keep on working. And I don't care either. Novels are easier to sell to readers than short stories, but I feel like if I can write something well, whatever it is, I ought to do that.

HG: Richard, thank you for talking to me.

RF: My pleasure. Thank you for taking such care with this.

A Conversation with Ford

Holditch

[1] Kristina Ford, conversations with the author over the past decade.

[2] Richard Ford, conversations with the author over the past decade.

Dupuy

[1] Alice Hoffman, in her review of *The Sportswriter,* was one critic who found Ford's tone ironic. She writes: "Bascombe's estrangement is charted with unsettling irony" (14). Hoffman, Weber notes, is in the minority. Robert Towers called Ford's tone "gentle and meditative" (38), and Rhoda Koenig says the book "has none of the pomposity or self-pity that usually inhabits such stories" (86).

[2] Rhoda Koenig characterized Ford's style as "lambent . . . as clear and cold as early-morning light over the water" (86).

[3] In an interview with Kay Bonetti, when asked about the fact that *The Sportswriter* has an ex-fiction writer telling us his story, Ford responded, "Odd isn't it, how literature has that double reflex? I would have to be a fool not to be aware of it, but you start looking in those double reflecting mirrors and you can look forever" (87). Following Ford's warning, I choose not to explore the double reflex. In that same interview, Ford says writing is telling (88).

[4] In the interview with Bonetti, Ford maintains that in saying literature is consoling, he does not "mean to say that literature is therapeutic. It *can* be consoling. It *can* say the thing not before said. But that's about all I really mean" (80).

[5] Towers, among others, has called Frank a survivor.

[6] See Bonetti, 84.

[7] I borrow this term from Fred Hobson's *Tell About the South: The Southern Rage to Explain.* Hobson uses Quentin Compson as the prototype of the southerner who possesses the "rage to explain." Hobson also points to a correlation between the rage to explain and suicide (8).

[8] Frank's views of relationships and life seem to derive, again, in part, from Ford's own. In a piece he wrote for

Harper's ("My Mother, in Memory") Ford tells us that after his father's death, his mother was "always . . . resigned somewhere down deep. I could never plumb her without coming to that stop point—a point where expectation simply ceased. This is not to say she was unhappy after enough time had passed. Or that she never laughed. Or that she didn't see life as life, didn't regain and rejoin herself. All those she did. Only, not utterly, not in a way a mother, any mother, could disguise to her only son who loved her. I always saw that. Always felt it. Always felt her—what?—discomfort at life? Her resisting it? Always wished she could *relent* more than she apparently could . . ." (53) (my emphasis).

[9] In the interview with Bonetti, Ford says this about Frank's decision to quit "real" writing: "To a literary audience, I think, for a writer to stop being a writer seems a kind of world-class defeat, and for him to say, 'Well, it's no big deal' is kind of ironic. Except that just isn't the way I mean it to be. I mean it to be all right. I mean it to be fine. Because he goes ahead and lives the happiest life he can live, full of mirth and tragedy and affection" (84).

Hobson

[1] One might contend, of course, that the items in mail-order catalogs are *not* the things themselves, but rather representations, abstractions. As concerns Frank's viewing of Johnny Carson—which he shares with Bobbie Ann Mason's Sam Hughes in *In Country*, among others—it is perhaps worthy of mention that in southern fiction of the 1980s Johnny Carson and Ed McMahon seem to be heeded, pondered, and quoted far more than Robert E. Lee and William Faulkner.

[2] One should probably draw the line, however, at claiming kin for Eugene Gant's Uncle Bascom Pentland in Thomas Wolfe's *Of Time and the River*—another questing expatriate southerner in the Northeast.

[3] In most of his work Ford demonstrates a sensitivity to place, even in a work so apparently rootless as *Rock Springs*, the first two stories of which, "Rock Springs" and "Great Falls," are not only connected to but named for place. In another story in that collection, "The Children," the narrator, looking back at his teens in northern Montana, considers that it was "the place itself, as much as the time in our lives or our characters, that took part in the small things that happened and made them memorable" (69-70).

Ford is hardly the only expatriate southern writer who cannot escape a fascination with place. It is hard to find a contemporary novel more concerned with place, for example (as well as family, time, and community), than Gail Godwin's *The Finishing School*, which is set in upstate New York.

[4] The town of Haddam, Ford writes, is a place "where it is not at all hard for a literalist to contemplate the world" (48). Whether the founder of Haddam was, in fact, named *Wallace* Haddam, as Frank tells us he was, I have not been able to ascertain, but Ford's brief description of the town includes references to Wallace

Haddam, Wallace Hill, and insurance brokers. Perhaps one can avoid thinking of Wallace Stevens, but given Ford's sly and allusive manner it is not easy.

5 Ford also shares with Percy a penchant for striking similes. His "dumb as a cashew," "dreamy as Tarzan," "dangerous as a snake," "distracted as a camel," "apprehensive as a pilgrim," and so on surpass—to choose just a couple of many in Percy's *The Last Gentleman*—"sweating like a field horse" or "life [which] seems as elegant as algebra."

Walker

1 Sartre's narrator, however, speaks only from the present moment, whereas Ford's narrators speak retrospectively about their lives.

2 A native of Mississippi, Ford and his southern background tempt readers and critics to find in his work characteristics that would ally him with a southern tradition in literature.

3 Walker Percy also read Marcel, Kierkegaard, Husserl, Heidegger, and Sartre, in addition to many linguistic and semiotic theorists. Perhaps one key difference between Percy and Ford is that Percy's philosophical apparatus is apt to be more apparent in his fiction. Ford's short fiction, particularly, is sparer in style, more likely to be favored to Ernest Hemingway's or Raymond Carver's work than to Percy's, though, again, in the longer novels, Frank Bascombe has reminded more than one reader of Will Barrett. (And fans of John Updike cite echoes of Harry Angstrom.) More to the point, often imbedded in so-called "minimalist" fiction are complex notions, and Ford is fond of quoting Sartre, Emerson, and Wallace Stevens in conversation.

4 Critics often comment that Ford's musing, "bigger" books, such as *The Sportswriter* and *Independence Day*, depart from his earlier more spare style. In these texts, however, the reader may find voices that complement Frank Bascombe's philosophizing one.

5 Jean has also uttered those words to Joe on the page preceding, illustrating her own despair and pent-up frustration.

6 Note again the syntactical separation of "my father and I, and my mother."

Folks

1 "Western" art was indeed often the creation of eastern writers who had little actual contact with the West—as in the case of Clarence E. Mulford, inventor of the Hopalong Cassidy figure, who never visited the West until seventeen years after his first published western story (Savage 143-44), or Rodgers and Hammerstein, who had not visited Oklahoma until the premiere of their now classic "western" musical.

2 The trail ride, from the southern plains to markets in the North, may have actually served the purpose of initiation for many young men, if we are to judge

from memoirs and historical accounts. The long trail ride provided the first extended period away from home for many young men from small towns and rural backgrounds, and it offered a memorable, and in many cases one-time, adventure for youths destined to return to their isolated communities (Savage 14ff).

Bonetti, Kay. "An Interview with Richard Ford." *Missouri Review* 10.1 (1987): 71–96.

Brooks, Van Wyck. *America's Coming-of-Age.* New York: Doubleday, 1915.

Chandler, Raymond. "The Simple Art of Murder." 1950. Reprinted in *The Simple Art of Murder.* New York: Vintage Books, 1988.

Christianson, Scott R. "A Heap of Broken Images: Hard-boiled Detective Fiction and the Discourse(s) of Modernity." In *The Cunning Craft: Original Essays on Detective Fiction and Literary Theory,* edited by Ronald G. Walker and June M. Frazer. Macomb: Western Illinois University, 1990. 135–48.

Clemons, Walter. "The Divorced Men's Club." *Newsweek,* 7 April 1986, 82.

Crouse, David. "Resisting Reduction: Closure in Richard Ford's *Rock Springs* and Alice Munro's *Friend of My Youth.*" *Canadian Literature* 146 (1995): 51–64.

Deleuze, Gilles, and Felix Guattari. *Kafka: Toward a Minor Literature.* Minneapolis: University of Minnesota Press, 1986.

Dunne, Michael. "Romantic Narcissism in 'Outlaw' Cowboy Music." In *All That Glitters: Country Music in America,* edited by George H. Lewis. Bowling Green, Ohio: Bowling Green State University Press, 1993.

Emerson, Ralph Waldo. "Self-Reliance." 1841. In *Essays.* Vol. 2. Reprint, New York: AMS, 1968.

Exley, Frederick. *A Fan's Notes: A Fictional Memoir.* New York: Random House/Vintage, 1968.

Faulkner, William. *Absalom, Absalom!* New York: Random House, 1936.

Fukuyama, Francis. *The End of History and the Last Man.* New York: Avon, 1992.

Ford, Richard. "Accommodations." *Harper's Magazine,* June 1988, 39–43.

———. "First Things First: One More Writer's Beginnings." *Harper's Magazine,* August 1988, 72–76.

———. *Independence Day*. New York: Random House/Vintage, 1995.

———. "My Mother, in Memory." *Harpers Magazine*, August, 1987, 44–57.

———. *A Piece of My Heart*. New York: Random House/Vintage, 1976.

———. "Reading." In *Writers on Writing*, edited by Robert Pack and Jay Parini. Hanover: Middlebury College Press, 1991.

———. *Rock Springs*. New York: Random House/Vintage, 1987.

———. *The Sportswriter*. New York: Random House/Vintage, 1986.

———. "The Three Kings: Hemingway, Faulkner, and Fitzgerald." *Esquire*, December 1983, 577–87.

———. *The Ultimate Good Luck*. New York: Random House/Vintage, 1981.

———. "Walker Percy: Not Just Whistling Dixie." *National Review*, 13 May 1977, 558–64.

———. "What We Write, Why We Write It, and Who Cares." *Louisiana Cultural Vistas* 4.1 (1993): 44–53.

———. "Where Does Writing Come From?" *Granta* 62 (1998): 250–55. Reprinted in *Why I Write: Thoughts on the Craft of Fiction*, edited by Will Blythe. New York: Little, Brown, 1998. 13–20.

———. *Wildlife*. New York: Random House/Vintage, 1990.

———. *Women with Men*. New York: Knopf, 1997.

Gornick, Vivian. "Tenderhearted Men: Lonesome, Sad and Blue." *New York Times Book Review*, 16 September 1990, natl. ed., sec. 7: 1+.

Heffner, Richard D. Foreword to *Democracy in America*, by Alexis de Tocqueville. New York: Mentor, 1984.

Hemingway, Ernest. *To Have and Have Not*. New York: Scribner's, 1937.

Hobson, Fred. *The Southern Writer in the Postmodern World*. Athens: University of Georgia Press, 1991.

———. *Tell About the South: The Southern Rage to Explain*. Baton Rouge: Louisiana State University Press, 1983.

Hoffman, Alice. "A Wife Named X, a Poodle Named Elvis." *New York Times Book Review*, 23 March 1986, 14.

Hyman, Stanley Edgar. *The Armed Vision: A Study in the Methods of Modern Literary Criticism*. New York: Greenwood, 1955.

Kakutani, Michiko. *New York Times*, 26 February 1986, sec.C: 21.

Kammen, Michael. *Mystic Chords of Memory: The Transformation of Tradition in American Culture*. New York: Knopf, 1991.

Keats, John. *The Selected Letters of John Keats*. Edited by Lionel Trilling. New York: Farrar, Straus, and Young, 1951.

Koenig, Rhoda. "The Sweet Shot." *New York*, 31 March 1986, 86.

Kreyling, Michael. *Figures of the Hero in Southern Narrative*. Baton Rouge: Louisiana State University Press, 1987.

Lasch, Christopher. *The Culture of Narcissism: American Life in An Age of Diminishing Expectations*. New York: Norton, 1980. Revised edition, 1991.

Lesley, Craig. Introduction to *Dreamers and Desperadoes: Contemporary Short Fiction of the American West,* edited by Craig Lesley and Katheryn Stavrakis. New York: Laurel, 1993.

Malone, Bill C. *Country Music, U.S.A.* Rev. ed. Austin: University of Texas Press, 1985.

Marin, Peter. "The New Narcissism." *Harper's Magazine,* October 1975, 46+.

Martin, Russell. Introduction to *New Writers of the Purple Sage: An Anthology of Contemporary Western Writers.* New York: Penguin, 1992.

Melville, Herman. *Moby Dick.* 1851. Reprint, New York: Signet Books, 1961.

Ngugi wa Thiong'o. *Decolonising the Mind: The Politics of Language in African Literature.* London: J. Currey, 1986.

Percy, Walker. "The Delta Factor." *The Southern Review* 11 (1975): 29–64. Reprinted in *The Message in the Bottle: How Queer Man Is, How Queer Language Is, and What One Has to Do with the Other.* New York: Farrar, Straus & Giroux, 1984.

———. *The Last Gentleman.* New York: Farrar, Straus & Giroux, 1966.

———. *Lost in the Cosmos.* New York: Farrar, Straus & Giroux, 1983.

———. *The Moviegoer.* New York: Knopf, 1960.

Sartre, Jean-Paul. *Being and Nothingness: An Essay on Phenomenological Ontology.* Translated by Hazel E. Barnes. New York: Philosophical Library, 1956.

———. *Nausea.* Translated by Lloyd Alexander. London: Purnell & Sons, 1949.

Savage, William W., Jr. *The Cowboy Hero: His Image in American History and Culture.* Norman: University of Oklahoma Press, 1979.

Simpson, Lewis P. *The Fable of the Southern Writer.* Baton Rouge: Louisiana State University Press, 1994.

Stevens, Wallace. "The Idea of Order at Key West." In *The Palm at the End of the Mind,* edited by Holly Stevens. New York: Random House/Vintage, 1972.

Sweeney, S. E. "Locked Rooms: Detective Fiction, Narrative Theory, and Self-Reflexivity." In *The Cunning Craft: Original Essays on Detective Fiction and Literary Theory,* edited by Ronald G. Walker and June M. Frazer. Macomb: Western Illinois University, 1990.

Tocqueville, Alexis de. *Democracy in America.* 1835. Reprint, New York: Mentor, 1984.

Towers, Robert. "Screams and Whispers." *New York Review of Books,* 24 April 1986, 3.

Updike, John. *Rabbit, Run.* New York: Knopf, 1960.

Walker, Elinor Ann. "An Interview with Richard Ford." *The South Carolina Review* 31.2 (1999) : 128–43.

Warren, Robert Penn. *All the King's Men.* 1946. Reprint, New York: Bantam, 1959.

Weber, Bruce. "Richard Ford's Uncommon Character." *The New York Times Magazine,* 10 April 1988, 50+.

Wylder, Delbert E. *Hemingway's Heroes.* Albuquerque: University of New Mexico Press, 1969.

William G. Chernecky is associate professor of English at Louisiana State University at Eunice. He has written articles on works by Connie May Fowler, Annie Dillard, Josephine Humphreys, and other contemporary American novelists.

Edward J. Dupuy is academic dean at Saint Joseph Seminary College in Saint Benedict, Louisiana, four miles north of Covington. His book, *Autobiography in Walker Percy: Repetition, Recovery, and Redemption*, was published by Louisiana State University Press in 1996. He has published several articles, primarily on writers of the South, and reviews.

Jeffrey J. Folks is professor of literature at Doshisha University in Kyoto, Japan. He has published three books, the most recent being *Southern Writers at Century's End*, with James A. Perkins, as well as articles in numerous journals.

Robert N. Funk is assistant professor of English at Louisiana State University at Eunice. He has published several articles on John D. MacDonald's work, as well as articles on Christopher Marlowe and Theodore Dreiser.

Huey Guagliardo is professor and coordinator of English at Louisiana State University at Eunice. He has published essays, interviews, and reviews in various journals, including *The Southern Review, The Southern Quarterly, The South Central Review, Notes on Mississippi Writers, Louisiana Cultural Vistas,* and *Forum.*

Fred Hobson is Lineberger Professor in the Humanities and coeditor of the *Southern Literary Journal* at the University of North Carolina at Chapel Hill. He is author of a number of books, including *Serpent in Eden: H. L. Mencken and the South* (1974); *Tell About the South: The Southern Rage to Explain* (1983); *The Southern Writer in the Postmodern World* (1991); *Mencken: A Life* (1995); and, most recently, *But Now I See: The White Southern Racial Conversion Narrative* published by Louisiana State University Press in 1999.

W. Kenneth Holditch is research professor of English emeritus at the University of New Orleans. His book, *In Old New Orleans*, was published by the University Press of Mississippi in 1983. He has published numerous articles, chapters in books, and reviews, as well as short stories and poetry. He is currently coediting two volumes on Tennessee Williams for the Library of America.

Priscilla Leder is associate professor of English and director of the writing center at Southwest Texas State University in San Marcos. She specializes in American women writers and has published essays on Kate Chopin, Sarah Orne Jewett, and Alice Walker.

Elinor Ann Walker received her Ph.D. from the University of North Carolina at Chapel Hill. She has published essays in *Mississippi Quarterly, Southern Literary Journal, Studies in the Literary Imagination,* and *The South Carolina Review,* as well as chapters in books and source books. Her research interests include southern culture and literature, especially the works of Walker Percy, Josephine Humphreys, Jill McCorkle, and Richard Ford.

Index

Adams, John, 163, 164

alienation: as literary tradition, xii; in modern world, 5; reversed by language, xvii, 6; and western settings, xiv, 156

All the King's Men (Warren), 94

American Adam: concept of, 165–66, 175

Anderson, Sherwood: "Death in the Woods," 6, 85; "I Want to Know Why," 179

Autry, Gene, 141

Avedon, Richard, 187

Babel, Isaac, "The Story of My Dovecot," 179

Barth, John, xiii; *The End of the Road*, 182

Barthelme, Donald, xiii; "The Indian Uprising," 185

Becker, Carl, *The Declaration of Independence*, 25, 172

Bercovitch, Sacvan, *The Rites of Assent*, 149

Blackmur, R. P., 193

Bonetti, Kay, "An Interview with Richard Ford," 15, 73, 75, 84, 148, 149, 197n, 197n, 198n

Bosch, Hieronymus, *The Garden of Earthly Delights*, 67

Brooks, Cleanth, 193

Brooks, Van Wyck, *America's Coming-of-Age*, 166

Browning, Robert, 5

Camus, Albert, xii, 34, 49

Carver, Raymond, xiii, 85, 199n

Céline, Louis-Ferdinand, 187

Chandler, Raymond, 54, 57, 58, 59, 61; *The Big Sleep*, 60

Cheever, John, xiii, 86, 157

Chekhov, Anton Pavlovich, 181

Christianson, Scott R., 58–59

Clemons, Walter, xi

Cool Hand Luke, 178

Cooper, James Fenimore, 62, 163

cowboy myth, 141–42, 154

Crouse, David, 98

cummings, e. e., 185

Davidson, Donald, 92

Declaration of Independence, 163, 168–69

Deford, Frank, 93–94

Deleuze, Gilles, 145, 146

Didion, Joan, 188

Dostoevsky, Feodor, 47

Dunne, Michael, 142, 152

Ecclesiastes, 114

Eliot, T. S., 58; "The Hollow Men," 93; "Tradition and the Individual Talent," 168; *The Wasteland*, 71

Emerson, Ralph Waldo, 166, 174, 199n; "Nature," 169; "Self-Reliance," 25, 163, 165, 169–71, 172

entrapment, images of, 45

Existentialism, French humanistic tradition of, xii, 49

Exley, Frederick, xiii; *A Fan's Notes*, 182

Faulkner, William, xiii, 51, 55, 72, 75, 83, 86, 94, 96, 148, 149; *Absalom, Absalom!*, 6, 72, 75, 85, 90, 121, 122; "Old Man," 85; *The Sound and the Fury*, 93

Fitzgerald, F. Scott, xiii, 55, 72, 94, 96
Ford, Kristina, xv, 47, 187, 189, 190, 197n
Ford, Parker Carrol, xiv
Ford, Richard: on affection, 15, 182–83; on America's future, 188; on art, 5; on European publishing, 195–96; on film work, 194–95; on language, xvi–xvii, 6–7, 72, 149, 183–85; on literature 5–6, 149; on narrative voice, 186–87; on New Orleans, La., 189–90; on the novel, 180; on the novella, 177; on the Pulitzer Prize, 191; on redemption, 182–83; on the short story, 180; on solipsism, 178; on teaching and the academy, 192–93; on Walker Percy, 54, 181–84, 189; on work habits, 193–94; on the writer's marginality, 5; on the writer's relationship to his reader, 181; on writing as a process of discovery, 179–80

Collections: *Rock Springs* (short stories), xii, xiv, 83, 85, 97–120, 121, 123, 141–56, 198n; *Women with Men* (novellas), xii, 83, 123, 177–80, 184, 186

Essays: "Accommodations," xiv, xv, 30; "First Things First," xviii; "My Mother, in Memory," xiv, xv, xvi, 84, 123, 198n; "Reading," xvi, 6, 11; "The Three Kings," xiii, 6, 31, 55, 72, 75, 85, 94; "Walker Percy," 54; "What We Write, Why We Write It, and Who Cares," 5, 6, 16; "Where Does Writing Come From?," xvi

Novellas: *Jealous*, 123, 177, 178, 179; *Occidentals*, 179–80, 184, 185, 186, 190; *The Womanizer*, 177

Novels: *Independence Day*, xi, xv, 3, 4, 6, 16, 21–32, 53, 83, 154, 155–56, 157–76, 177, 178, 186, 188, 191, 192, 195, 199n; *A Piece of My Heart*, xi, xii, 3, 4, 7–11, 33–51, 53, 83, 85, 154, 186, 190, 194; *The Sportswriter*, xi, xiii, 3, 6, 15–21, 27, 29, 49, 53, 71–81, 83–96, 151, 154, 155–56, 157–62, 181–82, 186, 188, 189, 199n; *The Ultimate Good Luck*, xi, xii, 3, 11–15, 16, 51, 53–69, 83, 85, 154–55, 186, 190, 195; *Wildlife*, xi, xiv, 51, 83, 121–39, 141, 154, 186

Screenplay: *Bright Angel*, 195
Short Stories: "Children," 100, 108–10, 119, 123, 146–47, 150, 198n; "Communist," 100, 106–07, 123, 147, 153–54; "Empire," 100, 112–15, 118, 120, 150–51; "Fireworks," 100, 119–20, 144; "Going to the Dogs," 100, 115–16, 144; "Great Falls," xii, 100–04, 105, 107, 121–39, 144–45, 198n; "Optimists," 100, 104–05, 107, 123, 147, 152; "Rock Springs," 100, 116–18, 143–44, 156, 198n; "Sweethearts," 99, 118–19, 146; "Winterkill," 100, 110–12, 119, 147, 151–52

Frazier, Charles, *Cold Mountain*, 191
Freud, Sigmund, 11
Fukuyama, Francis, 175–76

Gass, William, 193
Godwin, Gail, *The Finishing School*, 198n
Gornick, Vivian, 97
Guattari, Felix, 145, 146

Hammett, Dashiell, 54, 57, 58, 59; *Red Harvest*, 58
Heffner, Richard D., 173
Heidegger, Martin, 128, 138, 199n
Heller, Joseph, *Something Happened*, 182
Hemingway, Ernest, xii, xiii, 72, 85, 94, 96, 97, 101, 199n; "A Clean,